Jimmy Carter in the White House

Jimmy Carter in the White House: A Captain with No Compass

Robert K. Green

BLOOMSBURY ACADEMIC
LONDON • NEW YORK • OXFORD • NEW DELHI • SYDNEY

BLOOMSBURY ACADEMIC
Bloomsbury Publishing Plc
50 Bedford Square, London, WC1B 3DP, UK
1385 Broadway, New York, NY 10018, USA
29 Earlsfort Terrace, Dublin 2, Ireland

BLOOMSBURY, BLOOMSBURY ACADEMIC and the Diana logo
are trademarks of Bloomsbury Publishing Plc

First published in Great Britain 2024

Cover design: Paul Smith
Cover image © Chuck Fishman/Getty Images

A catalogue record for this book is available from the British Library.

A catalog record for this book is available from the Library of Congress.

ISBN: HB: 978-1-3503-5291-9
         PB: 978-1-3503-5290-2
       ePDF: 978-1-3503-5293-3
      eBook: 978-1-3503-5292-6

Typeset by Integra Software Services Pvt. Ltd.

To find out more about our authors and books visit www.bloomsbury.com
and sign up for our newsletters.

Dedicated to James, Matthew, Rebecca,
Ivy and May.

Contents

Acknowledgements

When I took early retirement to study for a master's degree, I never dreamed that I would end up writing a book. For this minor miracle, I have a number of people to thank.

First some great teachers all of whom are also distinguished authors. Professor Catherine Merridale who whilst at Queen Mary University of London (QMUL) was my course tutor and marked my very first essay after thirty-three years. She reassured me that it was not really that bad (I am afraid it was), and she convinced me that I could succeed after all this time. Iwan Morgan, Emeritus Professor at University College London (UCL), where his brilliant teaching on the American Presidency inspired me to do more. Finally, my mentor and friend Professor Mark White of QMUL whose help and encouragement convinced me that I could not only achieve a doctorate but had absolute faith that I could write this book.

The research and writing of this work have brought me into contact with the wonderful archivists at the Jimmy Carter Presidential Library in Atlanta, the Library of Congress and the National Archives in Washington DC. I would also like to mention the library staff at various libraries in London, in particular Senate House, London School of Economics, UCL and the British Library. Without all of their kindness and hard work this book would not have been possible. Thanks to all of you.

Finally, I would like to thank the people at Bloomsbury Publishing for not only supporting this project but guiding me through the process. In particular my thanks go to Atifa Jiwa, Nadine Staes-Polet and Saffron Forde for their patience and support.

Preface

Any writer embarking on a presidential biography is often asked 'why this president?' This particularly is the case when it is a president who has failed to win re-election as he is invariably regarded as a failure. Yet Jimmy Carter's presidency raises a number of issues that have not been resolved by the current historical literature. His ignominious defeat to Ronald Reagan in November 1980 appeared to signal political oblivion. A series of biographies wrote off his time in office. Burton and Scott Kaufman, in their 2006 work *The Presidency of James Earl Carter,* summed up this view of his presidency by stating:

> The events of his four years in office project an image to the American people of a hapless administration in disarray and a Presidency that was increasingly divided, lacking in leadership, ineffective in dealing with Congress, incapable of defending American honour abroad and uncertain about its purpose, priorities and sense of direction.[1]

This seemed to me neither a fair nor accurate picture of Carter's presidency. Also, a re-evaluation of Carter seems particularly relevant at this time given the challenges being faced by President Joe Biden. In the 2020 election Biden argued for his ability to be both competent and get things done but, much like Carter, has faced the challenges of stagflation, an energy crisis and a divided society. The Republicans have been quick to draw negative comparisons between Biden and Carter.

This book is a re-evaluation of the key domestic policies of the Carter presidency. Making use of a wide range of primary sources, including declassified materials from the Jimmy Carter Presidential Library, it discusses how he sought to reshape America in the 1970s at a time of ideological conflict, and how he tried to make government an effective vehicle for change. He believed that by providing comprehensive solutions to America's most deep-rooted problems he would win support across the political and ideological divide.

Early writers on Carter have criticized his leadership and his failure to deliver on his key domestic programmes. Even those who have taken a more sympathetic position have accepted that he had significant failings but have argued that these were due to external factors beyond his control. All have sought to understand his character and define his ideology in a wider context. However, it is striking how little consensus has been found in the enigma of America's thirty-ninth president.

Historians such as Burton and Scott Kaufman, as well as Haynes Johnson in *The Absence of Power (1980)*, have argued that Carter's failure was one of leadership. He failed to articulate a vision for America and provide a coherent agenda that could deliver meaningful change. His administration's poor relations with Congress, the press and even Washington as a whole were viewed as avoidable. They characterized Carter as a mediocre president who, despite understanding the will of the electorate, lacked the political know-how to carry the country with him.[2] The most critical of Carter were the political scientists who studied the office of the presidency.[3] They argued that effective presidents require a core set of skills such as being a good communicator, having a strategic view, being persuasive, having managerial skills, self-discipline and emotional intelligence. Measured against these criteria, except for self-discipline, they found Carter wanting. His inability to persuade the public of the soundness of his policies and to articulate a coherent vision for his administration were all characterized as a failure of leadership. To these academics Carter's failure as president therefore was viewed as inevitable.

The revisionists' view of the Carter presidency did not really challenge the idea that he was an unsuccessful president. Their argument was in effect a plea for mitigation that given the political, cultural and economic environment he faced it would have taken someone with the skills of a Franklin Delano Roosevelt (FDR) to succeed.[4] Revisionists highlighted his achievements such as the 1976 election victory, his record on the environment and his success in the Middle East. John Dumbrell, in *The Carter Presidency. A Re-evaluation (1993)*, argued that Carter was a 'post liberal' who sought to adjust liberalism to a new age, and although many of his policies were incomplete, they set the scene for legislation in the future.[5] Abernathy, Hill and Williams reasoned in *The Carter Years: The President and Policy Making (1984)* that Carter was a victim of the 'Age of Limits' in that he was the first modern Democratic President to operate where there was limited economic growth. This made it very difficult, if not impossible, to fund social programmes.[6] In *Jimmy Carter as President: Leadership and Politics of the Public Good (1988)* Erwin Hargrove believed that Carter recognized the issues that were critical for the future of the Democratic Party. He was therefore ahead of his time but as a president in office during a transition to a more conservative era, he lacked the skills to change the fortunes of his party.[7]

The improved public image of Jimmy Carter resulted from his post-presidential achievements, including the success of the Carter Center and his charity work. The election of Donald J. Trump in 2016 and the marked contrast in their characters prompted a nostalgia for a different, more moral leadership. This, along with his advanced years (he was ninety-nine in 2023), has resulted in a fresh re-evaluation of his presidency. This new revisionist impulse in the historical literature, led by authors like Jonathan Alter in *His Very Best, Jimmy Carter. A Life (2020)*, Kai Bird in *The Outlier. The Unfinished Presidency of Jimmy Carter (2021)* and Nancy Mitchell in *Jimmy Carter in Africa (2016)*,[8] has been more positive in their analysis than earlier revisionism which had largely fizzled out by the mid-1990s. This new interpretation portrayed Carter as a president who was both brave, decisive and ahead of his time in promoting policies on health and the environment. This new revisionism reinforced an image of Carter as a good man *not* out of his depth as president, as other historians have argued, but whose capabilities and achievements were not only underestimated but demonstrated a level of foresight not recognized at the time.

Whatever their approach, historians have not successfully addressed many aspects of the Carter legacy. Could he be described as such a failure when so many of the policies he attempted to implement also proved beyond the capabilities of his successors? What was his ideology, or indeed did he have one? What was the impact of his character on his administration? How far did his faith, his background as an engineer and his attitude to politics affect his presidency? Was his belief in government by experts even possible in an ideologically divided America?

This book seeks to address these issues and increase our understanding of Jimmy Carter by evaluating his policies on key domestic issues. One caveat: while the book provides a wide-ranging coverage of Carter's major domestic policies, it is not exhaustive. So certain issues, including deregulation, consumer affairs and government reform, are not explored in depth. In deciding which policies to focus on, I have taken several factors into consideration.

I chose his economic policies and energy reform because Carter himself had identified these as critical issues during his election campaign and transition to the presidency. To Carter, providing solutions to two of the country's most complex problems would fulfil his promise in the 1976 campaign of competence. To explore a major theme of this study, the effect of ideology on Carter's presidency, I have discussed his approach to health, welfare and labour policy, key priorities for liberal Democrats. On a similar ideological theme, the Culture Wars chapter reviews the major social movements of the 1970s linked to race, religion, gender and the environment, all of which buffeted the Carter presidency and influenced his administration's policy agenda. The book is completed by an analysis of the 1980 election as it sheds light on his domestic policy record. This was Carter's attempt to win a second term by maintaining a politically neutral ground in the face of liberal opposition in his own party and a conservative shift in American politics. The election reflected not only a popular verdict on Carter's policies, but on his leadership, his ideological position and his vision for America. In addition to exploring Carter's domestic policies in depth I start by analysing his rise to the presidency and how he sought to organize his administration so as to deliver the promises he made during the presidential campaign.

This book attempts to unravel the enigma of Carter. For a politician who famously put his character front and centre of his campaign in 1976, even his chief advisor Hamilton Jordan admitted that after four years in office 'the American people *still* do not have a clear picture of who he was'.[9] Historians such as Thomas Reeves, in his biography of John F Kennedy, focused on personality flaws, but no such analysis has been applied to a president like Carter, an overtly good man.[10] How did his character traits, both good and bad, impact on his presidency? Also, in a period when the country was becoming increasingly divided, much like it is today, was it even possible for someone who avoided ideology like Carter to deliver 'the best' solutions whatever the political cost: was it possible to run a technocratic government in a two-party democracy? Finally, how important is image for a national politician? Despite appearances to the contrary, Carter was acutely aware of his image and worked very hard to build and maintain an image of competence and trust that was perfectly suited to the post-Watergate/Vietnam era. But this could not be sustained as president without a track record of success. The Republicans were able to paint a very different picture of his presidency that not only was sustained in 1980 but is even being used to this day.

I will seek to answer these questions and put Carter's presidency in a proper historic context. I will also ask whether his technocratic approach to government can succeed in a modern America. It is a story of a president's belief in doing the right thing whatever the political consequences in the face of a sceptical press, a fiercely independent Congress, a wide range of competing interest groups, and, above all else, an increasingly divided country.

1

Jimmy who?

It is often forgotten how little-known Jimmy Carter was before his victory in November 1976. He lacked the national recognition of potential rivals for the Democratic presidential nomination like Senators Edward Kennedy, Walter Mondale and Frank Church, as well as Governors George Wallace and Jerry Brown. Early polling indicated Carter's recognition level was as low as 1 per cent, resulting in comments from poll respondents when asked about him to say, 'Jimmy Who?' Attempts by Carter to raise his profile included an appearance on the famous TV show 'What's My Line'.[1] As to confirm his outsider status, his mother Lillian, who was always good for a quote, when told by her son that he intended to run for president, was said to have responded, 'President of What?'[2]

James Earl Carter's early life and career helped shape his attitude to government and the role of the presidency. He was born in 1924 and brought up in a farming community in Plains, Georgia. His father, Earl, was a peanut farmer and a community leader whilst his mother, Lillian, had been a nurse. He was educated in Georgia, but he left home when he joined the Naval Academy in Annapolis in 1943, graduating three years later. He married a local girl, Rosalynn Smith, in 1946, starting the most long-lasting and influential relationship of his life. He served in various postings around the country before qualifying to command a submarine as a full lieutenant. He later joined the fledgling nuclear submarine programme under the legendary Captain Hyman Rickover. The illness and subsequent death of his father in 1953 forced him to resign from the Navy to return to Plains to manage the family business. During the next nine years Carter successfully developed the business and, following the footsteps of his father, he became influential in his local community. Carter represented a growing breed of southern businessmen focused on promoting economic and social reform and as such spoke strongly in favour of racial tolerance and integration. At one point he faced down the local white Citizens Council who boycotted his business because he refused to join them. In 1962 he successfully ran for the Georgia Senate and was re-elected in 1964.

There were three important influences on Jimmy Carter's adult life, both personal and philosophical, the first of which was his wife Rosalynn. She ran his home and business whilst he was away campaigning in Georgia and later became a highly effective campaigner on his behalf when he ran for both governor and president. Carter discussed decisions with her and as president arranged for her to sit in on cabinet meetings. She has remained throughout his life his co-partner, advisor and main supporter. A second major influence on Carter was his superior in the Navy, Hyman Rickover. Carter quoted him heavily throughout his presidential campaign. His campaign biography *Why Not the Best?* was a direct quote of Rickover's.[3] The training Carter received as a nuclear engineer was reflected in his approach to problem solving. His obsession with being right as a substitute for being political was a hallmark of Rickover's training and decision-making.[4] The third and the most important influence on Carter was his faith. In 1966 following an electoral defeat he became a 'born again' Christian. His religious beliefs were reflected throughout his political career in his determination to do the 'right thing' and in his speeches which were laced with moral themes. His faith gave him peace and detachment but also influenced a political element to his campaign. His critique of interest groups had a strong element of 'driving money changers from the temple of Washington'.[5] His faith reinforced his support in the south, but it also brought its disadvantages. Some argued that the drive for a moral argument in dealing with the nation's problems was a turn off for a public used to optimism and a political elite expecting to bargain.[6] Despite political disadvantages, Carter remained upfront about his beliefs. His campaign speeches, in which he described who he was, continued to finish with an affirmation of his Christian faith despite the numerous attempts of his advisor Stuart Eizenstat to discourage him.[7]

After an unsuccessful campaign for governor in 1966, Carter ran again successfully in 1970. He was a ruthless campaigner in the Democratic primary against the liberal former governor Carl Sanders. He repositioned himself to the right in running a populist campaign contrasting himself in television adverts with Sanders' alleged urbanity, aloofness and liberalism. He avoided controversial issues like Civil Rights but emphasized economic growth and improved efficiency in government. He argued for reform in education, criminal justice and particularly the state government. Whilst he avoided radical change as governor, he recognized the importance of symbolism. He used his inaugural speech in 1971 to announce that the 'time for racial discrimination is over'.[8]

This seemed a radical statement, it certainly appalled his more conservative supporters, but to Carter it was recognition of what was reality and that it was time for the south to move on. He followed this up with the symbolic gesture of hanging Martin Luther King's portrait outside his office in the state capitol. Carter wanted his time as governor to be seen as a symbol of his competence but also, he believed that his record in Atlanta demonstrated how he could manage Congress in Washington. Historian Gary Fink described Carter's general treatment of the Georgian Assembly as unthinking neglect.[9] His legislative success rate was as high as 90 per cent but he was never popular in the Assembly.[10] This was to be a sign of things to come.

In the passing of state government reform, Carter as governor demonstrated a range of effective strategies and skills to gain support from use of patronage, threats on pet projects as well as individual lobbying.[11] Government reform may not have been a controversial issue, but it had no natural constituency among the Georgia electorate. So, Carter worked very hard to establish an advisory committee to raise awareness and to lobby state officials and members of the Assembly. His tenacity coined a new phrase about him when he was likened to a South Georgia turtle pushing a log out of the way.[12] Many of the characteristics of the Carter presidency could be seen in his governorship with its emphasis on efficiency, comprehensive solutions, avoidance of radical change, his attraction to symbolism and his abhorrence of special interests. He could be stubborn but was able to craft an astute compromise, for example, over the proposed 'William Calley Day' (the officer associated with the My Lai massacre) which he replaced with 'America's Fighting Man's Day' which left both his liberal and conservative supporters content on the sensitive issue of Vietnam.[13] However, these successes did not make him popular. Bert Lance, a close friend and Georgia Commissioner, characterized his chances of re-election if he stood again in 1974 as very poor given that he had 'inflicted enough serious damage on himself that he was not viable' as a candidate.[14]

Carter's experience as governor of Georgia demonstrated to him what could be achieved in terms of reform and gave him first-hand experience of how the Federal Government operated. As governor he did not think that the Nixon Administration served Georgia well. He felt ignored by White House staff and was particularly unimpressed with the performance of the Corp of Engineers on Federal Water Projects in his state.[15] Carter's view of the role of the Federal Government was in many ways like that of his great rival Ronald Reagan. Both saw the government as too big, inefficient, and even corrupt but whilst Reagan saw government as 'the problem' that needed to be reduced if not eliminated, Carter saw it as a potential force for good. In his 1976 presidential campaign he kept asking two questions: 'Can our government be honest, decent, open, fair and compassionate' and 'Can our government be competent?'[16] To Carter the answer to both questions was an unequivocal yes. He also grew concerned about the influence of interest groups. He highlighted this in his 'Why not the Best' speech on 12 December 1974: 'The lobbyists who fill the halls of Congress, state capitols, county courthouses and city halls often represent well-meaning and admirable groups. What is often forgotten is that lobbyists seldom represent the average citizen.'[17] Carter held this view throughout his presidency; it had a strong moral dimension and affected how he operated politically in Washington. This was partially a response to a dramatic rise in interest groups during this period. In total the number of lobbyists rose from 2000 after the Second World War to over 15,000 in 1978, spending $2 billion.[18] Carter saw interest groups as nothing less than a challenge to his vision of an effective government. He said, 'Our commitment to these dreams has been sapped by debilitating compromise, acceptance of mediocrity, subservience to special interests and absence of executive vision and direction.'[19] He entered the White House in the firm belief that he held a mandate not from any special interest but *only* from the public.

In deciding to run for president in 1976 the Carter campaign had to consider the profound changes that were affecting America in the 1970s. The decade saw a decline in American prestige abroad and loss of public confidence at home. This was a result of two major events: the defeat in the Vietnam War and the Watergate scandal which ended in the resignation of President Richard Nixon. The loss of public confidence in political institutions, politicians in general and particularly the presidency was dramatic. This was reflected in the decline in voting in national elections which dropped to the lowest level since 1948.[20] The level of public disaffection also increased with a poll in 1975 indicating that 69 per cent of people felt that over the previous ten years America's leaders had lied to them.[21] The nature of reporting in newspapers and on television had also changed. News had become more immediate with a focus on investigation and reporters were sceptical in dealing with government information usually provided by White House staff. In this, journalists were aided by sources from expanded congressional staffs and leaks from low-level aides in the government, often reflecting different views to that of the White House.[22]

In response to presidential actions taken during Vietnam and Watergate, a revitalized Congress moved to end what was termed the 'Imperial Presidency' by restricting presidential powers to wage war, amend budgets and raise campaign funds. Changes to the political infrastructure were not confined to the presidency but impacted on Congress and political parties. Supreme Court decisions resulted in the enforcement of more geographically equitable congressional districts. The redrawing of these district boundaries resulted initially in an increased turnover of congressmen and women with most members in each House having less than six years' experience.[23] Those members of congress with more stable majorities became less likely to need presidential favours. Their success became based on delivering services for their own constituencies and they began to acquire more staff to do this. There were also significant changes in congressional governance as reforms resulted in the creation of 165 committees and sub-committees/special task forces to scrutinize legislation. In addition, congressional chairs were no longer appointed but elected by the party caucus.[24] All of this would result in the decline of White House influence on an increasingly complex legislative process.

The Fraser-McGovern reform of Democratic Party rules in 1971 sought to broaden the base of the party and improve participation at election conventions. It increased the number of delegates from women and minority groups whilst reducing the participation of ex-officio members from state party organizations.[25] These new party rules and the federal campaign funding legislation made it simpler for individual states to run primary elections rather than appoint delegates. The abolition of the unit rule in primaries meant that the result was no longer winner take all for delegates. This potentially gave any new candidate with limited financial backing the opportunity to build momentum and gain media attention by winning delegates in the early primaries. This would be the strategy that Carter used effectively in 1976.[26] At the convention itself the new rules reduced the participation and the influence of national and state party leaders over their fragmented state delegations. These changes were not without their disadvantages. As governor, Carter nearly failed to attend the 1972 Democratic Convention as he only just beat a local Black college student by fifteen votes in a state delegate election.[27]

There were other major changes in both parties that occurred during the 1970s. The traditional Democratic New Deal coalition built by Franklin D. Roosevelt (FDR) based on north-eastern industrial cities, labour unions, minority groups and southern states was continuing to fragment. The Republican Party (GOP) was gaining support among white voters in the south as Civil Rights legislation had damaged the Democrats politically. The traditional liberal base in the north-eastern states was being undermined by economic decline with industries moving to the southern and western states. The GOP became increasingly under the influence of conservative pressure groups. These initially focused on local protest, for example, against property tax in California. However, this concern over inflation on middle-class incomes developed into wider resentment against government spending, especially on welfare which conservatives felt unfairly benefitted minority groups. Such protests at the state level resulted in twelve states between 1978 and 1982 restricting state government spending.[28]

The decade also saw major changes in the US economy. The 1960s was the most successful period for America in terms of growth, both domestically and in foreign trade. However, by the end of the decade President Lyndon B. Johnson's attempt to fund his Great Society reforms and the Vietnam War caused the economy to overheat and resulted in increased inflation. A decline in productivity and increased competition from abroad resulted in a fall in economic growth coupled with major inflation (known as stagflation) and higher unemployment. Successive administrations struggled to strike the right balance of policies to control stagflation. The inability of economic advisors to resolve these challenges meant that each new administration faced the decision on whether to stimulate the economy to fix a recession or impose fiscal restraint to reduce inflation. Whichever option was followed had serious political and economic consequences. Most administrations after 1968 found it difficult to follow a consistent line. As a result, US financial indicators continued to deteriorate. The dollar fell in value in relation to other major currencies by 60 per cent between 1967 and 1980 whilst middle-class family income failed to grow for ten years after 1973.[29]

During this period of economic turmoil there was one sector of the American economy that continued to grow: a cluster of states in the south and west known as the Sunbelt. The growth of the Sunbelt originated in the Second World War when the government invested in defence industries in the region, and this continued in the 1950s and 1960s through the award of defence contracts because of the Cold War and investment in infrastructure such as highways. The boom in cheap housing after 1945 and the development of air conditioning made the south and west a more attractive proposition for young families from the big cities in the north-east. Incentives were provided to move South including a favourable state tax regime and 'Right to Work' laws which discouraged unions. This form of economic 'boosterism' under the leadership of Dale Bumpers, Terry Sandford and other southern politicians resulted in new industries flooding into the south and west. By the 1970s the economic success of the Sunbelt states helped change the negative image of the south, particularly in the north where racial tension caused by riots in the late 1960s and the issue of school busing in the 1970s had resulted in a more sympathetic attitude towards the southern viewpoint. The migration of professionals to the south and west not only provided a natural constituency for the GOP but also increased the political importance of states like Florida, Texas and California whose increased representation amounted to 20 per cent of the total electoral college vote.[30] This was matched by an electoral decline in the north-eastern states which were a natural constituency for the Democrats. This increase in economic power and consequently political influence was exploited by Carter as he came to represent a new, more positive perception of the South.

If the 1970s saw major changes in America, not all of these were accepted by the public at large. It was this conservative backlash that was to have a major impact on the effectiveness of the Carter presidency. However, it was equally fair to say that Jimmy Carter as a southern politician was able to make some of those changes work in his favour when campaigning to become president. His simple style, candour about religion and the 'I will not lie to you' promise all helped to create a calm persona that harked back to a simpler time of a stable America that was aimed at a more conservative electorate.[31] The impact of these changes became more problematic when he was in office and had to implement his programme.

A presidential candidate in the 1970s was defined ideologically not just by his campaign and his party allegiance, but by his political friends, his opponents and by a proactive press. Once such views were established about a politician's ideology it was assumed that the relevant policies would be followed. A failure to deliver on such expectations would create a credibility gap with key elements of the electorate. Jimmy Carter, however, did not accept any ideological badge. He refused to be categorized as either a conservative or a liberal. When cornered on this issue early in the 1976 presidential campaign he said, 'I never characterise myself as a conservative, liberal or moderate and this is what distinguishes me from them.'[32] He sought throughout the 1976 campaign to avoid ideology by standing on the question of his character, but as a national figure he found himself scrutinized on both.

His early political years gave few clues as to his ideological leanings. His aides Jody Powell and Hamilton Jordan were fiercely loyal to Carter but had no strong political views themselves, whilst friends Bert Lance and Charles Kirbo were apolitical. Carter himself conspicuously avoided mentioning his ideology during elections but adjusted his position depending on the opponent. He was often linked with the new breed of southern liberal politicians due to his stance on Civil Rights and integration. His position politically was, however, more nuanced. He always linked support for Civil Rights and integration with a defence of the south's record. He also stepped very carefully around the conservative segregationist George Wallace. He never directly attacked Wallace, supporting him on busing and speaking at Wallace Appreciation Day but he refrained from endorsing him as a presidential candidate in 1972.[33] There was little evidence of strong liberal leanings despite the emphasis on reform and good government. The symbolic launch of his presidential campaign from FDR's home in Warm Springs, Georgia, was less about reviving the old New Deal coalition and more about better TV coverage and avoiding the traditional union Labour Day launch.[34] Carter suggested that President Harry S. Truman was his role model,[35] but there is some doubt about this. When he had an opportunity to spend time with Truman's long-term aide Clark Clifford, he did not ask one question about Truman or his administration.[36] The press and his Republican opponents believed that Carter was attempting in 1976 to be all things to all men and failing to satisfy any particular group.[37] Even some Democrats believed that he constantly shifted positions for political expediency. Mark Shields, Congressman Morris K. Udall's advisor, quipped that Carter 'had more positions than the Kama Sutra'.[38]

He was certainly more attuned to the conservative mood of the 1970s than many in his party. Some argued that Carter was an early New Democrat, a forerunner of Bill Clinton. Clinton's approach had strong echoes of Carter's when he said, 'The change we must make isn't liberal or conservative, it's both and it's neither.'[39] Suggestions by his staff such as Les Francis from congressional liaison, that he was an early New Democrat, socially liberal but strong on defence and fiscally conservative, only demonstrated the benefit of hindsight. Some of the measures Carter sought to implement could be categorized ideologically, but many could not, and often his more comprehensive proposals divided the country regionally.

As the presidential campaign progressed his espousal of traditional policies of the Democratic Party created an expectation from liberals that he would support their agenda in office. But his commitment to many liberal issues in the election was driven by the need to secure core Democratic Party support in an increasingly tight election. Carter acted as if ideology did not matter, backing liberal legislation in some instances, and conservative in others, pleasing neither side. This frustration and confusion were shown by the press, often in the form of cartoons.[40] Democrats like Senator Moynihan were just bemused. He told a Carter aide, 'the problem with your boss is that he is conservative on domestic issues and liberal on foreign policy issues and he ought to be the other way around.'[41] Carter was often on the opposite side of the argument from the liberal majority in his party. He recognized this anomaly when he said, 'In many cases I feel more at home with conservative Democratic and Republican members of congress than I do with the others, although the others, the liberals, vote for me more often.'[42] Carter did take what appeared to be ideological positions on some issues, but he never talked about them in those terms and there was no evidence that he was guided by such thinking.

If Carter was not prepared to define himself ideologically, he was happy to stand on his character. This did not however result in any clarity about who he was. Clark Clifford, in his autobiography, used Winston Churchill's quote about Russia to describe Jimmy Carter as 'a riddle wrapped in a mystery inside an enigma'.[43] According to one source, he 'may have been the psychologically most complicated presidential candidate this century'.[44] Historians who have studied the question of presidential character have focused on negative aspects of presidential behaviour, for example, the infidelities of John Kennedy and Bill Clinton, and the psychology of Richard Nixon. Jimmy Carter, whilst lacking their vices, is an extremely complex man.

Carter encouraged this uncertainty about him by refusing to be categorized by the media. He defined himself to the electorate by the roles that he had played in the past. In his first major national speech to the National Press Club, in 1974, he described himself as 'a Farmer, an Engineer, a Businessman, a Planner, a Scientist, a Governor and a Christian'.[45] This description which he used throughout the 1976 presidential campaign conspicuously avoided ideology. He also, unlike every other major presidential candidate, did not emphasize his military service except in the context of being an engineer and a scientist. These roles meant something to him and helped define not just who he was but how he sought to achieve his goals. His frustrated campaign speechwriter Patrick Anderson described the enigma of Carter as, 'Our hope, our despair, leader, and loose cannon. Machiavelli and Mr Rogers.'[46] Carter himself did not see this complexity. He told *Time* magazine, 'I don't think that I am that complex. I am pretty much what I seem to be.'[47] He ran his presidential campaign on the issue of his character, but this had consequences for both his staff and the public. His outward image of calm was coupled with a certain ruthlessness, particularly with the press. Some believed that journalists like James Wooten of the *New York Times* were on a Carter enemies list.[48] His National Security Advisor Zbigniew Brzezinski wrote of the famous Jimmy Carter smile being in fact three smiles, including the one to hide his anger.[49] He was an ambitious politician, confident in himself and his political strategy. He believed in rational policies based on intense study and analysis that would result in comprehensive solutions. He pushed himself hard to understand complexity. As a Georgian senator, he prided himself on reading every draft of a bill.[50] This approach, he believed, would be enough to persuade the electorate that correct legislation was being proposed without any political lobbying. He believed that he could explain his policies to the electorate without simplifying issues or creating slogans or themes to sell the 'message'.

The most revealing aspect of Carter's character was his training as an engineer. He described himself as being 'A trained engineer who prided himself on making technical judgements unburdened by ideology.'[51] He admitted that because of this training he liked to be personally involved 'so I can know the thought processes that go into the final decisions'.[52] There is a revealing comparison here between Carter and another engineer in the White House, Herbert Hoover. Like Carter, Hoover sought technical solutions to problems but also was widely regarded as a failed president. It was a comparison that conservative commentators took delight in highlighting, calling him 'Jimmy Hoover'.[53] It was Carter the engineer who set the structure and the tone for the solutions he prescribed for the country's ills. He was much more motivated by the method rather than the outcome. He focused on a process that was comprehensive, delivered by experts with no political input. He believed that this would produce policies that were uniform, simple to carry out, predictable and that would support the public good.[54] In doing so he was undeterred by the technical or political complexity of the problem as he believed that all problems were fixable.[55] This philosophy, which was reflected in Carter's legislative programme, revealed a certain naivety on his part.

Carter's character, the perception of being a good man, became a political asset for the campaign and his administration. But there were traits in Carter that were less attractive and were visible even before he took office. His competitiveness could overflow into meanness, whilst his preachiness palled on the public after a time. Less noticeable but more apparent when he became president were his stubbornness and his vanity – his need to demonstrate his intellectual superiority. Both became issues as he tried to deliver his programme in office. However, the first issue Carter had to address in 1976 was his faith.

A major part of Carter's life was his religious faith. A president's religious background had not been a controversial issue since the election of the Roman Catholic John F. Kennedy in 1960. Since then, presidential candidates had downplayed their religious convictions during campaigns. The 1976 election, in the wake of Watergate and Vietnam, changed all of that. Carter always emphasized that he was a 'born again' Christian and that it had a daily impact on his life. As president he continued to teach Sunday school and was happy to talk about his personal faith at press conferences. Carter refused however to directly tap into the potential political support that being an evangelical Christian could bring. In 1976, 34 per cent of the population claimed to be 'born again'.[56] The growing political power of the evangelical movement saw Carter as their natural champion. But he came from a liberal Baptist tradition based around an altruistic social agenda whilst the evangelical movement was becoming increasingly conservative. By 2001 the Carters had become so alienated from the movement that they left their Church's hierarchy (Southern Baptist Convention) over the issue of women's rights.[57] Whilst Carter was open about his faith, he argued that it would not impact on his presidency. This approach would attract criticism from both liberals and evangelicals. He worked hard during the campaign to normalize his faith in the mind of the public by arguing that being 'born again' was a typical experience for Christians.[58] He was not always successful. A thoughtful interview about his faith became subsumed by arguments about the magazine he chose (*Playboy*) and his off-the-cuff comments which proved harmful to him during the election campaign.[59]

His faith provided him with a strong moral stance on all his political activities. His speeches always had a moral tone with his aversion to both ceremony and interest groups reflecting fundamental religious teaching. In government he ensured that his administration stayed ethical even at times at the expense of common sense. He unnecessarily vetoed Federal funding for a paved road in his hometown[60] and refused to sanction a personal birthday celebration as part of a fundraiser.[61] Whether it was standing up to the White Citizens Council over desegregation in the 1960s or his continued focus on doing the 'right thing' whatever the political cost, Carter's religious beliefs had a major impact on his political career. This would become an issue when Carter the 'born again' Christian conflicted with Carter the politician.

According to his aide Stuart Eizenstat, Carter saw a clear separation between the politics of campaigning and governing. He certainly enjoyed the former but characterized the latter, dealing with politicians and interest groups, as 'tawdry'.[62] It seemed to his aide Lloyd Cutler that 'Carter more or less had to fight himself to be a good politician'.[63] Yet for a politician who found at least some of the process distasteful he was by 1976 highly successful. He came to believe, naively, that he could transfer his success as governor and as a campaigner directly to the White House. His presidential bid appeared to the Washington press as coming out of nowhere as he was an obscure governor from the South, but it was a product of meticulous long-term planning which took advantage of the political climate of the time and reforms to the political system that came into force in 1972. Within ten years many of these reforms were reversed, so Carter took advantage of a unique set of circumstances to help get elected as president.

He made the decision to run nearly four years before the election and he never wavered in his belief that he would win. Carter used the two years whilst still governor both to widen his experience and to build a network of contacts across the country. As governor he initiated and led trade delegations abroad to build up his foreign policy experience.[64] In 1973 he joined an influential think tank called the Trilateral Commission, which enabled him to broaden his experience in foreign policy and gain several high-profile contacts; some twenty of these later joined his administration.[65] It was one such contact, the President of Pepsi Cola, who persuaded *Time* magazine to put Carter and no other Southern governor on its cover in 1971.[66] He used his appointment as Chair of the Democratic Campaign Committee to raise his profile across the country and recruit future campaign workers by campaigning for Democratic candidates in the 1974 midterm elections.[67] To help establish his network after these elections Carter wrote not only to the winners to congratulate them but also to the losers to solicit their advice.[68] These contacts once made were maintained. Mark Siegel, the Executive Director of Carter's campaign, told the *Washington Post*: 'At every wedding, birth and funeral in a Democratic family there were flowers from Jimmy.'[69] Carter and Jordan used the experience gained during the 1974 mid-terms to build the Carter campaign book for his presidential bid.

Carter entered the primaries with certain disadvantages. He was a relatively unknown southern governor with no major national backers, limited funding and no Washington experience. Carter was helped by being able to follow a detailed plan put together by Jordan. It established a centrally run campaign based in Atlanta with little party interference, which carefully managed his scarce resources.[70] There was also an effective media strategy that helped raise the candidate's profile in critical states. The early national coverage of Carter on the cover of *Time* magazine[71] and his later speech at the National Press Club in 1974 were the exceptions as his campaign team used the local media to raise Carter's profile during the primary races. He was also helped by a dearth of national rivals, who either did not run (Edward Kennedy), withdrew from the race early (Walter Mondale) or simply followed the wrong tactics. As a result, at no point did he have a consistent challenger throughout the primary campaign and his opponents failed to gain any momentum. Carter on the other hand used the new electoral rules in the acquisition of delegates through primaries to maximize his advantage.[72] He used his limited resources to establish momentum in the early primaries, and this enabled him to gain federal campaign funding. This was not without risk. Joel McLearly, Carter's National Finance Director, admitted that there was no campaign structure beyond the Florida primary, which Carter had to win.[73] Jordan's strategy was to build momentum and increase media attention early by defeating the conservative George Wallace in the South. The plan was to target Wallace's constituency and counter his populist appeal by being better qualified and a more responsible alternative.[74] He identified eighteen key journalists/opinion formers for Carter to woo. These individuals worked for national organizations, but many were southern born who wanted someone other than Wallace to succeed. Carter's defeat of Wallace in Florida was also helped by the more liberal candidates staying away. This enabled Carter to take more conservative positions and help focus media attention on Wallace's health (he had been shot in 1972). Carter's success was not just about campaign strategy. As a candidate he tapped into the anti-Washington sentiment across the country. He stood as an outsider, a new face with a track record as a governor and more than anything else someone who could be trusted.

He was also an excellent, resilient campaigner with a strong personal touch. This was highlighted on the Iowa campaign trail when talking to small groups at factory gates or on farms.[75] There is no doubting Carter's achievement in gaining the Democratic nomination given his lack of national status and major supporters. However, his primary campaign was not flawless. He lost nine out of the sixteen primaries he took part in and often when Carter visited a state to campaign his poll ratings went down.[76] The Democratic Party reforms had increased the importance of primaries which favoured Carter as an early starter, so even a surprise defeat in New York was quickly followed by a success in another primary in Wisconsin.[77] Jordan's planning coupled with Carter's tireless campaigning ensured he arrived at the convention in New York with his nomination secured. The convention and the subsequent campaign would prove a further test of Carter's political skills. Walking through the delegates at the convention to make his acceptance speech turned out to be the zenith of his campaign. Anderson commented, 'if he had gone home and stayed there, he might have won by a landslide. Unfortunately, he campaigned.'[78]

Once the presidential campaign proper started, Carter persisted with the strategies that had brought him success. He continued to stand as an outsider from Washington focusing on his own character ('I would never lie to you') and symbolic acts such as launching his campaign against President Gerald R. Ford at FDR's home in Warm Springs. Carter also continued to rely on the network of volunteers (dubbed 'the Peanut Brigade') that he had built up during the primaries, but these groups tended to bypass the state party apparatus. The campaign was still run centrally by a small team in Atlanta. This was to keep control of limited campaign funding; however, it resulted in organizational failings. This included many unanswered calls to party officials causing resentment that continued into his administration. The campaign team were slow to engage the key players in the Democratic Party. As head of his party, Carter needed their support and to campaign on behalf of local candidates, but this weakened his stance as a candidate who claimed to be an outsider. In the summer of 1976, President Ford had barely been in office two years. But although he was well liked personally, his administration was beset with problems. His economic record was poor with high inflation and unemployment. His pardoning of former President Richard Nixon was very unpopular, and many believed that this ultimately cost him his presidency. As a result, his campaign was in many ways similar to Carter's in that he focused less on policy but more on his personal qualities and his ability to unite the country. This approach was reflected in his television adverts.[79]

Carter steered away from controversial policy issues by straddling the positions of both parties. He only sought to be radical on non-controversial issues that did not define him ideologically such as government reorganization and ethics. These reforms were linked to creating a government 'as good as its people'[80] and resonated with the public disquiet arising from Watergate. President Ford's campaign and the newspapers highlighted Carter's 'fuzziness' on policy issues which increased pressure on Carter to change his approach, particularly as his poll lead, initially 35 points, had started to decline alarmingly. As the campaign progressed Carter was forced to move away from general themes towards specific campaign commitments that were very much in line with traditional Democratic Party values. He did try to reassure the public about his perceived vagueness on issues in his famous interview with *Playboy* magazine in September 1976. In this he argued that he was not an ideologue but tried to analyse each question individually on its merits. He further sought in the same interview to reassure the public, particularly in the North, about his religious beliefs as a 'born again' Christian and its potential impact on his presidency. Unfortunately, whilst his answers were both honest and thoughtful, the article will forever be remembered for his use of language at the end of the interview. Phrases like 'lusting in my heart' and 'screwing around' grabbed the headlines.[81] This language shocked his conservative supporters and reinforced an image of strangeness with the rest of the electorate. As a result, his lead in the polls was cut by 10 points within a single day.[82] The long-term impact of the *Playboy* interview has been exaggerated but it did reinforce an image of Carter as someone who was a little weird. This contradicted the image that Carter had carefully crafted throughout his campaign and would seek to maintain during his presidency. This was of someone who was honest, trustworthy and more than anything else competent. The ability to sustain this as president would become a major challenge for him.

The three televised presidential debates were an opportunity for both candidates to promote their agendas. The debates proved to be highly popular with the electorate, with approximately half of American households watching the first debate and over 90 per cent watching at least one of the three.[83] Carter acknowledged in the first debate that this was an opportunity to establish in the minds of the electorate exactly where he stood on issues. His acceptance speech at the Democratic Convention earlier in the campaign had continued his anti-Washington theme but had not focused on specific policies other than vague commitments on cutting government waste, tax reform and reducing unemployment.[84] Whilst the debate did not by any means cover all his commitments it did enable him to articulate the key ideas of his campaign. These included the reduction of unemployment to 3 per cent supported by increased economic growth, controlled inflation and a balanced budget by 1981. He proposed reform of the tax system which he labelled a disgrace, including tax cuts for the middle and lower incomes but also the closing of tax loopholes. He called for reform of the government structure, including the reduction in the number of agencies. He made further commitments on government finances, the pardoning of Vietnam draft evaders and mentioned as an aside a comprehensive energy policy.[85] Whilst it was generally accepted that the overall result of the three debates was a draw, it did give Carter a national platform to articulate policies that he would later seek to implement.

Despite accusations from his opponents of 'fuzziness' by the end of the campaign Carter had taken 51 positions and made 186 pledges, most of which were aligned to the party platform, including on health, welfare, childcare and social security reforms as well as housing subsidies.[86] This was in addition to his commitments on the economy, to restructure the federal government and reform energy policy. This was significantly more than any of his three presidential predecessors.[87] It would form the basis of Carter's domestic policy agenda and given his pledge of competence create the expectation from the electorate of a substantial legislative programme. It also secured him support during the campaign from key Democratic constituencies that enabled him to win in major industrial states. The American Federation of Labor and Congress of Industrial

Organizations (AFL-CIO) support alone provided 120,000 campaign workers, made 10 million calls and sent out 80 million pieces of literature.[88] To gain office Carter was prepared to compromise when necessary; his public embrace of the corrupt Democratic boss of Chicago, Mayor Richard Daley, ensured his support in Illinois although it damaged his image for probity.[89] As the presidential campaign progressed these more liberal commitments made Carter appear less of an outsider, more a mainstream politician. This damaged him in the polls as the gap between himself and Ford continued to close. Yet Carter did not seek to link the commitments of his campaign to an appealing overall theme. Walter Mondale, his running mate, wanted Anderson to do this for Carter but Anderson was unable to persuade him. Carter continued to campaign on himself, his character and his overall competence which he believed were in line with the voter's need for an efficient, honest government.[90] In the end the result on 2 November 1976 was closer than many had predicted. Carter beat Ford 50 to 48 per cent in the popular vote. Given Carter's control of the southern states, Ford needed to win six of the eight so-called battleground states; he won five. Carter won the Electoral College 297-241.

Getting elected president was Jimmy Carter's greatest political achievement. He demonstrated supreme confidence that he would win right from the start. This was supported by innovative campaign planning and an energetic, effective campaigning style. He fed off the 'national psyche' by appealing to voters' deeper needs for honesty and efficiency in government in the wake of the Watergate scandal.[91] However, it still turned out to be a close election given that he had a 35 per cent lead at the time of the Democratic Convention. Voter scepticism of both candidates was summed up by the acerbic William Loeb of New Hampshire's *Manchester Union Leader* in the headline announcing the result as 'Shifty beats Stupid'.[92] Commenting on his victory Jimmy Carter said, 'I owe special interests nothing. I owe the people everything.'[93] This was not how those interest groups, or a Democratic Congress, saw it. This would become a limit on the incoming president's room for manoeuvre in trying to deliver on his campaign commitments.

His campaign agenda was reformist but not radical, with an emphasis on good governance with policies that would demonstrate competence. Stuart Eizenstat, now Carter's domestic policy advisor, outlined in a speech to the Washington Press Club what good governance meant. He talked about openness, efficiency backed by a substantial reorganization, better targeting of government programmes and addressing long-term fundamental issues.[94]

These policies were to be driven not by ideology, but a process derived from careful analysis of objective data by experts.[95] The assumption by the president was that good policy would be accepted by legislators because the proposed solutions would be well researched and objective. However, such success would be dependent upon how effectively Carter could manage Congress and engage with the American people.

A question of competence

Jimmy Carter's inaugural address on a cold morning on 20 January 1977 was short (only fourteen minutes) and lacked the rhetorical flourish of his Democratic predecessors. But it highlighted many aspects of Carter's character. There was an emphasis on religious themes. He talked about the moral character of the nation and about the limits of American power – 'We cannot afford to do everything … We must simply do our best.'[1] Few if any critics regarded the speech as inspiring but many commented on his decision after his address to leave the motorcade and walk with his family up Pennsylvania Avenue. Lesley Stahl of CBS exclaimed the gesture was 'game changing'.[2] It was seen as symbolic of his presidency, one that was closer to the people. However, as a harbinger of the criticism to come, long-term critic William Safire of the *New York Times* described the speech as ranking, in comparison with previous presidents, as 'slightly above Millard Fillmore and not quite up to Calvin Coolidge'. He finished by describing the walk as a stunt.[3] Despite scepticism Carter had created during his campaign an expectation that he would be an honest and trustworthy president who would run a competent, efficient government.

Carter had given an early indication of his vision for his future administration in his speech to the National Press Club in Washington on 12 December 1974. He spoke of 'a government that is honest and competent with clear purpose and strong leadership can work with the American people to meet the challenges of the present and future'.[4] Competence, specifically his own, was to become an important theme for his campaign. To be a successful president he would not only have to become the nation's leader, but an effective legislator, an efficient head of his administration and its communicator-in-chief. As president he would be defined ideologically by his political friends, opponents and by a proactive press. Carter, however, did not accept any ideological badge, refusing to be categorized either as a conservative or a liberal, much to the frustration of journalists. Yet he was not afraid of labels and throughout his campaign went out of his way to define himself in terms of the roles he had played in his past. 'I am a Farmer, an Engineer, a Businessman, a Planner, a Scientist, a Governor, and a Christian.'[5] His life experiences had a profound influence on him personally and on his presidency. It affected how he managed his administration, implemented his legislative programme, dealt with the media and how he communicated with the public. Ultimately it shaped the development of his domestic policies.

As the election result became closer, Carter made additional campaign commitments.[6] This was not unusual but many of these largely liberal measures were forced upon him by his need to shore up support from his own party. Newly elected presidents were expected to utilize the period between their election and inaugural address to consult and establish a prioritized set of proposals that would turn campaign promises into concrete plans for legislation. Whilst Carter did consult widely during this transition, he displayed from the beginning a marked reluctance both to prioritize his commitments and to provide an overall theme for his new administration. He often quoted the religious philosopher Reinhold Neibuhr in his speeches. One of Niebuhr's most famous prayers was, 'God give us grace to accept with serenity the things that cannot be changed, courage to change the things which should be changed, and the wisdom to distinguish the one from the other.'[7] Throughout his administration Carter could not bring himself to do this. He freely admitted that 'Everybody warned me not to take on too many projects so early in the administration but it's almost impossible for me to delay something that I see needs to be done.'[8] His advisors, including Bert Lance, knew this was a problem as it was certain to create a legislative log jam in Congress.[9] However, attempts to limit presidential goals and delay some initiatives such as the Panama Canal Treaty to a possible second term were ignored. The historian James McGregor Burns believed that as far as his agenda was concerned Carter had 'strategic myopia'.[10]

A systematic process to consult within the administration and with Congress was not created until April 1977. This was to become the first in a series of comprehensive plans over the next two years, produced by Vice President Walter Mondale, to establish the administration's priorities. Objectives were broken down into 30-, 60- and 90-day plans involving Carter's personal commitments and communications.[11] There were several reasons why ultimately these attempts failed. The complexity of the legislation and the difficulty in gaining support in Congress represented one factor. Secondly, only Carter had the authority to delay any legislation, but he remained extremely reluctant to do so. Indeed, as the process developed those measures that were given priority tended to increase. Sixty per cent of proposed legislation that was sent to Congress had priority status, which resulted in many measures losing momentum.[12] As a consequence the agreed agenda was invariably unmanageable. For example, the 1978 agenda had thirty-eight items on it.[13] This can be contrasted with the Kennedy administration's focus on just five 'Must Bills'.[14] Thirdly, Carter did not attempt to articulate his agenda's key themes which often resulted in confusion over administration priorities. His Communications Director Gerald Rafshoon tried to persuade Carter in the autumn of 1978 to promote bills to reduce waste and fraud, but this conflicted with the work of the vice president who wanted priority given to themes of inflation and compassion.[15] This confusion was never fully resolved. There was also dissent within the administration with members continuing to argue that the president's agenda was overloaded. In November 1978, Jordan was expressing concern that the priorities for the following year would not give the president enough time to build momentum for the 1980 election.[16] The White House, however, was more interested in the promotion of the volume of its legislation than its quality or cohesiveness. This was also reflected in Carter's speeches which were in effect a check list of achievements rather than a vision of the changes he was trying to accomplish.

To be effective and to project his power as president, Carter was dependent upon his own abilities and how well his staff and cabinet operated in supporting him. He therefore had to decide on the structure of his team, picking the right people and managing them day to day. Carter, like any other new president, had personal qualities that would both help and hinder him as a leader. He was highly analytical, had excellent concentration and a passion for accuracy. His capacity for absorbing information became legendary; Carter wrote that he read 300 pages and five or six newspapers a day, helped by speed reading training he and his wife received early in his administration.[17] The White House files are filled with Carter commenting on everything imaginable, including the White House mail, staff grammar and even the subject of White House pens.[18] The press picked up on this theme, notably questioning Carter's involvement in allocating the use of the White House tennis court.[19] For Carter finding time to do 'homework' was a crucial element of the policy process because that gave him the detailed understanding of issues that would enable him to make the right decision. Critics of his administration argued that it was impossible for any president, even Carter, to be involved in that level of detail. The increase in paperwork did cause problems. Carter's initial plan of working a 55-hour week with 15 hours reading had by April 1977 risen to 80 hours with 30 hours reading. Carter recognized the problem and was regularly complaining to his staff who in response kept providing information on his workload. He admitted that although he had advice from Democratic congressional leader Tip O'Neill to cut back, he could not do it.[20]

Carter exacerbated the problem because of his management style. He preferred communication on paper to face-to-face discussion and as a result his aides like Jordan found writing memoranda was the most effective way of influencing him.[21] This resulted in an increase in the volume of memoranda sent to him as, except for his Press Secretary Jody Powell and the First Lady, all his staff put their cases in writing, knowing the prodigiously hard-working Carter would read them and send them back promptly. Aide Harrison Welford said, 'The memos we send in sometimes come back with more comments than our original text. I don't know how long he can keep this up, but he has a passion for getting involved in the details of a lot of these decisions.'[22] After his first year, comments on internal White House and non-policy matters declined but the flow of paper to him did not. This developed into a long-term perception of Carter's leadership style in the media. Journalists equated his undoubted attention to detail and his extraordinary ability to absorb information quickly with an inability to delegate and a tendency to micromanage the creation of policy. This perception was simply not true as with the possible exception of energy policy, Carter delegated the development of policy entirely to his cabinet. In initiating new policies his often-vague guidance to his cabinet secretaries, followed by a hands-off approach, was to become the norm for Carter. Ironically, it was often this lack of interference in the development of policy that was to cause problems as cabinet members struggled to understand Carter's wishes.

Carter was not a natural manager of people; he was by nature solitary. He admitted that 'When I am now in the White House in Washington, my greatest hunger is to be alone, away from the security officers, away from the press, and to be in the fields and woods again.'[23] Bert Carp, a member of the Domestic Policy Group (DPG), said that Carter rarely talked to aides below Eizenstat or cabinet secretary level and he believed that Carter did not really like having staff.[24] Even with people whom he had worked with for a long time he rarely complimented them on good work but always criticized sloppiness.[25] In keeping with his complex character, the Jimmy Carter who berated Jordan for the poor organization of his staff meetings would banter with Powell over an amusing article.[26] He wrote many warm personal notes to politicians, members of the public and even on occasion a journalist.[27] Whatever his personal qualities Carter entered the White House with limited governmental experience and a long list of campaign commitments. He recognized this: 'I have a substantial lack of experience and knowledge about the history of government here in

Washington, the interrelationship among agencies, the proper division of authority and responsibility between Congress and the President.[28] To help overcome these disadvantages, he had to manage an effective transition to office, agree a working structure and pick staff and a cabinet with relevant experience.

Carter was the first presidential candidate to put significant resources into transition planning. He appointed a Georgia lawyer, Jack Watson, as its leader with fifty staff, many of whom had Washington experience.[29] Carter heavily promoted the work of the team to the press. They worked on draft policies, and established a talent advisory group which made twenty-seven recommendations on appointments as well as advice on staffing structure.[30] They operated in isolation from the campaign which unfortunately proved to be the team's undoing. When the election was over it was perceived that Watson's recommendations on White House structure, which included appointing a chief of staff and a raft of policies, were a threat to Jordan as campaign manager and Eizenstat who was head of the campaign policy team.[31] Carter was forced to arbitrate and found, not surprisingly, in favour of his campaign staff. This resulted in the rejection of virtually all the work done by the transition team and the potential advantages gained by early planning were lost. Carter did not even read Watson's proposals on White House organization.[32] Carter's Democratic successor, Bill Clinton, was to make the same mistakes over his transition in 1992. There were also delays in the appointments process caused by Carter's insistence that there were to be a woman and a minority candidate on the shortlist for each job.[33]

The role of the vice president was resolved quickly. Walter Mondale, after the election, presented Carter with a detailed paper which not only defined a substantial role for himself but the integration of his staff into the main White House structure.[34] Carter accepted his recommendations without amendment, paving the way for a meaningful role for Mondale in the new administration. This was a major departure from previous practice and would set a precedent for future vice presidents. When Joe Biden was elected as vice president to Barack Obama in 2008, the first public figure he called was Walter Mondale.[35]

In establishing how his staff were to operate in the White House, Carter was driven by one major concern: access. He did not want intermediaries between himself and any of his advisors because 'they fractured his concept of comprehensive policy making'.[36] He therefore replicated a similar model of decentralized staffing to the one he had operated as governor. This was the 'spokes of the wheel' model with key aides being given access to the president both face to face and by memorandum. Carter's ability to absorb information would, he believed, prevent confusion in the policy process. From his viewpoint, it maximized his personal control because his aides worked closely under his direction and therefore only the president knew everything.[37] Carter did not look at the White House in organizational terms. To him his staff were not there to help with the business of government but to be more a family unit to support him.[38] He was always more comfortable dealing one to one with staff he knew and trusted. He never liked staff meetings and did not meet his senior staff team in his first two years in office.[39] He was very concerned that if he recruited a chief of staff as an alternative approach, which was recommended by his transition team, he would be replicating the maligned structure under Nixon. This would not sit well with the image of Open Government. Carter may have said that he did not want a 'Sherman Adams in his office' but it was being seen to have a 'Bob Haldeman', that really concerned him.[40] In addition, the natural choice for the chief of staff role was Jordan who was his key advisor, but he was both unwilling and lacked the administrative skills for the role.[41] Finally, having no chief of staff gave Carter a sense of being in control and he was supremely confident in his ability to deal with ten direct reports as well as cabinet members, the vice president and his wife. He said that 'Unless there is a holocaust, I'll take care of everything the same day it comes in.'[42] The success or failure of White House staff structure was inevitably linked to Carter's concept of cabinet government. As part of his approach to Open Government he believed that cabinet secretaries should initiate policy and manage subsequent legislation. This would, in theory, limit the role of White House staff but even in these circumstances there were concerns expressed about the risks of honouring a campaign pledge for a 20 per cent cut in staff by April 1977.[43] The later head of the Office of Management of the Budget (OMB) James McIntyre believed this cut caused major disruption.[44]

Carter sought to replicate his experience as governor when he had a close working relationship with cabinet members, but the size of the task prevented such relationships developing. Carter's belief in cabinet government did not extend to collective responsibility. Despite the large number of cabinet meetings, fifty-nine in the first two years, there were no collective discussions or debates on issues. Meetings quickly deteriorated into 'show and tell sessions'. Cabinet members were however given a wide range of discretion. They were expected to run their own departments with no interference from the White House and they could be free to have the final say on appointing their own staff.[45] As to the policies they were to follow, at Carter's request, Cabinet members were given copies of all his major speeches[46] but otherwise they were left to their own devices. Carter believed that 'the staff and Cabinet Officers would prefer to have minimal participation by me until the final decision point is reached.'[47] He was to follow this maxim with the possible exception of energy policy throughout his administration.

Carter's relationships with individual members of the cabinet were cordial but not warm. Secretary of Agriculture Bob Bergland said it was nearly three years before he and his wife were invited to dinner at the White House.[48] While many cabinet members had complaints about White House staff none had any about Carter personally. All at various times were asked about how easy it was to gain access to him, and none had complaints on that score. He picked individuals from a range of backgrounds with only two, Cecil Andrus at the Department of the Interior and Bergland at Agriculture, representing any sort of interest group. Ray Marshall at Labour was picked against the direct advice of George Meany, head of the AFL-CIO. Carter described his cabinet appointments in terms of geographic diversity.[49] He was also one of the first presidents to appoint women and minority groups throughout his administration. In terms of ideology the Carter cabinet represented a range from the liberal Secretary of Labor to the conservative Attorney General, Griffin Bell. Most were picked for their administrative skills rather than innovation and only one was a friend, Bert Lance, who was chosen to head up the OMB. James Schlesinger was selected as his special advisor on energy because Carter got on with him despite reservations from his team.[50] Given his later sacking in July 1979 one would assume that the relationship between Joseph Califano, Secretary of Health, Education and Welfare (HEW), and Carter would have been difficult but despite policy differences they were on cordial terms. There were numerous examples of Carter writing notes of praise and support for Califano's work at HEW.[51] Califano did receive criticism from the president but as Carter himself admitted, it was the relationship of Califano and Mike Blumenthal, the Secretary of the Treasury, with White House staff that proved critical in the eventual decisions to sack both men in July 1979.[52] Their departure was to signify the escalating conflict between cabinet members and White House staff.

The degree of independence given to each member of the cabinet resulted in disputes with the White House. The situation was made worse by the president's failure to give specific political guidance on the broad policy issues that he asked the departments to resolve. According to Jordan the only place where politics and policy came together in the White House was with the president and that proved far too late in the process to prevent mistakes.[53] Carter assumed that a comprehensive solution to policy issues would naturally win public and congressional support, but his staff were fighting political fires from his first day in office. Cabinet members were appointing individuals into departmental positions without consulting the relevant member of congress. After prompting from Mondale, Carter instructed his cabinet to check any appointments with Jordan,[54] but the complaints persisted. There were also problems over communication, with each department issuing conflicting messages on policy. Carter wrote a personal note to the cabinet in April 1977 requesting one lead spokesman on major issues[55] but this was not fully implemented until the following year when Jerry Rafshoon was appointed as Communications Director. Cabinet members were accused of leaking to the press and there was often counter leaking from White House staff. Press comments forced Carter on more than one occasion to deny in public that he was unhappy with certain cabinet members.[56] Discontent from White House staff culminated in a highly critical personal memorandum from Jordan to Carter. He listed the cabinet's failings, including inability to notify the White House of decisions, systematic leaks to the press, not responding to Congress, and lack of support for presidential polices. Jordan described Transport Secretary Brock Adams, as well as Califano and Blumenthal, as being disloyal. He further suggested that the whole cabinet was working against Carter's policy on the budget.[57]

Carter's practice of telling policy makers not to worry about the political implications of their proposals quickly became a problem. For example, the Department of Health's launch of an anti-smoking campaign had major political consequences for Carter in North Carolina where Governor James Hunt was a key supporter. A consequence of these organizational failures and a decline in the polls was the Camp David Domestic Summit of May 1978. Carter agreed to White House staff demands to give them a major role in coordinating policy and handling the political issues arising out of cabinet policies through the process of Presidential Review and Decision Memoranda.[58] Jordan began running meetings of policy staff to improve coordination across the administration, although Carter continued to maintain that a chief of staff was unnecessary.[59] Whilst approving these changes Carter did not appear to be very active in the debate. Despite this weakening of cabinet independence there was agreement that the reforms brought improvements in both coordinating policy and managing the political consequences.[60] The development of Anne Wexler's outreach role and her use of 'Task Forces' was also regarded as a major success. This approach, which brought together relevant cabinet departments, White House staff and external support for individual policies, had its signature success with the passage of the Panama Canal Treaty bill in 1978.[61] All of this did not result in the end of cabinet government, but it curtailed the power of individual secretaries to act independently. It did not stop, however, the leaks or suggestions that staff were deliberately trying to undermine members of the cabinet and so mutual mistrust remained.[62] This situation continued until July 1979.

Carter's insistence on cabinet government had a detrimental effect on White House efficiency but to many in the Washington press the problem was with the quality of his staff. Journalists and politicians often claimed that the Georgians he appointed lacked the crucial experience of working in Washington.[63] Once these opinions formed, they were very difficult to shift. This was particularly true of Frank Moore and his congressional liaison team.[64] Even the more positive cabinet members like Bob Bergland regarded the administration as 'loaded with honest amateurs'.[65] The experienced aide Anne Wexler said of Jordan 'he is a very nice courteous young man who is about as far out of his depth as anybody I have ever known'.[66] Others questioned staff competence. Clark Clifford, a Washington insider brought in to advise Carter and Attorney General Bell, blamed the Bert Lance resignation over financial irregularities on poor staff work.[67] Carter was criticized for appointing Georgians to six of the nine special assistants' posts. What really mattered to Carter was not that they were from the same state but that they had personal experience of working with him. Eizenstat may well have had experience of working in Washington for Hubert Humphrey but as Carter said, 'he didn't really have those four years of experience and training within state government to know exactly how I did things.'[68] There was some recognition of a shortage of DC experience and 'wise men' were brought in on an ad hoc basis. Such discussions were held with senior figures, notably Clark Clifford and Averell Harriman, but this was not sustained.[69] To the press, however, much was made of the Georgian influence and some of this criticism smacked of regional prejudice and outright snobbery. The high-profile Jordan and Powell on one occasion were described by speechwriter Patrick Anderson as 'a couple of raw boned, narrow eyed South Georgian thugs'.[70] Not to be outdone, Meg Greenfield of Newsweek described the Georgians as 'bare-chested peanut feeding yahoos'.[71] By 1979 Carter had hired several senior staff with DC experience but the tone of the criticism persisted.

Carter saw himself as a leader who was taking on Washington and believed he had the skills to evaluate options and make the best decisions. He had only two real friends in politics and after Charles Kirbo declined to take a job in his administration that left only Bert Lance. He made no new friends whilst he was president[72] He and Rosalyn did not participate in the Washington social scene which was noted in the Washington press.[73] The First Lady commented, 'If there is one thing Jimmy dislikes more than anything it is a cocktail party or reception or dinner party every night.'[74] He did bring with him into the

White House two long-term associates, Hamilton Jordan and Jody Powell. As press secretary, Powell saw Carter daily, but he had no influence on policy. Jordan's role, at least initially, was vague given Carter's rejection of the chief of staff model. Jordan focused mainly on the appointments process but his access through memoranda was important and unlike other staff members he was sufficiently confident of his relationship with Carter to be critical of the operation of the White House and Carter personally.[75] But Carter's major source of personal advice within the administration was Bert Lance. Over and above access to Carter's office, Lance had a weekly lunch with the president as well as regular games of tennis. He was able to use his influence, for example, to tone down Carter's performance at budget meetings, where his detailed knowledge often intimidated staff, and to abandon plans to save energy by turning off the lights on the Lincoln Memorial.[76] Lance said that he and long-term supporter Charles Kirbo were Carter's only two sources of candid advice.[77] This was not quite accurate given Jordan's influence but with Kirbo visiting Washington infrequently, the resignation of Lance in September 1977 due to alleged financial irregularities in his bank dealings in Georgia was a personal blow to Carter. He acknowledged at his press conference that he did not believe that Lance could be replaced.[78] Lance had credibility both within and beyond the administration and was seen as a fixer. Kirbo described Lance as being 'best at cementing ties with key members of congress, with Cabinet members and with Business and Finance leaders'.[79] Carter lost the option of saying to staff 'talk to Bert about that'.[80] His departure also curtailed the influence of the OMB because while his successor, Jim McIntyre, was trusted for his mastery of the detail and grew in influence, he lacked Lance's political skills.

When Lance resigned the role of fixer was mainly taken up by Vice President Mondale. He had a regular weekly lunch with the president and was to play an influential role firefighting on Carter's behalf. As Carter ran into trouble with Congress, he used Mondale as a bridge builder to facilitate deals, for example on the Water Projects and the Farm Bill.[81] A measure of how Carter valued Mondale was his swift response to articles in the press suggesting that his vice president was losing influence. He called journalists from the *New York Times* and *LA Times* to deny this.[82] However, after Lance, Carter's only source of personal advice was his wife Rosalyn who remained his political partner throughout his term in office. The indications of how he valued her role came in his decision to send her to South America on his behalf, her sitting in at cabinet meetings and her involvement with issues like mental health and the Equal Rights Amendment (ERA). No archival evidence is currently available that confirms the extent of her influence other than the word of Carter and his aides. But for Carter there was no doubt about her importance. Speaking in 1978, he said that 'We've been married 31 years and the personal partnership has been there all the time.' He confirmed that he discussed almost every major issue of his presidency with his wife.[83]

In terms of morale one of Carter's more experienced staff, Anne Wexler, believed that the White House was the 'least turf conscious place she had ever worked'.[84] But there were some tensions between the Domestic Policy Group and OMB. Jim McIntyre thought Eizenstat's team represented the views of the interest groups they used to work for.[85] Eizenstat, whilst accepting OMB's technical competence, thought that they were politically naive. More seriously some of this disagreement spread into fundamental areas of policy. The administration's increasing emphasis on fighting inflation was often undermined by leaks from White House staff.[86] Carter's attempts to distinguish his personal views on abortion from his neutral public stance were undermined by an open rebellion led by Midge Constanza, the Special Assistant for Public Liaison, who organized a petition of White House staff.[87] The main cause of tension, however, came from the failure of Carter to deliver a coherent policy development process. Initially cabinet secretaries and their advisors could largely ignore White House staff but as they became aware that their policies required support across the administration, the role of Eizenstat's team in coordination became important. This increase in their power following the Camp David Domestic Summit of May 1978 resulted in a reduction in cabinet secretaries' authority.[88] These reforms did bring about improvements in White House efficiency. Yet tensions and problems persisted until the cabinet government model was finally abandoned in July 1979 and a chief of staff appointed. The new structure and the appointment of three experienced 'outsiders' – Lloyd Cutler, Hedley Donovan and Alonzo McDonald – further improved the effectiveness of the White House. Whether an earlier implementation of these changes would have significantly improved the administration's record seems unlikely given the serious problems Carter faced when dealing with Congress.

One of the main challenges for Carter if he was to be seen as competent was to ensure the passage of his legislative programme. To succeed he needed to have clear legislative goals, the skills to build support in Congress and across the country, and an effective congressional liaison team. Carter started his term of office with perceived weaknesses in all these areas. He inherited a Congress with a Democratic majority but one that was fractious with a new leadership and a complex structure of 165 committees and sub-committees that would make passage of all but the simplest legislation difficult.[89] His electoral mandate was perceived in Congress to be limited and his lack of any consistent ideology meant that he had no natural constituency within the legislature that would provide consistent support. Consequently, the White House had to build a new coalition for every major piece of legislation it proposed. This made Carter dependent upon his own political skills and the quality of staff around him. Not even his greatest supporters would claim that Carter was a successful legislator in the Lyndon Johnson mould. He did not understand how Washington politics operated or the consequences of ideological conflict. He made mistakes but, as Bergland argued, part of the reason Carter could not control Congress was that Congress could not control itself.[90]

A critical factor in legislative success was how well relationships with members of Congress were managed. It is here that Carter's role as a politician was crucial. Once the campaign was over Carter did not believe that politics in terms of deal-making had a role in government. Zbigniew Brzezinski, his national security advisor, commented that 'Carter made hardly any effort to disguise his disdain for domestic politics.'[91] He spent on average thirty hours a week in meetings with members of congress, but this was regarded as not enough.[92] Eizenstat commented on dealing with Congress, 'You have got to like dealing with politicians … and it just takes enormous energy,'[93] but Carter neither liked nor understood politicians. He emphasized that congressional constituencies were also his, as president, which challenged their legitimacy.[94] He refused to accept that he owed Congress a debt from the election and he believed that they should back his proposals because he had studied each issue and, unlike Congress, was unaffected by special interests.[95] Whilst Carter did accept that he lacked Washington experience, there was little effort to adjust to his new environment. Recognizing the problem, Lance tried to coach Carter on his lack of inter-personal skills in dealing with politicians and his staff. He often asked Carter to 'Repeat after me. Thank you for your good work.'[96]

Attempts by senior legislators in Washington to argue for Carter to pay them more attention had the same outcome as in Georgia. Carter was always prepared to meet them, but it was usually in groups, and he appeared to lack affinity with them or understand their viewpoint. Senator J. Bennett Johnson of Louisiana said that Carter 'didn't have any friends who were in Congress who you'd think of as being warm and friendly. He just didn't have any kind of relationship with anybody.'[97] When he gave an important speech at Notre Dame University, he failed to mention the local Democratic congressmen in the audience.[98] Another attempt at relationship building became almost comical when Rafshoon persuaded Carter to play tennis with Senators Lloyd Bentsen of Texas and Ernest 'Fritz' Hollings of South Carolina at the White House. Rafshoon's expectation was that the game would be followed by drinks and political discussion. Carter finished the game and left them standing there, assuming this was all that was required.[99] Although Carter was conscientious in making calls to congressmen at the request of his staff, he was reluctant to do so. Jody Powell stated, 'It's the damndest thing about him. He went all over the country for two years asking everybody he saw to vote for him for president, but he doesn't like to call a congressman and ask for his support on a bill.'[100] Senator Joe Biden from Delaware, one of Carter's earliest supporters, summed up the dilemma of a relationship with the president. After failing to get White House support for his busing proposal, Biden commented, 'Nixon had his enemies list and President Carter his friends list. I guess I'm on his friends list and I don't know which is worst.'[101]

Carter was not totally lacking in political guile. He could sometimes be pragmatic and when as governor his government reform bill was going through, he had ordered that no liberal measures be put forward so as not to antagonize conservative supporters of the bill.[102] He was also prepared to compromise to get legislation through but he was extremely reluctant to do deals that related to other policies.[103] Exceptions were his successful intervention with key Senators to enable the passage of the Panama Canal Treaty and when he ensured Congressman Mo Udall of Arizona's support for Government Reform by appointing one of Udall's friends to the Civil Aeronautics Board.[104] However he vetoed funds for a nuclear carrier sponsored by Senator Henry 'Scoop' Jackson of Washington despite needing his support on the Energy bill.[105] When Pennsylvanian Congressmen threatened to vote against all his legislation unless he approved their choice for a US Attorney role in Philadelphia, he told them 'to go to hell'.[106] Carter's need to do the right thing over political expediency would make his relationship with Congress problematic. Carter needed the support of senior members of congress if his legislative programme were to succeed. He did not expect problems because his party had majorities in both Houses.[107] He was disabused of this by his first difficult meeting with the Democratic Chairman of the Government Operations Committee, Jack Brooks of Texas, over Government Reform in January 1977.[108] Frank Moore, Carter's assistant for congressional liaison, advised Carter weeks before the inauguration that he 'must decide early your first initiatives and work with the leadership prior to January in making them feel they are part of it'.[109] For Carter the leadership referred to was House Speaker Thomas P. 'Tip' O'Neill and Senate Majority Leader Robert Byrd.

Tip O'Neill was a liberal congressman from Massachusetts and newly elected to the position of Speaker. Carter and O'Neill developed an effective working relationship. This was despite some ideological differences on the economy and O'Neill's fractious relationship with Carter's staff, particularly Jordan. Carter in his diaries talked of O'Neill as a friend whose loyalty he valued despite O'Neill's natural support for Teddy Kennedy.[110] This relationship was reflected in several warm personal notes from Carter.[111] O'Neill ensured that key measures passed the House, including the Energy bill, and he also influenced Carter's compromise on the Water Projects. O'Neill had no illusions about Carter's failures with Congress, but he later said that 'I miss Jimmy Carter. With his intelligence and energy and his tremendous moral strength, he would have been a great leader.'[112] No such sentiment was ever likely to be expressed by the newly elected Senate Majority Leader Robert Byrd.

Byrd made it clear from the start that his first loyalty was to his state, West Virginia, then to the Senate and finally to Carter.[113] Carter was prepared to defer to Byrd on the tactics he employed to get his legislation passed but it did not always work as Byrd often gave way to the will of the committee chairmen. Frank Moore's team were always conscious of the need to massage Byrd's bruised ego when he felt that he was not getting the attention he deserved.[114] To Byrd, however, Carter did not treat the Senate with due respect. He believed, with some justification, that Carter and his advisors still thought they could treat the Senate as if it were the Georgia legislature. He was unhappy about Carter's reversal of his decision in April 1977 on the $50 tax rebate which was taken without proper consultation or warning. Disturbingly for the administration, such decisions made Byrd question whether it would be wise for the Senate to support such policies if the president were going to undercut them by changing his mind.[115] There were also arguments with Byrd over the administration failing to consult him properly on local issues and appointments.[116] These were similar to disputes with Tip O'Neill but Byrd's anger and threats to withdraw support from key legislation were more direct.[117] Byrd, unlike O'Neill, fundamentally disagreed with much of the legislation that Carter sent to the Senate, but he did play a key role in helping Carter on some issues such as the Clinch River Reactor, the Korean Amnesty and auto pollution.[118] But Byrd did not prove an effective champion of the administration in passing legislation in the Senate as O'Neill had been in the House. In the final year of Carter's term, relations with the president had deteriorated to the point that Byrd was openly talking of removing Carter as Democratic nominee for the presidency.

Carter's failure to influence key members of Congress was a product of his inexperience and his attitude to making deals with politicians. He expected that a Congress led by his own party would follow his lead and accept his proposals. He believed that his experience as governor would be sufficient to deal with any issues. But Congress was proud of its own prerogatives and had an agenda of its own. The success or failure of any legislative programme was dependent upon the ability of the White House to mobilize support. This was more difficult for the administration because of the complex committee and sub-committee structure and the fragmented nature of the political parties. In addition, the Carter administration's predilection for comprehensive solutions placed increased strain on the legislative process. To be successful therefore Carter needed a proactive congressional liaison team.

Frank Moore made recommendations to Carter during the transition about the role his team should play. Nearly all of them were ignored and in general the president expressed little interest in how Moore's team operated.[119] In the Carter White House congressional liaison officials were to have no influence on policy development as that was to be the remit of cabinet departments that also had their own liaison staff. Moore initially had only 7 people compared with HEW which had 40, and Commerce 30 staff in this role.[120] Moore's team were picked for their ability to serve the president, not support Congress. Hence, they were organized under specific policy areas. This was against the advice of President Kennedy's Legislative Liaison, Lawrence J. O'Brien, who recommended that staff be aligned to build relationships with members of congress.[121] Moore did benefit from daily access to the president and had Carter's backing whether it was fending off criticism or him conscientiously making calls to key congressmen at Moore's request. Moore's prime role was to keep Carter informed of congressional views whilst at the same time maximizing the president's independence.[122] However, this method of operation soon ran into problems. Moore's appointment was perceived as a negative sign by Congress given his lack of Washington experience. His staff were overwhelmed by the legislative programme and a backlog of politically sensitive appointments. Their focus on policies resulted in issues raised by individual congressmen being mishandled. Attempts to devolve work to cabinet departments failed because congressmen felt fobbed off. They wanted access to the president and, if not him, either Jordan or Moore. The president was not inclined to talk to congressmen, and Jordan had agreed with Carter that he would step back from dealing with Congress. To Moore this was simply a numbers issue; the president's commitment to a 20 per cent cut in White House staff made the situation worse. There was also criticism of the lack of legislative experience within the White House. But this was not reflected in the administration as a whole because liaison staff working in ten out of the eleven government departments were led by staff with congressional backgrounds.[123]

Delays in transition resulted in avoidable errors at the start of his administration. Even before he began in the role, Moore had acquired a reputation for ignoring queries from congressmen. This was due to an initial misunderstanding about his role in the campaign,[124] but was made worse by the continued failure of his staff to deal with congressional requests.[125] There were several high-profile mistakes over appointments and the award of government grants. This was often caused by decisions made by cabinet departments but nevertheless Moore got the full force of congressional anger. During the first year there were a series of high-profile complaints by Senators James O. Eastland of Mississippi, Daniel Patrick Moynihan of New York, William D. Hathaway of Maine and the Chair of Ways and Means committee Albert C. Ullman of Oregon.[126] In addition Califano quoted Congressman Daniel D. Rostenkowski of Illinois, Chief Deputy Whip and one of the Democratic leadership team, about Moore stating that 'Every time he comes up here he costs us votes.'[127] The most serious falling out was with Tip O'Neill who found out from the newspapers that one of his key supporters Bob Griffin had been removed from the General Services Administration. Moore was banned from the Speaker's offices and Carter had to placate O'Neill and force Moore to apologize.[128] This incident was less Moore's fault than it was the administration's inability to coordinate its actions. For whatever reason, members of congress felt neglected. As a senior congressman put it, 'Two classes of people who don't want to be ignored, beautiful women and politicians. If you ignore them, you must be doing it on purpose because it is so obvious to everyone, they are singular people. They don't care for that kind of treatment.'[129] The frustration was often mutual. The Democratic leadership frequently blocked attempts by Carter to replicate tactics that had worked for him in Georgia. O'Neill and Byrd vetoed attempts by Carter to engage with the GOP even when there was a natural constituency of support on specific legislation.[130] To the Democratic leadership an invitation to key senators to discuss the energy bill, without consulting them, demonstrated ignorance of protocol but to the administration it was merely attempting to get the job done.[131]

The gradual move away from cabinet government resulted in increased resources and improved credibility for Moore's team. The recruitment of the experienced Bill Cable as House Liaison in May 1977 and Dan Tate as lead for the Senate in the following year resulted in a better understanding of Congress.[132]

The team also became important members of the task force approach to legislative challenges. Used successfully for the Panama Canal Treaty bill, this became the norm as a means of managing important legislation in the second half of the administration. This approach under Anne Wexler's Outreach team brought together the relevant cabinet departments, the press office, members of Moore's staff and departmental liaison to deliver key legislation. This was a recognition that with no natural coalition in Congress all major pieces of legislation required specific planning to enable passage. This coupled with regular Tuesday meetings between Carter and the Democratic leadership ensured that there was a more coordinated approach as his presidency unfolded.[133]

Despite the problems it encountered, Moore's team did provide a flow of valuable information to Carter. This took the form of weekly reports on congressional activity, which Carter continued to read and comment on assiduously.[134] They also provided briefings for when the president met members of congress which provided political and personal guidance to enable him to maximize his effectiveness.[135] Moore worked hard to persuade a reluctant Carter to spend more time in different environments with legislators to put across the administration's goals but also, Moore admitted, to educate Carter himself.[136] The introduction of more experienced staff and the realignment of the team won more plaudits. The move of Moore's team to the West Wing in 1978 also brought a more important benefit by integrating them with senior White House staff.[137] In the run up to the Camp David Domestic Summit, Moore's team conducted a review with the Democratic whips following the failure to pass the Consumer bill. The criticism moved beyond that of congressional liaison to the whole administration approach to Congress.[138] Many of the recommendations were endorsed by the president and implemented. Coordination improved, and the Democratic leadership were consulted more frequently. In October 1978 Byrd was moved to say that he had never seen such achievement and harmony between President and Congress in twenty-seven years.[139] Yet the question of Carter's perceived attitude to Congress remained an issue, particularly after his decision early in his administration to take on Congress over the authorization of water projects.

Carter's attempt to cut back on government investment in water projects demonstrated many of the key themes of his domestic presidency. It highlighted his determination to do the right thing, fight special interests, reduce waste in government and to protect the environment. It was also seen as an early test of his administration's competence and his ability to stand up to Congress. For many members of congress, it was a direct attack on their patronage because such projects provided help to their constituents. There was however no universal support for such investment. Many of the projects were not financially viable and there were often major environmental concerns. Carter believed that he had the support for his actions of the American people (as he was fulfilling a campaign promise), of Democrats in Congress,[140] key GOP leaders, the OMB, the Water Resources Council and the Council of Environmental Quality.[141] Carter expected a Democratic Congress to fall into line, but he underestimated the political impact of his proposals. Senator Russell Long of Louisiana, Chair of the Finance Committee, was baffled by Carter's actions because to Long the president 'was asking for a fight when he didn't have the votes to win to begin with'.[142] The proposal affected congressmen across the political spectrum and many of them held key committee and sub-committee positions. Carter received little advice about the political consequences of his decision. Only Secretary of Interior Andrus raised it as a potential issue.[143] The announcement was due on 21 February 1977, but it was leaked beforehand with affected congressmen being misinformed by the newspapers that their projects were cancelled (as opposed to postponed).[144] No attempt had been made to warn these congressmen with Moore being quoted in the *New York Times* as saying that he did not know that it was tradition to tell congressmen in advance.[145]

The reaction on Capitol Hill was immediately hostile with congressional committees holding up key legislation and appointments. A senator who was delaying a foreign aid bill and noting that it included a dam in Pakistan said, 'Once I get my dam, you can have your dam.'[146] Carter and his team made various attempts both at compromise and 'hanging tough',[147] but many of the proposed cuts were reinstated as Carter was forced to accept a compromise brokered by O'Neill. This may have been the right decision, but Carter's staff were unaware of what in effect was a U-turn and therefore it further damaged the president's and their own credibility.[148] Despite a much-improved performance from White House staff in dealing with the political realities, Congress continued to reinstate the remaining cancelled projects with subsequent annual budgets. Lance argued that the Water Projects policy was Carter's worst mistake, as the negative effects lasted the rest of his term. He believed it 'doomed any hopes we ever had of developing a good effective working relationship with Congress'.[149] The administration grossly underestimated the ferocity of the local and regional forces that they were taking on.[150] The initial ham-fisted attempt in February 1977 made limited gains but at the cost of alienating key members of congress and creating the impression that if pressure was applied, the president could be 'rolled' on legislative issues.

As Carter's popularity began to decline in late 1977 one of the major reasons given in the polls was his perceived inability to control Congress. At first, he continued to insist that relations with Capitol Hill were good.[151] but his lack of understanding was evident as he continued to express surprise at the 'inertia of Congress'.[152] Many of the problems centred on his attitude and his failure to treat Congress as a partner but most related to the sheer logistics of what his administration was trying to achieve legislatively. Many of the main bills put forward were extremely complex, as Carter himself recognized, often having to involve up to seventeen committees and sub-committees. Mondale's review of Carter's agenda for 1978 highlighted the limited amount of 'floor days' available for new initiatives.[153] This workload imposed on Congress was a factor affecting the administration's success rate. The other issue was the lack of a consistent base of support. Attempts to build support with the GOP were vetoed by the Democratic leadership which forced Carter to rely upon an increasingly volatile Democratic Caucus.[154] Analysis by Les Francis of congressional liaison indicated an overall level of support for Carter's legislation of 68.5 per cent amongst Democrats in the House but that varied amongst the regions with support from Texas legislators as low as 29 per cent.[155] There were various attempts to quantify the administration's 'success rate'. The consensus suggested that after a relatively poor first year Carter's success rate increased to around 78 per cent. Although this compared favourably with previous presidents, it did not consider bills withdrawn to avoid certain defeat or the importance of the legislation that failed.[156] If Carter's legislative record was regarded in general as a failure this view was largely a result of expectation and public perception. For the former, Carter admitted that one of the biggest mistakes he made was to build up expectations that he did not fulfil.[157] If direct influence on Congress was not working there was always the option of shaping public perception of his programme by taking the administration's case directly to the American people.

The ability of modern presidents to communicate effectively with the public has been a critical factor in the overall assessment of their performance. By the mid-1970s the communication channels available to presidents had expanded to include national newspapers, press conferences, television (interviews and speeches), radio as well as various face-to-face meetings with the public usually at town hall events. All of these were used by administrations to create an image of a successful presidency, to inform and on occasion persuade the public on critical issues. When Carter was elected, he did not have a very clear image and the Washington press, who had mainly supported Ford, largely based their expectations on the style of previous Democratic presidents. Hence the press believed that Carter would present a vision to the country supported by a coherent agenda, and he would work effectively with Congress. Carter fulfilled few of those expectations. He regularly was criticized for his 'fuzziness' and confusion over his ideology on issues. Journalist James Wooten summed up their frustration with Carter: 'It was so damned hard to bracket the man ... He is a quicksilver bubble, a living breathing grinning paradox maddening for those who tried to define him.'[158] HIs attempt to address this and other concerns about his religious beliefs in the *Playboy* interview had failed spectacularly. In addition, the press, generally more cynical since Watergate, were at best sceptical over Carter's statement 'to never lie' to the public and this, coupled with his obvious intelligence, became a challenge for them to catch him out.[159] The media, particularly the White House press, were negative about Carter throughout his term in office. Carter believed his administration had only one month of positive coverage in the media out of forty-eight and that was the first month.[160] James Reston of the *New York Times* agreed with this view when he said that 'The press was primarily responsible for destroying Carter's political reputation.'[161] Mistrust existed on both sides as Carter's advisors were equally suspicious of the Washington press. This was particularly the case with Frank Moore who bitterly resented criticism in the *Washington Post* of his team almost as soon as they arrived.[162] There was to be much criticism of the Carter administration's lack of understanding of Washington but many in the White House felt that part of this was due to regional prejudice.[163] To the Carter White House some of the coverage around Lance's financial difficulties reinforced this suspicion.[164]

Carter recognized that as president he was required to use his office to inform and influence the public and he believed that to carry out his mandate he needed to maintain contact with the people who had elected him. He was supremely confident in his intellectual ability, so he preferred this contact to be interactive where he could answer questions in an open and honest manner. He was therefore at his most comfortable and effective in campaigning, town hall meetings, radio phone-ins, television interviews and despite his reservations about the audience, press conferences. The editor of the *Atlanta Constitution*, Reg Murphy, by no means a Carter supporter, said of him that 'one to one, he's probably as convincing as anybody I've ever seen.'[165] He was much less effective in front of large audiences, especially on television. Early in his 1976 campaign, Charles Kirbo insisted that Carter took a television test. He was told by the experts that the maximum time he would be effective on TV was five minutes. Carter ignored this advice.[166] His most regular and most important channel to the public was through the press and, unfortunately, he simply did not trust them. In his *Playboy* interview he argued that the press had 'zero interest in any issues unless it's a matter of making a mistake … What they are looking for is a 47 second argument between me and another candidate or something like that.'[167]

He believed that the *Washington Post* conducted a vendetta against Lance and that the 'so called Lance affair, was a DC only story'.[168] By late 1977 Carter was writing in his diary that 'distortions in the Washington press are absolutely gross,'[169] and by the following year in a television interview with Bill Moyers he was talking about being surprised by the 'irresponsibility of the press'.[170] Carter's defensive attitude hampered his staff's attempts to improve media coverage. Efforts to increase contact between the president and members of the media were met with resistance from Carter,[171] culminating in his much-criticized refusal to speak at the Annual White House Correspondents Dinner in 1978. This was a major media event which the president always attended; Carter refused despite the efforts of his staff and Mondale to dissuade him.[172] His stubbornness as far as the press was concerned was a barrier to any media strategy his staff tried to implement. The natural response of blaming the press for every negative story was not challenged by White House staff until the appointment of a former editor Hedley Donovan as senior aide in 1979. Drawing parallels with behaviour he saw as a journalist in the Nixon White House, he tried to warn Carter in October 1979 of the risk of a paranoid-like response to every negative story.[173] But Carter did not think that all the press was irresponsible. In discussions with editors, he lauded the work of the *New York Times* and *Time* magazine, and even praised the editorials of the *Washington Post*.[174] He also continued to read the major newspapers and take notice of what they said. Articles, both 'good and bad,' regularly appeared in Carter's In-Box and, negative or not, he still demanded a response to the issues raised. For example, he demanded action be taken over an article in the *Washington Post* that reported that White House Staff numbers were going up at the time when 20 per cent cuts were being implemented.[175] Any media strategy that his staff developed needed to consider not only Carter's prejudices but his strengths and weaknesses as a communicator.

In the 1970s the main communication channel with the public remained the press. The Washington-based press was crucial because they shaped the agenda of those regional and state papers which did not have DC-based journalists. His staff shared Carter's suspicion of the White House press but equally he enjoyed and was an effective performer at press conferences, so the administration followed a dual strategy. Carter made a public commitment to hold news conferences every fortnight, but these events were opened to the journalists, editors and owners of newspapers across the country.[176] This attempt to reach a national audience was popular with those invited to the White House and Carter did receive a more sympathetic hearing. His standard press conferences were not confrontational, and he gave relaxed performances which demonstrated his in-depth knowledge of the subjects discussed. It was what journalists reported afterwards that Carter thought was the problem. His administration did have a 'honeymoon' period with the press, backed by favourable polls and perhaps lasting as long as seven months until the Lance affair.[177] However, by the end of 1977 Powell, Carter's Press Secretary, was recommending an emphasis on television for 1978 based on the assumption that fair treatment from the written press was unlikely.[178]

A second theme of the administration's media strategy was linked to the president's commitment to communicate with the public about his policies. This was called within the White House the 'People Programme'. Coordinated by one of his aides, Greg Schneiders, it covered a series of events from Carter's first fireside talk in February 1977, to town hall meetings, radio phone-ins (his phone-in on 5 March 1977 with Walter Cronkite attracted 25 million listeners)[179] and visits to people's homes.[180] In addition, ordinary members of the public were invited to White House dinners and the public were encouraged to write to him personally. He also asked his cabinet to go out and meet the people.[181] This fitted in with Carter's image of himself as an open and honest president who listened and was answerable to the people. During the early phase of the programme the president was perceived as a breath of fresh air. David Broder of the *Washington Post* commented after the Clinton Town Hall event on 16 March 1977 that 'In his first two months as President Jimmy Carter has achieved a triumph of communication in the arena of public opinion. He has transformed himself from a shaky winner of a campaign into a very popular President whose mastery of the mass media has given him real leverage with which to govern.'[182] For this strategy to be successful, however, direct communication with the public had to be not only sustained, which it was not, but also his staff needed to use public support for his policies to influence legislators. Although this approach was eventually adopted to gain public backing for the Panama Canal Treaty, it was not fully implemented until Anne Wexler replaced Midge Constanza as Special Assistant for Public Outreach in September 1978. This established an outreach strategy that linked together all aspects of the administration's operations in a task force to support specific policies.[183]

A third element of the media strategy, which was perfectly in tune with Carter's style, was the administration's attempts to increase informality and reduce ceremony around the presidency. Best symbolized by his decision at the inauguration to get out of the car and walk to the White House with his wife and daughter, Carter calculated that this act would symbolize his closeness to the people who elected him. This was also reflected in his rhetoric, a plain and simple style of a man talking to his neighbour.[184] Other actions initiated by the White House included reducing the use of 'Hail to the Chief' music whenever Carter appeared at events and the selling of the White House yacht. This image helped him be a successful presidential candidate but became less beneficial as his term progressed. Carter soon discovered that once in office the public expected him to act as the leader of their country. Attempts to reduce ceremony and his informality were used as examples of him lacking the qualities of a leader. Helen Thomas, the veteran DC journalist, argued that Carter 'stripped out of the office some qualities that give it that sense of awe that many of us are still moved by'.[185] This was recognized by the White House and informality was gradually replaced by the need for Carter to be seen as acting 'presidential'.

A major problem for Carter was the message he was trying to communicate. The issues he wanted to address were by their nature complex and controversial. He had difficulty in explaining in simple terms the solutions he was offering to the public at a time when he faced opposition both inside and outside Congress. Another consequence of the confusion around his message was that Carter began to be seen as indecisive. This was in sharp contrast to his image as governor as someone who was hard-headed, stubborn, inflexible and opinionated.[186] The situation was not helped by confusion arising from Carter's policy of cabinet government. There was no one in the White House who was able to coordinate an overall message on policy with each department having its own Publicity Information Officers issuing their own statements.[187] Carter was seen as the deliverer of bad news whilst he allowed cabinet members to give any good news to the public. Esther Petersen, the veteran Assistant for Consumer Affairs, contrasted this with Lyndon Johnson who insisted that any good news had to come through the White House.[188] Jerry Rafshoon was brought in to oversee Communication strategy in an attempt by Carter's advisors to improve coordination and control of his message. Rafshoon was successful in ensuring that communication was more co-ordinated, and he worked hard to reduce the president's personal exposure to the media, particularly on television. He told Carter that 'you are running the risk of boring the people and you have 3 ½ years to go'.[189] He also ensured that cabinet members became more involved in 'selling' the administration's policies. Always conscious of the president's image, Rafshoon was very concerned about jokes about Carter's indecisiveness on the Johnny Carson Show as it could indicate that criticism in the Washington press was going nationwide.[190] He continued therefore to encourage a somewhat reluctant Carter to court newspapers from outside Washington.

The staff who worked in the press and media offices of the White House were subjected to the little criticism from journalists. This was surprising given Press Secretary Powell's lack of Washington experience, but he was well regarded by the media who recognized that his history with and regular access to the president made his comments authoritative. The press office, unlike congressional liaison, was well staffed from the beginning and media liaison, based on Ford's operation,[191] became highly successful in engaging with non-DC based media outlets.[192] They also played a significant role in the task forces being established to support key policy initiatives. There was an improvement in the information provided to the press about Carter's speeches, both formal and informal, as well as more effective planning of how the administration dealt with the media.[193] However, partly because of Rafshoon's approach, the press came to believe that everything the president did was politically motivated and that proved damaging to Carter.[194] The *Wall Street Journal* for example suggested that Rafshoon had persuaded Carter to veto the Aircraft Carrier bill so the president could look tough to the public.[195] Furthermore Carter's television appearances became less appealing as the networks began declining to broadcast events like town hall meetings.[196] Carter and his aides remained convinced that the Washington media was biased against them. Powell stated, 'He received credit for almost nothing.'[197] Journalist Hugh Sidey's comment after Carter lost the 1980 election that 'Now maybe we'll have a little class',[198] did suggest an anti-southerner prejudice. On the other hand, White House defensiveness did help create a negative reaction from the press. In addition, Rafshoon admitted that many of the negative stories in the Washington press came from members of Carter's own party in Congress and his White House staff.[199]

The ability to deliver an effective speech to a range of audiences face-to-face and on television is an important skill for any president. Until relatively late in the campaign Carter had written his own speeches and was not used to working with speechwriters. To be successful, most speechwriters attempt to build a direct relationship with their president, Theodore C. Sorensen's relationship with President Kennedy being a good example. This did not happen with Carter as most of the speeches were developed in correspondence.[200] He was also vague in specifying what he wanted because he was 'not used to transferring his thoughts to other people'.[201] His insistence that other members of the administration should comment on a draft before he saw it was also unsatisfactory from the speechwriting viewpoint as it delayed and complicated the process.[202] Carter would often comment in detail on grammar and punctuation. He was not the first modern president to give detailed comment on a speechwriter's grammar; Eisenhower was equally pedantic.[203] Often, Carter would reject the draft and end up writing the whole speech himself. Rafshoon said, 'There are no speeches given by Jimmy Carter that aren't anywhere from 50 to 99 per cent his.'[204] Commenting on his role as Carter's senior speechwriter, James Fallows remarked sardonically that it 'was as rewarding as being FDR's tap-dancing instructor'.[205] Furthermore, the messages Carter tried to convey were complicated and often controversial. As he said in his *Playboy* interview, 'I've taken positions that to me are fair and rational and sometimes my answers are complicated.'[206]

Complexity was only part of the problem as Carter was reluctant to simplify or use any rhetorical device that added emotion to his argument.[207] He refused to project optimism or to sugar-coat his message. Speeches often started with phrases like, 'Tonight I want to have an unpleasant talk with you about a problem that is unprecedented in our history' (energy), or, in a similar vein, 'I want a frank talk with you about one of our most serious domestic problems (inflation).'[208] There was also no underlying theme which would lift or inspire the public. Fallows argued that Carter 'thinks he leads by choosing the correct policy, but he fails to project a vision larger than the problem he is tackling at the moment'.[209] Criticism of Carter's unwillingness to articulate a vision came to the fore during his presidency but he argued that the issues were too broad for slogans and that his speeches were aimed at building a relationship with the public not for the 'entertainment of the press corps'.[210] The closest his staff came to developing a theme in one of his speeches was the 'New Foundation' element of his 1979 State of the Union address. This had been well received but when questioned about this new theme at a news conference, Carter squashed the idea, and it was not further developed.[211] All of this would prove a marked contrast with his Republican rival in 1980. Ronald Reagan's messages were simple, optimistic, embedded in a coherent vision for America and delivered by a master orator.

The outcome was that his speeches came across as dry and uninspiring. Fallows said that 'You can't inspire people with a jigsaw puzzle.'[212] Not all of Carter's speeches were underwhelming. After his presidency he said of his oratorical difficulties, 'I have never been at ease with set speeches or memorized text … I like to speak from a few notes, and the more I am embedded in an element of rigidity, the more uncomfortable I feel.'[213] When speaking off-the-cuff to new congressmen or in his speech at the memorial for Hubert Humphrey, Carter could be warm and witty.[214] He also could be passionate when attacking what he perceived as the unfair behaviour of interest groups. Two notable examples of this were his speech on justice on 4 May 1978 and his earlier more famous Law Day Address at the University of Georgia on 4 May 1974 where he shared the stage with Ted Kennedy. This latter speech, improvised from notes, was immortalized by the journalist Hunter Thompson who memorably described it as 'one King Hell Bastard of a speech'.[215] But criticism of Carter's speeches was widespread and related not only to content but also to delivery. *New York Times* journalists Robert Novak and Rowland Evans described his style as, 'Allergic to all efforts at eloquence'.[216] More famously, former Senator Eugene McCarthy dubbed Carter the 'Oratorical Mortician who inters his words and ideas beneath a pile of syntactical mush'.[217] Carter was not receptive to coaching to improve his oratorical technique and Mondale believed that 'Carter had contempt for orators'.[218] Fallows said that Carter refused not only to receive training but to practise – other than talk into a tape and listen back. Carter was concerned that any coaching would tarnish his unvarnished style, which may have been code for his southern accent.[219] His reluctance to practise was not finally overcome until Rafshoon persuaded him to do a video practice for his July 1979 energy speech.[220] All of this hampered Carter's ability to communicate his message and get the public behind his legislative programme. Without their support putting pressure on Congress, many of the administration's bills were doomed.

In the 1976 presidential election Carter promoted himself through his abilities and character as the deliverer of competent government. It followed therefore that his inability to control Congress was seen as his personal failure by the public. Some of this was not Carter's fault and the performance of his administration improved as experienced was gained or in some cases hired. However much of the failure could be laid at Carter's door. He was hampered by his negative attitude to politics and politicians, his inability to prioritize his legislation realistically and more than anything else his failure to persuade the American people of the need for the sacrifice he was asking of them. All of this would undermine his ability to deliver on the public expectation of a competent government.

For most Americans, the measure of a president's success was the management of the economy. This would prove to be Carter's greatest challenge.

3

The economic challenge

Carter's failed economic policy has been identified as one of the main reasons for his defeat to Ronald Reagan in 1980. Poor economic performance of presidents has often been linked to their subsequent failure to be elected to a second term: Herbert Hoover in 1932, Gerald Ford in 1976 and George H. W. Bush in 1992. Equally, improved economic performance helped re-elect Ronald Reagan in 1984, Bill Clinton in 1996 and Barack Obama in 2012. Other than in time of war the economy has invariably been a key issue for presidential elections. Bill Clinton was famously reminded 'It's the economy stupid' by his campaign team in 1992. Carter campaigned in 1976 for tax reform, controlled inflation without high unemployment and free enterprise with minimal government intrusion,[1] but above all he stood for competence. His government would be efficient and solve the problems left by the Ford administration. Unfortunately, the economic difficulties of the United States went far beyond the failures of one administration and would take all of Carter's personal and political skill to try and resolve.

Carter inherited an economy that after a slow recovery in 1975 had stalled. Inflation was rising, and unemployment was at 7 per cent. To most economists all the indicators suggested that there would be a recession in 1977.[2] A fall in productivity masked underlying capacity issues in the economy resulting in much less room for stimulus measures than the experts believed.[3] The stagnation in the world economy, external pressure on oil prices from the Organization of the Petroleum Exporting Countries (OPEC) and the financial crisis in New York City presented a picture of an economy in a parlous condition. America's long reliance on a balance of trade surplus to fund internal investment ended in 1971 when it posted its first trade deficit since 1883 of $1.3bn. This had risen to $27bn by the time Carter took office.[4] Despite this, Carter, as with all presidents, wanted his economists 'to provide a blueprint for high growth, low inflation and a guaranteed re-election but without offending any important constituency'.[5]

Unfortunately for Carter he arrived in office at a time when the consensus amongst economists on how to address these problems had broken down. The prevailing economic theory of the 1960s, espoused by prominent economists like Walter W. Heller, argued that it was possible to maintain a balance between economic growth and unemployment. Known as neo-Keynesians, Heller and his disciples such as Arthur Okun held key positions in all administrations from 1960 until Reagan's election in 1980. Okun and Charles Schultze, who became Carter's Chief Economic Advisor (CEA), maintained that it was possible using fiscal measures including controlling government spending to continue economic growth whilst holding unemployment and inflation down to 4 and 2.5 per cent, respectively.[6] However, the neo-Keynesian economic models failed to consider the decline in productivity with the result that any fiscal stimulus overheated the economy and increased inflation.[7] By the 1970s such theories were coming under attack from economists like Milton Friedman who argued that the economy could be controlled only by adjusting the supply of money. This critique was to take on a political dimension with an aide to conservative Congressman Jack Kemp calling Keynesianism 'not just wrong but corrupt. A ramp for the expansion of the interests of Government.'[8] By the mid-1980s there would be a new economic orthodoxy espoused by Republicans based around fiscal restraint, monetary policy to control inflation, deregulation and tax relief to stimulate growth. But in the 1970s, as Frank Morris, President of the Federal Reserve Bank of Boston, stated, 'It is probably fair to say that economic policy is now being made in at least a partial vacuum of economic theory.'[9] As a result the solutions that Carter's experts recommended failed to deliver the forecast outcomes, particularly on inflation. Not all of this was due to a failure in policy. External factors such as the OPEC oil price increases and the inability of Congress to implement budgetary restraint also had a detrimental effect on the economy. This uncertainty over policy resulted in disputes within the administration over the twin objectives of promoting growth and fighting inflation. Such conflict was reflected in pressure from congressional Democrats on the administration to fund social programmes. This tension often resulted in Carter and his economic team seeking alternative advice from organizations such as the Brookings Institute. This air of uncertainty around economic policy was to continue throughout Carter's term in office.

Carter was not interested in theoretical debate over the economy. His campaign speeches focused on moral issues such as protecting the poor, reducing unemployment and providing efficient government. His approach was based upon his experience as a businessman and governor when he concentrated on reducing the fiscal deficit and balancing the budget. His support for Zero-Based Budgeting (ZBB) should be seen in this context. This was a discipline that ensured that all budgets were built from the ground up and not based on what had been spent the previous year. This fitted in with Carter's emphasis on good government, cutting waste and reducing regulation. He believed that by concentrating on small (micro) economic issues the big (macro) economic problems would be solved. His key advisor Charles Schultze thought Carter was a top rate micro-economist but that his eyes just 'glazed over on macro-economics'.[10] Carter was therefore dependent on his economic advisors for solutions to long-term problems and he became frustrated by their failure to agree. He referred to one meeting with economists as a waste of time as each one expounded his or her own theories.[11] As with all government policy Carter wanted his advisors to provide comprehensive solutions that he could study and implement. However, on the economy he found himself zigzagging between the conflicting priorities of avoiding recession and fighting inflation. This made it difficult for him to build a political coalition as each faction had different solutions to the country's economic ills. Carter often managed to find money to support social programmes but his rhetoric on economic policy remained conservative, all of which alienated both wings of the Democratic Party.

If Carter cut a frustrated figure on economic policy in general, he did believe that he could contribute personally to fiscal policy by encouraging reduced government spending. White House files are littered with Carter demanding cuts on a range of expenses from periodicals, staff travel costs and the selling of the presidential yacht.[12] This extended to interest in the budget where his mastery of the minutiae was such that it often intimidated Bert Lance's staff.[13] This degree of involvement did not continue after his first year in office,[14] as he began to devolve the decision-making to his economic team. His lack of expertise meant that Carter did not always recognize the economic implications of his decisions. His insistence on the development of a new energy policy without any input from his economic advisors nearly proved disastrous. He did recognize his inexperience and continued to ask basic questions about areas of personal concern on the economy.[15] This involvement contradicted Lance's view that Carter was not interested in economics but it did confirm that he neither mastered nor developed a coherent view of the subject.[16] It is often argued that Carter was a fiscal conservative, but this interest was based more upon his moral stance against waste and his view that government should lead from the front in making sacrifices rather than any economic ideology. He therefore remained dependent upon his economic team and invariably accepted their advice.

Carter's first appointment was Charles Schultze as CEA. Schultze followed a line of neo-Keynesian economists from the Brookings Institution who had gone into government. His practical background in economics appealed to Carter and they met at least once a week although this declined when inflation breakfasts were established in 1979.[17] His early appointment resulted in Schultze being influential in shaping the administration's initial economic policies. He provided Carter with regular written briefings on the state of the economy, and although Carter was frustrated with the failure of experts to improve the economic outlook, he rarely criticized his CEA. Schultze was frank with Carter about the financial situation, flagging his concerns early and often using his political judgement to persuade Carter to change course.[18] Schultze was grateful for both Carter's support against negative press coverage and his straightforwardness.[19]

Communication between Carter and his Secretary of the Treasury never reached the same level of trust. W. Michael Blumenthal had worked in the Kennedy and Johnson administrations and held senior positions in industry. As Treasurer he was chair of the Economic Policy Group (EPG), but he was criticized because he often failed to find a consensus with its members. Whilst his personal relationship with Carter was cordial, relations with White House staff were poor. Blumenthal quoted their lack of support in his resignation letter in July 1979.[20] The level of mutual suspicion often resulted in both sides leaking to the press. Lance believed that Blumenthal's jealousy of his access to Carter resulted in details of Lance's fraud case being leaked to the press by Blumenthal's staff.[21] White House staff in the run up to the Camp David Domestic Summit argued that Blumenthal deliberately undermined Carter's position on tax reform by leaking to Congress in advance of the public announcement, and he circulated details of the New York financial rescue plan before Carter had approved it.[22] Such infighting reduced Blumenthal's influence with the president but this did not restrict his access, and as late as March 1979 he was writing thoughtful memoranda to Carter on economic strategy. Some of his ideas were implemented after he resigned.[23] Carter, after his presidency, acknowledged Blumenthal's difficulty with his staff and defended his record.[24] Yet it was Carter's view that his successor, G. William Miller, was a conciliatory and therefore more effective figure.[25]

The third arm in Carter's economic organization was the Office of Management and Budget (OMB). This was important to Carter for two reasons. Firstly, his friend Bert Lance had been appointed as its head, and secondly, even after Lance's resignation in September 1977, the OMB was critical to delivering

Carter's campaign commitment to fight inflation by eliminating the fiscal deficit by 1981. Lance's personal relationship with the president and his political skills did increase the OMB's prestige within the White House. This influence was limited by Lance's lack of technical expertise and an initial suspicion of many OMB staff because they were holdovers from the previous Republican administration.[26] Lance's early departure weakened the OMB's influence but as the administration struggled to control inflation, Carter became focused on fiscal restraint which made him a natural ally of Lance's successor, Jim McIntyre. McIntyre lacked Lance's political skills but he was technically capable, and Schultze argued that the OMB and himself represented the 'realistic hair shirts' of Carter's economic team.[27] McIntyre felt that Carter's long-term commitment to a balanced budget was not shared by his administration and that his economic strategy was undermined by leaks from White House staff.[28] His complaints about lack of support from agencies often prompted counter-claims from Eizenstat that the OMB lacked the political skills to deliver on its programmes.[29] This would become a recurring theme as the Domestic Policy Group (DPG) gained more influence over economic policy.

All three organizations came together in the EPG. Inherited from the Ford administration, it quickly grew to over twenty members, including cabinet representatives from Labour, State and Commerce as well as the vice president, members of the National Security Council (NSC) and DPG. This proved to be unwieldy with Carter receiving papers from individual departments but with no summary of issues from the short-staffed EPG.[30] The president made the situation worse by insisting that Secretary of Housing and Urban Development (HUD) Patricia Harris be added to represent the inner cities, minorities and, as a concession, to the Black caucus.[31] The EPG was initially jointly chaired by Schultze and Blumenthal, at Carter's suggestion, but Schultze stepped down after six weeks, concerned about a conflict of interest with his role as CEA.[32] But Blumenthal proved to be an ineffective chair and within weeks alternative approaches were being discussed. The debate centred on the EPG's lack of resources and the unwieldy nature of the group. Blumenthal made proposals to centralize and give the EPG its own staff, so it could develop policy. Jordan and Eizenstat challenged this as they did not trust Blumenthal to oversee a centralized body.[33] The final decision by Carter gave the EPG more power and established a smaller steering group comprising just the three key economic advisors (Blumenthal, Schultze and McIntyre). In addition, Eizenstat was given a wider role of policy coordination which enabled the DPG to oversee economic proposals sent to the president. The steering group disagreed on major aspects of policy for the first eighteen months of the administration until it finally agreed to prioritize the fight against inflation. This policy continued to be challenged by cabinet members who were part of the main committee.[34] The appointment of Miller as Secretary of the Treasury and EPG chair in August 1979 did improve coordination. Carter admitted that he did not feel well served by the EPG and late in his term in office felt the need to question its track record on forecasting.[35]

Carter's economic advice did not just come from the EPG. Following the recommendations of the Camp David Domestic Summit of May 1978, the DPG became more influential in its advice on the political implications of economic policy. McIntyre resented the DPG's influence and argued that it represented interest groups and used its influence on Capitol Hill to undermine OMB policies on fiscal restraint.[36] As head of the DPG, Eizenstat did represent a more liberal view on economic policy, highlighting the political consequences of fiscal restraint as the 1980 election drew nearer.[37] But he was by no means the only liberal who argued for alternative policies. Ray Marshall, as Labor Secretary, was also criticized by McIntyre as having a negative influence on Carter's policies.[38] As the economic situation deteriorated the administration cast its net wider for advice. As early as October 1977 a paper from economist Arthur Okun, which argued for new policies to fight inflation, had been copied to Carter and was circulated to his economic team.[39] This practice continued throughout Carter's term in office. Although he had a formal structure to advise him on economic policy, Carter continued to encourage direct communication from his senior advisors.[40] This often hampered the ability of his administration to reach consensus.

There was one other organization that would influence Carter's economic policy, the Federal Reserve (Fed). Congress had established the Fed to control the banking system and specifically the money supply. Control of the money supply was one of the means available to government to reduce inflation, but it also had a consequence of increasing interest rates which damaged confidence and could potentially push the economy towards recession. The difficulty for any president was that the Fed was independent, and its chair could follow what policy he deemed appropriate. In practice presidents formed a relationship with each chair and sought to influence their actions indirectly. Carter established regular dialogue with his first chair, Arthur F. Burns, and his successor William Miller, seeking and receiving advice on economic policy and reassuring them on his administration's fiscal goals.[41] Burns and later Miller followed a relaxed policy of monetary controls but there were times when the White House sought to influence the Fed to prevent interest rate rises. In August 1977, the EPG feared that the Fed would respond to an increase in money supply by raising interest rates and so Carter was advised to talk to Burns.[42] Fed policy changed in the summer of 1979 when Carter appointed Miller to replace Blumenthal at the Treasury and picked Paul Volcker as his replacement. Volcker believed that the only way to fight inflation effectively was to control the money supply.[43] Such a strategy would prove to be very damaging for Carter politically, but he did not publicly attack Volcker for this policy. Despite what seemed conflicting strategies on fighting inflation, cooperation between the Fed and the White House increased with Volcker attending budget meetings, which was unprecedented.[44] The White House did try to use its influence on Volcker by appointing one of their own men to the Fed board[45] and applied pressure to hold down interest rates.[46] However, in the final weeks of the 1980 election with inflation still rising, Schultze, and by implication Carter, had accepted the inevitability of the Fed's monetarist strategy and had ceased to resist it.[47]

If control of the Fed proved difficult, the relationship with key members of congress on the economy was even more challenging for Carter and his team. Under the Constitution all revenue-raising measures had to pass the House. In practice this required the approval of the Ways and Means Committee, under its Chair Albert C. Ullman of Oregon. Ullman had been instrumental in reforming the congressional budget process and tax laws. He was to prove a key player in supporting Carter's stimulus package in February 1977. Senator Russell Long's Finance Committee, along with Ways and Means, dealt with between 80 and 90 per cent of the administration's legislation.[48] Long, unlike other Senate Chairmen, had not devolved any of his powers to sub-committees. He had a strong personal influence over each of the members and as a result over the committee as a whole.[49] The White House eventually recognized the importance of Long, and under pressure from Mondale, Eizenstat and Moore, Carter agreed to a series of personal meetings and dinners with the influential senator. But there was no meeting of minds. Long had not campaigned for Carter and saw himself as a reluctant teacher of an inexperienced president.[50] He spoke of admiring Carter's values,[51] but he expected deals to be struck which was not Carter's way of operating. This resulted in a frustrated Senator saying: 'I never knew if I could count on him or not.'[52] So he used the cover of Carter's U-turn on the $50 tax rebate in his Economic Recovery Plan of 1977 to sneak into the bill an exemption on oil drilling costs that would help his home state of Louisiana; the sort of deal that would appal Carter.[53] Long's committee blocked the administration's attempts at tax reform, and Carter's perceived inability to stand up to Long was seen as a personal failure.[54] In the end Carter's frustrations boiled over. He told

Califano, 'I never can understand him and then I never know what he is going to do except screw me most of the time.'[55] This attitude to Long was known to Carter's staff, with David Rubenstein of the DPG commenting that the one way to influence Carter against a proposal was to tell him that an interest group or Russell Long was in favour of it.[56] The failure of this relationship was to have a critical impact not only on Carter's economic policies but any legislation that had a financial dimension.

Whilst the Carter election campaign may have lacked specific proposals on the economy, the new administration was committed to a package of measures that would reduce unemployment, increase growth and control inflation.[57] Briefings Carter received in November 1976 claimed that the economy was moving towards a recession with a growth forecast at 4 per cent that would be insufficient to reduce unemployment below the current level of 8 per cent. The recommendation from his advisors was for a plan that would create jobs, incentivize the private economy, implement tax reform and establish prudent measures to balance the budget when recession was beaten.[58] Work on the plan's components started before Blumenthal had been appointed, so it was developed, at least initially, by Schultze. The stimulus package had all the hallmarks of a Carter solution. It was a comprehensive proposal that was designed to address many of the economic problems that the country faced. The complexity of the package meant that components were integrated with each other so a change to one area would have a detrimental effect on the whole plan. It was a conservative proposal with the total value of the stimulus less than President Ford's package of 1975.[59] The mix of tax cuts and job creation was a compromise between liberals and conservatives within the administration, with Carter straddling the debate. He was supportive of job creation but wanted the emphasis placed on training rather than public works. This was to be achieved by the expansion of the Comprehensive Employment and Training Act (CETA). On the issue of the tax cut Carter, whilst accepting it was necessary, was insistent that it would only be temporary because he wanted to protect his commitment to a balanced budget by the end of his term in office. The structure of the proposal suggested an 'all or nothing' negotiating strategy with Congress, which was not usual practice.

The package of measures was called the Economic Recovery Plan (ERP) and was submitted to Congress on 31 January 1977. Carter, in a fireside broadcast two days later, emphasized the balanced nature of the plan which included proposals that dealt with both inflation and unemployment.[60] He recognized that his proposals were not perfect and that many groups would want a different emphasis but argued that it was the best chance of producing steady, balanced, sustainable growth. His broadcast proved prescient as ERP was attacked by all interest groups as not doing enough for their sectors. The AFL-CIO and the conference of mayors who had campaigned for Carter wanted more done to create jobs.[61] This opposition was reflected in Congress with Ullman presenting his own alternative proposals on tax credits with the aim of stimulating employment. Carter, already frustrated by the House leadership breaking up the package and sending it to different committees,[62] now faced a proposal that his staff believed would destabilize ERP.[63] Despite an attempt by Blumenthal to dissuade him,[64] Ullman continued to promote his plan and within three weeks of its submission $1.6bn worth of spending had been added to the package.[65] The administration was also struggling to coordinate negotiations with Congress as each department was responsible for different aspects of the plan. This resulted in Eizenstat and Moore having to issue briefings to White House staff and cabinet secretaries to keep track of the plan's status in Congress.[66] The chances of ERP passing Congress deteriorated further when the White House announced cuts in the programme of water projects. The congressional reaction was hostile. Carter's attempts to reassure were to no avail as the Senate retaliated by delaying passage of ERP with Long threatening to put legislation in 'deep freeze' until the results of a review of the water projects that Carter had ordered stopped were known.[67] The delay in the legislation not only gave its opponents more time to resist elements of ERP which they did not approve but also allowed uncertainty to develop in the White House over the tax cut.

The $50 tax rebate was designed to boost consumer spending and the economy as a whole. At $11.9bn it represented by far the largest cost element of the plan with a further $4bn to be spent on tax simplification and a business tax cut. The rebate was unpopular with both Congress and business. Frank Moore, Carter's legislative liaison, was reporting in early February that Democratic support on the Senate Finance committee was wavering whilst the GOP wanted a permanent tax cut.[68] Further uncertainty was created by unexpectedly favourable unemployment and growth figures in March 1977,[69] resulting in some questioning the economic necessity for the rebate.[70] In April Carter received a brutally frank briefing from Dan Tate, congressional liaison, on the Senate vote on the rebate and Carter's overall congressional strategy. Tate stated that Democrats were voting against him across the spectrum, knowing that it would be personally embarrassing to Carter. They criticized him for not negotiating and being either naive, selfish or stubborn. Although they respected a hard-headed president, what they feared most was one who was high handed. According to Tate, Byrd believed that only Carter's personal intervention could save the rebate whilst Tate himself warned that this political battle would be key for his future relationship with Congress.[71] Despite this warning Carter continued to rally his administration and his supporters to back the rebate. He wrote to senators on 6 April laying out the arguments for this policy.[72] The turning point was a briefing from Mondale who had talked to Senator Alan M. Cranston of California and was now convinced that the administration was going to lose the vote and that any compromise would not necessarily succeed or be worth the price paid. Mondale also reflected the growing view that the economic conditions had changed and that many people whom Carter respected were opposed to this proposal.[73] Following further discussion with his economic team, Carter decided to drop the rebate in mid-April 1977. Given its unpopularity in Congress this should have been a win for the administration, but unfortunately poor communication resulted in many of his staff, cabinet and key congressmen being given no warning of Carter's change of heart. Blumenthal was left to make a speech to the National Press Corps without being apprised of the change of policy. Senator Edmund Muskie of Maine, a close ally, who had fought hard for the rebate, was also not told, prompting him to say, 'You can't trust these people.'[74]

The fate of ERP highlighted the issues that Carter was to face early in his presidency: the difficulty in proposing a comprehensive package that would be scrutinized piecemeal by different committees in Congress and a White House lacking the coordination and experience to manage such a process. A consequence of the reversal of policy on the tax rebate was the damage to key relationships in Congress, particularly with Byrd.[75] The failure of his economic advisors to predict the early upturn in the economy and more seriously the inflationary aspects of ERP was to prove a continuing problem for Carter. Although the size of the stimulus effect had been reduced by the withdrawal of the tax rebate, the later improvement in unemployment and growth figures did suggest that ERP had been successful. Carter was to see the biggest twelve months rise in employment since the Second World War.[76] However, even the more optimistic advisors like Blumenthal were raising concern about inflation and this was to become the focus of Carter's economic thinking from the summer of 1977 onwards.[77]

This was not the only attempt by the Carter administration to stimulate the economy. The Full Employment and Balanced Growth Act (also known as the Humphrey-Hawkins Act) was signed by Carter into law on 27 October 1978. This legislation was an attempt by liberals to tighten congressional control of economic policy by committing the government and the Fed to achieve specific targets on all key economic indicators. The aim was to force the government to achieve 'full employment' by developing job creation schemes. The bill was sponsored by former Vice President Senator Hubert H. Humphrey of Minnesota and a leading member of the Black caucus, Representative Augustus F. Hawkins of California. Both men had been important supporters of Carter during the election and passing this legislation had been a campaign commitment. Unfortunately for Carter the bill represented economic theory that was under attack and tied the White House to actions that Carter felt were inappropriate for the economic climate. The neo-Keynesian faith in government action to control growth, employment and inflation was proving ineffective and the administration was forced to prioritize its actions on fighting inflation at the expense of unemployment. Furthermore, whilst the bill had the support of liberals, the unions and minority groups, there were conservatives even within the Democratic Party that had strong reservations about its inflationary aspects and the enlarged role the bill gave government in the economy. They saw Humphrey-Hawkins as a symbol of excessive government spending.[78] The draft bill was submitted to the House in January 1977, but the EPG had raised fundamental objections. Blumenthal believed that the targets set on unemployment were not achievable, that insufficient attention was paid to inflation and the government had not been given enough flexibility to achieve its goals. He was also worried that proposed monetary controls would face objections from the Fed.[79] In an early example of the DPG intervening on economic policy, Eizenstat raised concerns with Carter that a draft letter from Schultze to Hawkins which proposed changes to the bill would alienate supporters.[80] Eizenstat warned of the frustration in the party: 'We are sitting on a timebomb here which will explode unless we move quickly.'[81] There followed a series of attempts by the White House to reach a compromise, initially with Hawkins and later with a more flexible Humphrey. Carter sought Tip O'Neill's advice who argued that the bill was unlikely to pass in its current form and urged compromise.[82] The bill's sponsors, fearing declining support in the House, accepted a White House proposal that softened the unemployment target to 4 per cent by 1983, removed many of the detailed restrictions and placed more emphasis on fighting inflation.[83] The compromise bill passed the House in March 1978 and the Senate to become law in the following October. Hawkins called the final bill 'A modern Magna Carta of economic rights'.[84] But many of Carter's economic team did not believe that even the watered-down targets were achievable.[85] This proved to be the case as by June 1980 Schultze was recommending the unemployment target date be extended by more than five years. Carter could argue that he had fulfilled a campaign promise, but it had little practical effect.

Another campaign commitment proved even more difficult to achieve, Carter's promise to reform the tax system. He may have been vague with many of his campaign promises but on tax reform he was very clear. In his acceptance speech at the Democratic Convention in New York, he said, 'It is time for a complete overhaul of the taxation system. I still tell you it is a disgrace to the human race. All my life I have heard promises about tax reform, but it never quite happens. With your help, we are finally going to make it happen. And you can depend on it.'[86] In his Fireside Talk on 2 February 1977 he confirmed that his advisors were working with Congress on a reform that would give a fairer, simpler tax system. He talked of a comprehensive package by the end of the year.[87] Carter did not give his advisors any specific guidance on reform, but this did not mean that he did not have views of his own. In his campaign speeches he talked about fairness where the taxation burden was to be shifted from lower- and middle-income families to the well off, and the closing of tax loopholes which gave allowances for activities such as lunches and entertainment that favoured the rich.[88] He also expressed an interest in reducing the level of taxation as a proportion of GDP, something Ronald Reagan would campaign for in 1980.[89] Carter looked to the Treasury to produce tax reform proposals. Blumenthal raised concerns that other administration initiatives, particularly on energy, would cut across his work but a deadline of the end of July 1977 was agreed; this proved to be optimistic.[90] By mid-May Carter expressed disappointment at the Treasury's early proposals, characterizing them as 'too timid'.[91] As a consequence Carter sent Eizenstat to brief Larry Wordworth, who was leading the Treasury team, on Carter's views. Eizenstat emphasized that Carter wanted a comprehensive solution based on first principles that would produce a fairer, simpler, progressive system that eliminated tax shelters. His mandate was for reform and not for a proposal that was watered down to suit Congress. For good measure Eizenstat went through statements Carter had made on the campaign. He stressed what Carter wanted from the Treasury was the best solution at zero cost and to leave how Congress might react to the president. Eizenstat expressed major concerns about the Treasury proposals which did not fulfil many of Carter's criteria, and having talked to Long and Ullman, he concluded that September 1977 was a more realistic target date.[92]

White House dissatisfaction with Treasury proposals continued through the summer of 1977. Carter's speechwriter Jim Fallows raised concerns about whether the current proposals fulfilled the presidential campaign promises, quoting from Carter's convention speech.[93] Carter was also receiving criticism from liberals like Califano and Senator Kennedy who had his own ideas on a new progressive tax system where the rich contributed more.[94] Carter wrote to Blumenthal and Woodworth, requesting changes with greater progressivity and the closing of more loopholes. Frustration with his Treasury team resulted in Carter looking for alternative sources of advice. This included Joe Pechman from the Brookings Institute whose ideas were to continue to receive a favourable response from the White House throughout Carter's term in office.[95] He was also concerned about quotes in the press attributed to Blumenthal that directly contradicted Carter's views on progressivity.[96] Blumenthal denied this was his view, but there did appear to be a lack of trust between them. When he met Ullman on the proposed bill, Carter did not want anyone from the Treasury present, preferring Eizenstat.[97] Early discussions with congressional chairmen in August had flagged concerns that the proposals were too complex, and many elements would be opposed. The Democratic leadership suggested splitting the bill, delaying the unpopular measures to the next session.[98] By September 1977 many of Carter's advisors, inside and outside the White House, recommended a postponement. Their main argument was that Congress would use the Tax Reform bill as an excuse to delay the passage of the Energy, Hospital Cost Containment and Welfare bills.[99] Blumenthal, supported by Eizenstat, still argued that the bill was deliverable, particularly if Ullman's committee sat during the winter recess. The risk was if the window was missed the chances of Congress passing a reform bill would be reduced and Carter would only get a tax cut.[100] This had become the most likely outcome as liberals in Congress became pessimistic that a reform bill would pass and were reluctant to take criticism for the unpopular elements of the bill. Mondale advised Carter that a modified bill, focused on tax relief with limited popular reform options such as cutting allowances for business lunches and entertainment, should be submitted in January 1978. Reluctantly Carter agreed.[101]

By April 1978 even this strategy was in disarray with a majority on the Ullman committee voting against every aspect of the bill. An evaluation of the administration's performance in promoting reform by one of Eizenstat's staff was highly critical, suggesting that the Treasury was even unaware of a major Senate amendment.[102] The Steiger amendment on capital gains tax which only benefitted the top 1 per cent and a more restricted version backed by Ullman, the Jones amendment, signified that Congress had taken control of the legislation. White House was forced to find a compromise on capital gains tax whilst the reform agenda was gradually being weakened. Lobbying of the key Ways and Means Committee had improved by July 1978 but by then Carter had lost the support of its chair, Ullman.[103] The search for a compromise on capital gains tax also revealed tensions between Blumenthal and the White House, with articles in the press suggesting he was compromising against Carter's wishes.[104] This may have been exaggerated because Blumenthal remained proactive in advising Carter in the final months before the bill was approved.[105] The final bill, whilst similar in terms of total cost, $21.4bn, bore little relation to Carter's original concept. Despite attempts to secure improvements, Eizenstat still described it as the 'worst tax bill since the 1940s'.[106] Schultze, in a rare intervention on this issue, argued that despite its faults it would be difficult to justify a veto economically as a tax cut, which was what this bill had become, was needed in 1979.[107] Carter accepted his advice and signed the bill on 6 November 1978.

On tax reform Carter wanted a comprehensive solution from his advisors, free from any political considerations. His Treasury experts either would not or could not follow his wishes. They argued that their view of accommodating Congress stood a better chance of success, but Carter had a mandate for reform and there was a window of opportunity in 1977 to pass such legislation. However, the administration was dealing with a Congress that was overloaded with government initiatives that were equally complex and whose members were very angry about Carter's policy on water projects. The GOP Senator Bob Packwood was highly critical of Carter, complaining that 'he didn't understand the power structure of the Congress or the interrelationships of economic issues'.[108] If Carter was to be left to deal with the political consequences as he wished, then he did not achieve his stated goals. The final bill had little reform left in it. The tax cuts were skewed towards the rich, many of the loopholes were not closed, it contained nearly $3bn in capital gains tax cut which Carter did not want, and at best progressivity was merely maintained, not improved as promised.[109] The administration had failed in its reform goals. After June 1978, the passing of Proposition 13 in California prompted a mood in the country, led by the GOP, which was largely focused on tax cuts. For Carter, his economic priority had moved onto fighting inflation. His tax reform was a missed opportunity. Carter came to believe that his policy failed due to the influence of lobbyists: 'a pack of ravenous wolves determined to secure for themselves additional benefits at the expense of other Americans.'[110] But he failed to give his proposal the priority that was necessary, alienated key members of congress with his water projects proposals and overloaded the legislative agenda which enabled opposition to coalesce. The final act contained no elements of reform and merely cut taxes. Ted Kennedy speaking for the liberals described it as 'the worst tax legislation approved by Congress since the days of Calvin Coolidge and Andrew Mellon'.[111] The opportunity for reform was delayed until the Reagan Tax Reform Act of 1986.

Carter saw deregulation as a means of making government more efficient and facilitating increased competition in the economy. Although he had the strong support of his economic advisors and the Federal Reserve, Carter faced opposition from interest groups, particularly the unions. But he was able to pass substantive legislation which included the deregulation of airline, banking, communications, railroad and trucking industries. This was followed by the eventual removal of restrictions on oil and gas pricing. Carter claimed that this legislative programme was 'the greatest change in the relationship between business and the government since the New Deal'[112] and certainly such reforms transformed the lives of many Americans. It was one of the few areas of economic policy where the administration was able to win support from both conservatives and liberals, notably Ted Kennedy. Deregulation was to become a major plank of the GOP presidential campaign in 1980 but Carter was able to point to his own record in this area. This policy trend initiated during the Ford presidency and expanded under Carter was to be continued by the Reagan, Bush and Clinton administrations in the 1980s and 1990s.

Inflation was not a problem unique to the Carter administration. The Ford presidency had struggled with the aftereffects of the OPEC price rises and had run its own ill-fated anti-inflation programme – WIN (Whip Inflation Now). Inflation, unlike unemployment, was not traditionally a key issue for the Democratic Party, but it was having a major impact on the middle classes and higher-income working families by increasing property taxes, college fees and non-unionized wages. The subsequent impact on tax thresholds was to trigger tax revolts in Colorado and New Jersey as early as 1976, well before Proposition 13 in California.[113] Carter had been warned during the transition of the dangers of inflation to consumer confidence.[114] But, at the beginning of his term, his focus and that of his advisors was on dealing with the risk of recession. If anyone had concerns about the inflationary aspects of an early stimulus package, Carter's economic team were quick to reassure them.[115] Carter kept Ford's Council on Wage and Price Stability (COWPS) but proposed no new initiatives on inflation until much later in 1977. Given that inflation had been prevalent throughout the 1970s the new administration had a number of options to tackle the problem. These ranged from mandatory controls of wages and prices to varying degrees of voluntary agreements with or without presidential involvement. What was striking throughout Carter's presidency was how little discussion there was of alternative approaches to reducing inflation when ideas such as control of fiscal and monetary policies were being advocated by economists such as Milton Friedman.[116] Mandatory controls were discussed during the transition and rejected, a decision that was maintained right until the end of the administration.[117] All of this limited the options that were available to Carter and his economic team to deal with a problem that from the autumn of 1977 began to dominate their priorities.

During the early phase of his administration inflation was between 5.8 and 6.5 per cent but there was much more concern about declining growth and unemployment at 7 per cent.[118] Elements of the stimulus package, increasing the minimum wage and proposed reforms of energy and social security policy, had an inflationary impact. Fred Kahn, who would later lead the fight against inflation, argued that changes in agricultural policy in the stimulus package, which reduced acreage, also contributed to food inflation over the next eighteen months.[119] Carter remained concerned about inflation but as long as wage increases kept pace there was no pressure on him from either his advisors or his supporters to deal with this problem. Schultze did not believe that the stimulus package would add to inflation, and at this early stage of the administration Blumenthal, who lacked macro-economic experience, did not intervene. Schultze's first draft of an anti-inflation policy on 29 March 1977 accepted that inflation would get worse before it got better but aimed to reduce it to 4 per cent by 1979. He ruled out any wage or price controls and encouraged dialogue with labour and business. COWPS's prime role would be to gather information.[120] Carter, who accepted Schultze's approach, was not without alternative views. Chair of the Federal Reserve Burns recommended more direct action to curb Federal spending: tax incentives to modernize plant, deregulation and vigorous implementation of anti-trust legislation.[121] There was also criticism of Schultze's proposals from Eizenstat who wanted tougher action on food prices.[122] He argued for clear inflation targets to win public support, and for speaking out against those in breach of them. A spike in inflation of 1.1 per cent in March 1977, due mainly to food prices,[123] was the catalyst that prompted some tightening of Schultze's proposals. This 'tougher' approach was reflected in Carter's first anti-inflation statement on 15 April 1977.[124] Additional measures included wider responsibilities for COWPS on monitoring, more action from government (including spending controls) and establishing a framework for co-operation with business and labour.

Whilst Carter's speech indicated more focus on inflation the approach by the White House remained low key and fundamentally ineffectual. Inflation grew to 9.8 per cent by the end of 1978, but food inflation was running much higher at 16.4 per cent.[125] His advisors continued to search for alternative approaches, but mandatory controls remained off the table. This enabled Carter to reassure

Republican Senator John Tower of Texas whose fear of mandatory controls caused him to hold up the renewal of COWPS in the Senate.[126] New proposals from the EPG were sent to Carter at the end of 1977. These included for the first-time numerical guidelines like those used by Presidents Kennedy and Johnson and an income policy which relied upon government persuasion.[127] Although he appeared to endorse these recommendations, Carter expressed disappointment that the proposals lacked specifics and appeared to be mostly wishful thinking.[128]

Further attempts at tightening controls were outlined in Carter's speech to the American Society of Newspaper Editors on 11 April 1978. It contained few specifics outside Federal government actions, but he emphasized in a typical downbeat manner that 'There were no easy answers. We will not solve inflation by increasing unemployment. We will not impose wage and price controls. We will work with measures that avoid both these extremes.'[129] One change that Carter did announce was the appointment of his special trade representative Robert S. Strauss to take on the additional role of special assistant on inflation. Strauss quickly was dubbed the 'Inflation Czar'. Whilst he did not have a significant impact on policy, it did symbolize Carter's advisors' increasing concern over inflation. In May 1978 Schultze wrote to Carter with some 'disturbing thoughts about the economic outlook'. He was beginning to recognize that the underlying problem was that inflation was being fuelled by a drop in productivity and started lobbying for further cuts in the Federal budget.[130] By June 1978 inflation had reached double figures. Carter received a range of proposals. George Meany of the AFL-CIO, afraid of wage controls being implemented, lobbied for credit controls which Carter rejected.[131] Strauss wanted budget cuts but also a new Federal committee on efficiency and cost reduction. This was again rejected as it increased bureaucracy and cut across the work of COWPS and the EPG.[132] By September 1978 there was recognition as inflation continued to rise that a further change of policy was required. It was Blumenthal who argued for more robust measures, and it was his proposals, despite reservations from Mondale and Eizenstat, that were mainly reflected in Carter's new policy announcement.[133]

Carter's speech on 24 October 1978 was an important moment for his economic policy. He publicly declared that fighting inflation would be 'a central preoccupation of mine' but again he went out of his way to dampen expectations: 'I cannot guarantee that our efforts will succeed. In fact, it is almost certain not to succeed if success means quick or dramatic changes.'[134] This partly demonstrated the pessimistic aspect of his character, but it was also a realistic reflection of his advisors' lack of confidence that a solution could be found. But he did outline a series of concrete proposals and specific targets. Measures included reducing the budget deficit to $30bn, cuts in Federal hiring and action on deregulation. He established guidelines both for wage settlements at 7 per cent and prices at 5.75 per cent which were to be monitored by COWPS. Despite continuing to reject mandatory controls, sanctions in the form of withdrawal of government contracts were threatened against those companies in breach of these guidelines. He also appointed Fred Kahn as Special Assistant to the President and Chairman of COWPS. The move of the former Chair of the Civil Aeronautics Board was a high-profile appointment. Kahn would have direct access to the president and joined the EPG. Reaction to the speech, however, was lukewarm. Wall Street did not think it was tough enough and foreign markets reacted with a run on the dollar.[135] Kahn did have difficulties coordinating with Carter's economic team. He complained of a lack of resources and felt that he was not getting cooperation from cabinet secretaries.[136] Kahn was also frustrated by his inability to get his ideas across, describing the EPG as 'an agency for systematically eliminating and weeding out any possibility of imaginative innovation'.[137]

The success of the new policy was dependent upon the ability of Kahn and Carter to persuade non-governmental bodies to accept the guidelines without any statutory powers to support them. Despite failure to follow up and communicate previous initiatives,[138] a more organized effort was made under Anne Wexler to convey the new government policy.[139] The impact of oil price increases in February 1979 caused Kahn to warn Carter that the policy was not working.[140] Carter's advisors were searching yet again for alternative approaches. Schultze believed that Carter's options had narrowed to fiscal restraint, credit controls or use of the Federal Reserve to raise interest rates.[141] Carter was even receiving advice from his political rival Edward Kennedy who recommended tougher sanctions such as legislation against companies that did not comply with the guidelines and even hinted at mandatory controls.[142] Kahn had become increasingly frustrated and in September 1979 threatened to resign. This was smoothed over by Carter and Eizenstat, but it was a symptom of Kahn feeling that he was being ignored on policy.[143] The inflation debates up until July 1979 continued to be limited by the administration's refusal to countenance a recession, mandatory wage-price controls and use of monetary policy. This changed when Carter appointed Paul Volcker as Chairman of the Federal Reserve.

Volcker was not Carter's first choice, but it was the one action that he did take to address inflation effectively. Inflation had reached 13.7 per cent in July 1979 and Volcker made no secret of his intention, if appointed, to tighten money supply.[144] He was determined to prioritize the fighting of inflation, even at the risk of recession. He quickly imposed tighter monetary controls which resulted in higher interest rates, but this would prove to be the long-term solution to the problem. Volcker ensured that the Fed's controls remained in place for the remainder of Carter's term of office, albeit with a brief respite in the summer of 1980.[145] This imposed a high political cost on Carter's re-election ambitions. His aides were already warning of the danger of a weak economy with the primaries only six months away.[146] Schultze viewed Volcker's policies as the 'only show in town' on inflation and he soon began a regular dialogue with him.[147] In the meantime the administration continued its efforts to find its own solutions to what seemed to be an intractable problem.[148] There was recognition that whilst wage settlements continued to fall within the guidelines set down by the government, tightening controls remained necessary. Further policy initiatives announced on 14 March 1980 contained no new controls on wages and prices but called for further cuts in the budget, the passing of oil conservation legislation and the imposition of credit controls.[149] However, within the White House there was scepticism as to whether this policy would succeed. Al From, who worked for Kahn, believed that the 'new' programme would not be effective because inflation was approaching a psychological tipping point at 20 per cent. The only policy that would work was the Fed's control of money supply but that was driving up mortgage rates and keeping traditional working-class families out of the housing market.[150]

Attempts by Kahn, with Carter's support, to penalize companies which breached administration guidelines through government contracts failed because both unions and business threatened to withdraw co-operation.[151] This left only the option of using presidential influence in private meetings or negotiations with major business and union leaders. Wexler's Outreach programme did give Carter the opportunity to meet with these leaders but unlike his Democratic predecessor, Johnson, Carter was not adept at such negotiation. Known as 'jawboning' this involved the president in face-to-face dialogue with business and union leaders and applying pressure to achieve the government's targets on wage and price settlements. Despite the urging of his staff Carter did not make the most of these opportunities to influence the behaviour of the country's economic leaders.[152] By April 1980 Kahn was reporting that with the renewed rise in oil prices and increase in mortgage rates, inflation had risen to 18 per cent in the previous three months. He feared that wages which had been restrained up to that point would soon accelerate to keep track. He also complained that commitments in Carter's 14 March speech to increase monitoring had not been implemented as Congress had failed to authorize the recruitment of 100 additional staff.[153] The administration's anti-inflation strategy was not working.

In November 1979 Kahn had what he described as a heart to heart with Carter about inflation. He argued that whilst the administration attempted all the right or orthodox actions, none of them were working. Carter's economic advisors had consistently got their inflation forecasts wrong which had damaged the administration's credibility.[154] Policies on minimum wage, farm price supports and protecting some organizations against competition had added to the inflationary spiral. Kahn argued for radical solutions and tough political choices on the budget. Carter appeared to sympathize but little of this was done.[155] Kahn could have added that it took eighteen months for the administration to recognize that inflation was the number one problem; up until then Carter's economic advisors' main concern had been avoiding recession. It could be argued that on inflation, Carter was an unlucky president and point to the OPEC price increases, but these were not a new phenomenon. His predecessor had suffered from substantial rises in 1974–5 and Schultze had told Carter that oil prices had had a negligible effect on inflation until late 1979.[156]

Carter's team tried alternative strategies to tackle the problem, but they were largely boxed in by their own policy decisions and the actions of Congress. The eventual solution, controlling money supply, was not discussed until Volcker imposed the policy on the administration. Any form of sanctions or mandatory policy to control wages and prices was rejected but more significantly the underlying decline in productivity was only vaguely understood and not addressed. This coupled with poor forecasting and the increasingly desperate actions of his advisors as they changed policies damaged Carter's credibility with the public. The impact of inflation was not just economic but psychological. Unlike unemployment it affected everyone and added an aura of uncertainty to every personal economic decision. Rafshoon warned Carter, 'It is impossible to overestimate the importance of the inflation issue to your presidency. It affects every American in a very palpable way. It causes insecurity and anxiety. It affects the American Dream.'[157] Carter's numerous initiatives and speeches on the subject did nothing to re-assure the public or give hope for better days ahead. He almost seemed to want to make the point to the American people that his solutions might not work. To the electorate Carter did not seem to be in control of the economy and his management of the budget only confirmed this view.

The budget process was something Carter understood from his time as Governor and from his experience as a businessman. Control of government spending was not only a key element of fiscal policy but a demonstration of the competence that Carter had promised the public when he was elected. Unfortunately to pass a Federal budget he needed the support of members of congress who had their own views on how money should be raised and where it should be spent. For a Democratic President, as far as the budget process was concerned it was politics not economics which dominated congressional thinking. A leading Democrat, Tom Foley, summed it up with 'Tight budgets strain the natural fault lines of the Democratic Party.'[158]

The process of building the budget was controlled by the OMB but to pass Congress its success was dependent upon the support of government departments and congressional liaison. Carter initially immersed himself in budgetting. It was something he felt he understood, and he hoped to reform the process with the introduction of ZBB helping to bring about a more rational approach. He had implemented this as governor and made major claims for its effectiveness during his presidential campaign. Carter argued that ZBB focused on objectives and needs, helped combine budgetting and planning, promoted cost effectiveness and finally encouraged management participation in the process.[159] Whilst it was implemented across government departments, extravagant claims of savings were soon toned down by the OMB.[160] ZBB was symbolic of Carter's approach to policy – if you build a budget by the best means possible then the legislature would accept it. Nothing could have been further from the truth. To succeed the administration needed to understand the detailed workings of Congress, in particular the committee structure. This was emphasized in a report from Douglas J Bennet, assistant secretary for legislative affairs. He highlighted the importance of building long-term relationships with key financial committee chairmen and to integrate them into the budget process. When the government failed to do this with its first budget, Bennet commented, 'if the administration shows the same contempt for orderly fiscal policy that Congress used to show, why bother with Budget Committees?'[161] This report was not followed up by Carter who was much more focused on agreeing a budget internally than how it was going to be sold to Congress.

Carter was hampered by conflict between a Democratic House which was determined to pass the social legislation that had been denied by his GOP predecessors and an administration attempting to fight inflation by fiscal restraint. Carter believed that fiscal irresponsibility was the 'Achilles heel' of the party.[162] Liberal Democrats demanded that Carter pass the reforms he 'promised' during the election, but such reforms increased expenditure when nearly 70 per cent of the budget was already fixed in areas like social security and health entitlements, defence and debt repayments.[163] This reality was to effect many of Carter's most cherished campaign pledges and put his administration in a war of attrition with Congress. This started in the first months of his presidency as Carter's request for a modest increase in the draft Ford 1978 budget was overridden by Congress which added a further $5.1bn.[164] There were also problems resulting from the White House losing influence over key congressional appropriations committees.[165] Recognition by Carter's advisors that constraining the budget was an important element of the administration's anti-inflation policy[166] had caused by mid-1978 conflict with congressional Democrats who were facing re-election that autumn. Proposals to cut back on spending were heavily criticized by liberals led by Ted Kennedy at the mid-term Democratic Conference.[167] Carter maintained the policy of fiscal constraint whatever the political cost, vetoing a $10.2bn public works bill in the run up to the mid-term elections because of its inflationary impact.[168] Carter's staff were concerned that members of the cabinet were expressing opposition to fiscal restraint, some being quoted as describing the draft 1980 budget as a 'Nixon-Ford budget which no Democratic president should sign up to.'[169] White House staff feared that a decline in Carter's approval ratings had been caused by a perceived lack of leadership in delivering a reduced budget.[170] Carter publicly committed to reduce the burgeoning deficit in the 1980 budget to under $30bn. This was despite pressure from his own party, a 3 per cent increase in defence spending above inflation, his own plans to deregulate oil and entitlement indexation (against inflation).[171] This proved not to be achievable.

The 1978 mid-term elections were a setback for his party, but the Democrats maintained their majority in the House despite an increase in the number of fiscally conservative congressmen elected. This should have helped Carter in achieving a balanced budget by 1981 but a review carried out by Moore's team found that whilst the majority of congressmen supported budget cuts in principle no one wanted to be associated with unpopular measures in an election year unless they were certain such changes would pass Congress.[172] By the end of 1979 Carter's advisors had accepted that a balanced budget was not a feasible goal.[173] Eizenstat argued that not only was this not achievable in a recession but such proposals would not pass Congress.[174] Congressional proposals for the 1981 budget were costlier than the White House's, which had included an additional $7bn for defence in response to the Soviet invasion of Afghanistan. This was despite efforts by Carter to make further savings by reducing the costs of social programmes, including welfare reform.[175] On the advice of his team he vetoed the proposed congressional budget as inflationary, alienating Byrd in the Senate who withdrew all support from Carter.[176] With the 1980 presidential election only five months away, Carter had failed in his budgetary goals and did not have an agreed budget for 1981.

McIntyre argued that Carter was successful in managing government spending, but this was based largely on technical issues such as establishing a three-year budget process and the use of budget reconciliation.[177] The public, however, saw constant haggling with Congress and a president who had failed to get to grips with a burgeoning Federal budget.[178] This was a harsh judgement given that much of government expenditure was fixed. Also, the administration had been affected by crises beyond Carter's control and by a Congress which continued to promote its own agenda. But this was a president who had campaigned on his competence. He looked anything but as his continued public commitment to a balanced budget became less credible with the passing of each financial year.

Many historians in writing about Carter's economic policy have stated that he tried to balance the liberal policies of his party with the fiscal realities of a weak US economy. His objective to move his party to the centre away from expensive social programmes to greater fiscal responsibility, ultimately, they argued, failed because his administration could not control inflation.[179] Others like Ann Mari May used a comparison of the key performance indicators of the Ford, Carter and Reagan administrations to argue that Carter's economic record was largely successful, particularly in relation to growth.[180] Iwan Morgan has stated that Carter's economic policies of giving priority to fighting inflation, fiscal conservatism, deregulation and supply-side economics anticipated the approach of his New Democratic successor Bill Clinton.[181] This coupled with his use of monetary policy and deregulation laid the groundwork for what became known as 'Reaganomics'.[182] Carter's fundamental differences with Reagan were not over economic policy but in their views on government. Reagan famously saw government as 'the problem' and wanted a free-market economy whilst Carter believed in the power of government to do good and correct faults in the economy. The underlying assumption in the historical literature implies that Carter had a coherent view on economic policy but there is little evidence to support this. His lack of expertise and involvement meant that decisions were made by his experts who failed to develop a consistent economic policy throughout his term of office, often zigzagging between fighting recession and inflation. The administration's economic forecasting was at best problematic, underestimating the economic recovery in 1977 and inflation rates throughout his presidency. His advisors did not grasp the significance of the decline in productivity or the importance of monetary policy until late in the administration.

Carter's interest in the budget and government spending may have indicated that he was a fiscal conservative, but he never articulated his views in any coherent economic philosophy, unlike his Democratic successor. His fiscal policies were more influenced by his business background and a moral sense of the importance of a country living within its means. The contention of being socially liberal had little meaning as he was unable to fund reform. His failure to convince his party and ultimately the country of the benefits of a balanced budget left his administration with little to offer other than austerity.[183] To the liberals in the Democratic Party, Carter's economic policies were little different from the Republicans, and this contributed to their support for Kennedy in the race for the 1980 Democratic presidential nomination. By the 1980 election the economic outlook indicated the continuation of high inflation and an imminent recession. The media compared Carter with Herbert Hoover, 'dawdling at the onset of the Great Depression'.[184] This was not the message of competence that Carter had presented to the public in 1976. None of his economic policies appeared to work and his most specific economic commitment, reform of a tax system he described as 'a disgrace', had been gutted by a Congress controlled by his own party.

It is worth considering how Carter influenced the way economic policy was developed in his administration. He did actively involve himself in his first year in office in micro-economic matters around the budget, ZBB and saving money in the White House, but contributed little to the macro-economic debate. Whilst he did get frustrated with his economic team, sometimes seeking alternative advice, he usually followed their guidance. His main role as president was to 'sell' his policy in Congress and to the public; unfortunately, this did not play to his strengths. Clinton, who was Arkansas's governor when Carter was president, described Carter's economic speeches as him sounding more like a '17th Century New England Puritan than a 20th Century Southern Baptist'.[185] Clinton was to learn from this experience. Carter 'preached' self-sacrifice but did not articulate a positive view of his policies that would justify in the minds of the public the sacrifices that he was asking them to make. His dealings with Congress were hampered by his marked reluctance to build relationships and do deals, something experienced congressmen had been used to under his Democratic predecessor, Lyndon Johnson. His distaste for the hard bargaining involved in passing legislation damaged his relationship with Congress. His decision to appoint Volcker to be chair of the Federal Reserve highlighted one of the positive elements of his character, the determination to do the right thing whatever the political cost – although this in effect passed control of America's anti-inflation policy to the Fed. Pressure from his advisors to sanction a politically popular tax cut in the run up to the 1980 election was met with Carter's 'I cannot just flip-flop' response.[186] Was he standing on principle or was he just being stubborn? The tightening of money supply was the eventual, if painful, solution to inflation. Carter recognized this would cost him politically in the run up to the election but as was often the case he did it anyway because he saw it as the right thing to do. His economic policy was in many ways a failure of presidential influence. He could not through his speeches and his conversations with members of congress and other leaders persuade decision makers and the American people that his economic policies would work and were worth the price he was asking them to pay. Public frustration with Carter's management of an economy with a very uncertain outlook was summed up by a New York librarian: 'The whole situation is frightening, and I don't know when it will end.'[187]

The energy crisis

America's oil production had been declining since it reached its peak in 1950 and its share of the world's production had fallen from 52 per cent to 16 per cent in 1974. In contrast oil imports had risen ten times in five years and represented an increase of $10bn on the US trade deficit.[1] The concept of an American energy 'crisis', however, was by no means unchallenged. The US public throughout the 1970s continued to believe that any crisis was caused by the greed of the oil companies or the incompetence of government. A Central Intelligence Agency (CIA) report stated that whilst dependence on OPEC imports represented 40 per cent of US domestic consumption, the opening of new fields in Alaska, Mexico and the Arab peninsula would remove the threat of shortage by 1980.[2]

The options for the government in dealing with an energy shortage were either to increase local production or reduce consumption by conservation. To increase production required initial investment to find and develop new oil and gas fields. In America, major suppliers had control of all stages of the production cycle from exploration, production, refining and distribution. Profits from increased prices in oil and gas were restricted by regulation which kept prices artificially low for the US consumer but did nothing to stimulate new production. Deregulation as a solution, strongly favoured by conservatives, would raise prices, increase both inflation and supplier profits but would not necessarily guarantee increased local production as producers often received a better return by investing in overseas oil fields. The alternative approach to address the country's profligacy in energy consumption was conservation. In the 1970s America was consuming 2.3 times more than the European Economic Community (EEC) and 2.65 times more than Japan.[3] A conservation strategy would include bringing US prices up to the real cost of production, fuel efficiency measures and incentivizing alternative sources of energy like coal, nuclear power and solar energy. There were two opposing views about resolving the energy problem. The first was the belief that the free market would be the most effective means of stimulating production and stabilizing prices. Alternatively, there was the acceptance of some form of regulatory control to protect poorer families against profiteering and reduce pollution.[4] Both options needed to be considered against a background of an American public who were used to cheap, easily available energy and had been unused to any restrictions on their consumption since the Second World War. In addition, there were powerful interest groups representing energy suppliers, environmentalists, business and consumer groups, all expressing divergent views on the best energy strategy for the country.

Although America's energy security had been deteriorating steadily since the 1950s, it was not until the Arab Israeli conflict of 1973 that energy problems began directly to impact the public. The OPEC price increases in 1973–4 presented a challenge to the administrations of Presidents Nixon and Ford. In his first State of the Union address, Ford unveiled policies to deal with the problem. This included deregulation, incentives for coal and nuclear power plants as well as an oil import fee. His policies were largely anathema to a Democratic Congress and Ford found himself in a year-long battle before his legislation, the Energy Policy and Conservation Act, passed on 22 December 1975.[5] This bill reinstated price controls originally brought in by Nixon but allowed the president to increase prices by 10 per cent a year over forty months. There were also some conservation measures including establishing a Strategic Petroleum Reserve and an average fuel economy standard for cars.[6] This legislation was regarded as having fallen short of Ford's stated objectives. The Carter campaign team therefore entered the presidential race in 1975 expecting that energy policy would be a major issue.

The decision to prioritize his new administration's efforts on resolving America's energy crisis was Carter's. It was not forced upon him, but he chose it over other substantive issues. Recent writings from revisionist historians like Jonathan Alter have sought to portray Carter's decision as an example of his far-sighted recognition of the problems America would face in the next century. Carter's reasoning, however, was more to do with his character. Energy had many of the components of a problem that he liked to address. It was an issue that was highly technical, complex and fundamentally impacted on American society. Energy policy cut across political ideology with possible solutions dividing Democrat from Democrat, liberal from liberal and region from region. Carter was influenced by writers like Robert Bellah, Christopher Lasch and Daniel Bell who wrote about the dangers of consumerism and were invited to the White House by Carter soon after his election.[7] Hence there was a moral element in his approach of seeking to promote energy conservation with consumers.

It was also a challenge that Carter saw as an opportunity to demonstrate that government could be a force for good, despite the failure of his predecessors. For James Schlesinger, who would become the President's Assistant for Energy, the choice highlighted two of Carter's character traits: the engineer who wanted to solve complex technical problems and the moral leader who wished to curb the country's wasteful use of energy.[8] Carter was to find this opportunity to demonstrate both the government's and his own competence irresistible.

Energy turned out not to be a major issue in the 1976 presidential campaign. Carter did not mention it in his speech accepting his nomination on 15 July 1976. The Carter-Ford Presidential debates in September and October 1976 did offer him the opportunity to promote his energy proposals. During the 23 September debate Carter argued strongly for an energy policy that would include moving production from oil to coal and support for solar energy. He emphasized the importance of conservation and criticized Ford for 'yielding every time to the special interest groups [who] put pressure on the President'.[9] This early indication of Carter's mistrust of interest groups was to have a major impact on how his administration's energy policy was developed. Another sign that Carter was considering a new initiative on energy was the involvement of Democratic Senator Henry 'Scoop' Jackson and his staff in the transition. Jackson had been a rival of Carter in the primaries but was a strong advocate of a proactive energy policy and chaired the important Senate Energy and Resources Committee. Jackson and his staff provided advice on energy to Carter and his transition team. This advice was for Carter to be cautious on energy policy. Grenville Garside, who was Jackson's staff director and counsel for the Senate Energy Committee, recommended that Carter should just focus on recruiting top quality people to the Federal Energy Administration (FEA) and the Energy Research and Development Administration (ERDA), and appointing an Energy Czar. He made no recommendations for specific polices but wanted the new administration to concentrate on education, consultation and policy formulation.[10] The reasons for this caution were expressed in a memorandum to Jackson from Arlon Tussing, chief economist on the Senate Energy Committee, who argued:

> Energy Policy was not a promising area for early policy innovation by the new Administration. No crisis is imminent and there are no bold dramatic steps that can quickly assure long-term security of our energy supply or bring down fuel and electricity prices. Most bold moves would at least in the short run increase uncertainty and result in higher costs and prices. We can afford to spend a year or more reconsidering the whole spectrum of energy issues without the aura of crisis and confrontation that have surrounded them since 1973.[11]

Carter did act on some of this advice from Jackson's staff, particularly on the eventual scope of the new Energy Department,[12] but ultimately, he wanted his administration to produce a comprehensive solution to the energy problem and he was not prepared to wait.

Carter may not have followed all of Jackson's advice on policy, but he did try to ensure that his key advisor on energy would be of the right calibre and be someone he trusted: he chose James Schlesinger. This was a critical appointment not just because Carter expected Schlesinger to become the Secretary of the newly formed Department of Energy but because he would delegate most of the policy development to him. He took an instant liking to Schlesinger. As well as giving him regular access during the week he also met frequently with him on early Saturday mornings.[13] This helped ensure that Carter was involved in the detail of the proposed legislation. Schlesinger proved to be one of Carter's most controversial appointments. He had been Ford's Secretary of Defence but had been fired because of his covert opposition to the second Strategic Arms Limitation Treaty (SALT II) and his condescending attitude to Ford over the president's relations with Congress.[14] Carter was also aware of concern from his staff about Schlesinger's suitability for the role.[15] The perception of Schlesinger being a difficult character was subsequently borne out by his actions over appointments, where he tended to ignore recommendations from the White House.[16] Tensions with White House staff would persist until his resignation in July 1979. The relationship with Carter remained cordial but Schlesinger was not above criticizing the president for spending too much time on the detail and not enough on leadership.[17] If Schlesinger was important to his administration's policy development it was Congress and the American public whom Carter needed to persuade to support his policy proposals. It was essential that Carter and his team were able to influence key congressional leaders and committee chairmen if their legislation were to pass. But this was to be affected by the inexperience and naivety of Carter and his staff. Energy policy divided Congress not on party or even ideological lines but more in terms of a state's natural resources and geography. In addition, the very complexity of the proposed legislation resulted in the involvement of a wide variety of powerful interest groups. For example, there were 117 groups alone involved in decisions on the pricing of natural gas in 1978.[18] Carter's deep mistrust of interest groups and their influence would be a major factor in how his administration decided to develop the new policy and how he dealt with individual members of congress and the public.

Carter's inaugural address on 20 January 1977 gave little indication that he was going to give energy such a high priority. Indeed, there were many alternative policies that were regarded as equally urgent, not the least of which was dealing with the parlous state of the US economy. The decision may have been triggered by a winter fuel crisis in eleven states east of the Rockies caused by the coldest winter in 100 years. This crisis prompted lobbying of Carter from such diverse individuals as Senator Jackson, the consumer lobbyist Ralph Nader and his mentor Admiral Rickover. Carter began to see energy not just as a complex technical problem to be solved but also, in seeking to reduce waste, a moral one.[19] To Carter, the policy's degree of complexity justified careful study and analysis. He wanted a comprehensive solution that would be for the public good and not for the benefit of interest groups. The winter gas shortages were resolved by effective cooperation between the Federal government, Congress and private industry. It resulted in the passage of the Emergency Natural Gas Act on 2 February 1977. In his statement on the energy shortage on 21 January 1977, Carter signalled action: 'Today's crisis is a painful reminder that our energy problems are real and cannot be ignored. This Nation needs a coherent energy policy, and such a programme of energy action will be formulated promptly.'[20] Carter's promise of action was confirmed in his 'Fireside Talk' on 2 February. Energy was not the only issue covered by this address, but it was the first one he raised. Carter set a deadline of ninety days for his administration to report back to Congress on a new energy policy. This would include recommendations for a new Department of Energy as well as a focus on conservation, reduced dependency on oil and use of alternative energy sources, particularly coal and solar power. He acknowledged that the public might not believe that there was an energy crisis but hoped that the winter gas crisis would have changed their minds.[21]

Two decisions proved critical in how Carter's final proposals were received: firstly, the creation of a ninety-day deadline; and, secondly, the decision to keep the development of the plans restricted to a small group of 'experts' under Schlesinger. An artificial deadline had been used by Carter before as governor to drive through proposals with the legislature and lobbyists who, given the short timescales, found it more difficult to disrupt his legislation. He also hoped to replicate the cooperation that enabled the passage of the Emergency Natural Gas Act earlier in the year. He was concerned that any consultation prior to announcement would just be an opportunity for special interests to delay and sabotage his proposals. So, he insisted that the plans be developed by experts in secret even from other government departments which Carter believed had relationships with interest groups. This had the effect of restricting the expertise available to Schlesinger's team and consequently limiting the scope of their analysis of the problem.[22] This decision also caused concern among

White House staff and resentment in Congress. Eizenstat became involved in March 1977, acting on behalf of advisors from the CEA and DPG who were growing concerned about the potential economic and political implications of any energy proposals.[23] Economic advisors eventually saw the proposals two weeks before publication and immediately raised objections about the impact on growth and inflation. Fortunately, there was time to resolve this before Carter's speech in April, but this opportunity was not available to Congress. Major supporters like Jackson felt excluded and as early as 3 February 1977 Dan Tate from congressional liaison described Jackson's behaviour as 'bitter' and that he had 'made life in the Senate Liaison pretty miserable lately'.[24] The use of an artificial deadline and secrecy did hamper the progress of the new policy. Carter's approach would draw striking parallels with the doomed attempt by the Clinton administration to pass healthcare legislation sixteen years later. The health taskforce of experts also working in secret under Hillary Clinton aimed to create a comprehensive healthcare system, but it ultimately failed due to pressure from interest groups they initially sought to exclude and opposition in Congress. A lesson that Clinton had failed to learn from Carter.

Although there were tensions caused by the secrecy within the White House during the ninety-day deadline, many issues were resolved. Schlesinger was able to agree with Cecil Andrus, Secretary of the Interior, on the structure of the new Department of Energy.[25] As the deadline approached Carter, prompted by Eizenstat, accepted that the new energy plan should be integrated with other programmes so as not to hamper the administration goal of a balanced budget by 1981.[26] The concerns expressed by the EPG over the plan's impact on inflation were also addressed.[27] There was pressure from liberals within the administration such as Secretary Califano to do more to protect the poor from the aftereffects of the fuel crisis and use energy taxes to reform social security but these ideas were resisted.[28] Carter also rejected attempts by Schlesinger to include more individual 'sacrifice' in his plans with taxes on commuter parking and luxury cars.[29] Overall whilst the imposed deadline and secrecy did bring disadvantages, especially with Congress, Carter believed that a broad package of well-thought-out measures would not have succeeded without the restrictions he imposed. He now wanted to use his current high approval ratings to convince the American people of the benefit of his Energy Plan, thus enabling him to defeat the formidable interest groups that would inevitably align against him.[30]

Carter understood that on energy policy his main task was to convince Americans of the seriousness of the crisis and the fairness of his solution. The launch of his Energy Plan was carefully choreographed. He continued the use of symbolism that he had followed in the winter fuel crisis with a Saturday cabinet meeting and the staged helicopter visit to Pittsburgh prior to his speech. He spoke to the nation on 18 April 1977, followed by his address to Congress two days later and a televised press conference on 22 April.[31] The administration attempted to engage the public as part of the ninety-day period by sending out over 450,000 postcards asking for suggestions on energy.[32] Carter had also used the Town Hall meetings to raise awareness of energy issues. Early ABC polling indicated that whilst there was initially an increased level of public concern about energy this was not sustained.[33] Carter's speech was remembered for the acronym MEOW which was derived from his phrase the 'moral equivalent of war', wording he had taken from Admiral Rickover.[34] Carter sought to convince the American public that the country faced a situation that was worse than the gas crisis of eight weeks earlier and even the OPEC crisis of 1973. He attempted to promote moral and social responsibility for the common good. He argued that 'we must not be selfish' and wanted to 'test the character of the American people', all of which was aimed at encouraging individual self-sacrifice in the use of energy.[35] In presenting Schlesinger's comprehensive package to Congress, he was much less 'preachy' but was certainly downbeat: 'This cannot be an inspirational speech tonight. I don't expect much applause. It's a sober and a difficult presentation.'[36] In his televised press conference, Carter was forced to defend the use of the phrase MEOW which had been criticized as an overreaction. He later claimed that his bill had raised energy awareness by 20 per cent, but it did not get the response from the American people that he had hoped. Three months later a frustrated president was saying that 'the public is not paying attention, voluntarism is not working'.[37] Carter's desire for an honest assessment of the energy problem without any 'spin' came across as so pessimistic that it failed to motivate the American people. This was to continue throughout his term in office. A participant at a later Town Hall Meeting in Portsmouth, New Hampshire, summed up public scepticism when he asked Carter 'I would like to know if the situation of the shortage of gas is really true or is it being built out of proportion?'[38] If the US public were not responding, how would Congress react to the complex set of proposals submitted by Carter?

The National Energy Plan, submitted on 20 April 1977, covered 113 separate but interlocking initiatives, the clear majority of which were not controversial. The objective of the proposed legislation was to reduce energy demand, increase supply and distribute costs equitably between the consumer and industry. Measures included a Crude Oil Equalisation Tax (COET) which would allow the domestic price of oil to rise to world levels by the ending of price controls by 1981. The first-year tax revenues were to be redistributed to poorer families. Oil consumption targets were to be established and if missed by over one per cent, a five cents gasoline tax was to be imposed. There were incentives for mass transportation and alternative sources of energy such as coal and solar power. Conservation was to be encouraged through incentives for major buildings and house insulation, and a national 55-mph speed limit was proposed.[39] Carter's Energy Plan was comprehensive and complex, and he recognized the difficulty he would face in passing such legislation given the number of congressional committees that could be involved.[40] He also had no natural constituency either in Congress or the country that would support his proposals in full. This resulted, for example, in environmentalists being natural supporters of his conservation measures but in opposition to the proposed move to 'dirty' coal-fired power stations. The administration would have to build separate alliances for each aspect of the plan. In addition, the comprehensive nature of the plan meant that any change to a component of the bill would affect its overall objectives. To be successful would require the White House to run a sophisticated operation to manage the legislative process and muster public support.

The initial public response, according to a Gallup poll on 26 April 1977, was overwhelmingly in favour of the Carter plan (87 to 13 per cent),[41] but there were few if any groups that supported the whole package. Democrats were split not only in terms of ideology but to a large extent geography. Natural supporters like the environmentalists favoured restricting energy growth but Carter's labour constituency wanted a plan that would increase jobs. Supporters such as the Urban League believed that aspects of Carter's proposals would hit the poor whilst unions like the Teamsters regarded the standby tax as an imposition on working people.[42] These were just some examples of the response from within the Democratic Party and did not include the views of the GOP or the energy industry which would be lobbying to support or change parts of the plan that they did not favour. Carter hoped that by developing the plan in secret he would avoid such pressures until it was announced but he knew that he could not avoid opposition indefinitely. He did hope that he could counter the interest groups by mobilizing popular opinion but whilst the overall plan had high public approval ratings, these were never translated into active support. This encouraged congressional intransigence. The struggle with Congress over energy also had a negative impact on Carter's personal popularity with a 10 per cent drop in his approval ratings reported as early as 5 May 1977.[43]

Carter's performance in supporting the Energy Plan was also subject to criticism in the press and even from Schlesinger. The conservative press continued to argue that there was no crisis, just government incompetence. Jordan summed up the problem for Carter by saying, 'We cannot create an atmosphere of sacrifice that is politically meaningful if the American people persist in thinking the crisis is not real.'[44] It was suggested that he 'dropped the ball between April and September' by not being sufficiently proactive.[45] This was unfair as up until August 1977 the bill was being steered successfully through the House by Speaker Tip O'Neill and it was only when it transferred to the Senate that those problems occurred. It was at this point that Carter became heavily engaged in lobbying by going on the road, making three televised speeches and encouraging cabinet members to speak out in favour of the plan.[46] In a rare occurrence the workaholic Carter recognized that he had to prioritize his time: 'It's become obvious to me that we've had too much of my own involvement in different matters simultaneously. I need to concentrate on energy and fight for a passage of an acceptable plan.'[47] There was some recognition that he was more effective after that point, but criticism remained about his ability to influence key members of congress. Schlesinger regarded him as a failure at lobbying, quoting an unsuccessful meeting with Senator Lloyd Bentsen of Texas as an example.[48]

The passage of Carter's Energy Plan took eighteen months despite his personal efforts. Although this legislation contained many significant measures, it was not the all-encompassing solution that Carter had promised the American people. The parts of the original plan that involved price increases like the oil standby tax and the COET (also called the Wellhead Tax) had little support in Congress and the country. Carter's appeal for self-sacrifice came up against the hard realities of electoral politics. An unnamed Democratic Representative from New York bleakly summed up the problem in supporting Carter: 'You are asking me to vote for something that will cost my constituents money and make life less convenient, and they won't see any benefit from it for the next 5 years. And I'll tell you something else if I do what you want ... I will be out.'[49] The White House and the party leaders in Congress faced different coalitions of members for every aspect of the legislation. Carter's most effective champion in Congress was Tip O'Neill. He did not break the bill down and send it to different committees as was customary but by using one super committee created an 'Omnibus Bill' and successfully managed its passage through the House.[50] This radical approach ensured that following the bill's introduction in the House on 2 May 1977, it passed three months later.[51] Only the standby gasoline tax proposal failed due to opposition from a coalition of liberal and conservative legislators, neither of whom was convinced by the administration's case.[52]

The Senate would prove to be much more of a challenge. The momentum created by the passage of the House Omnibus Bill was lost during the summer recess and the impact of the Lance Affair. Senate Majority Leader Byrd was a traditionalist and so, unlike Speaker O'Neill, he broke the bill up and sent it to the various Senate Committees. The two key committees were Finance under Russell Long and Energy and Resources under Henry Jackson. The administration's difficult relationship with Long has already been discussed but it should be added that Long's home state, Louisiana, was oil producing and so he was naturally opposed to many of the bill's provisions. Jackson, on the other hand, had long campaigned for a national energy policy and had contributed to the Carter transition discussions on energy. However, relations between Jackson and the White House were never cordial. Jackson had mounted a late challenge to Carter in 1976, and Jordan had made derogatory comments about him in an interview during the campaign. The president had also rejected Jackson's cautious approach on energy and his advice on the inclusion of natural resources in the new Department of Energy.[53] Schlesinger argued that it was the White House's failure to build an alliance with Long and Jackson that damaged the Energy bill in the Senate.[54] Long, whilst supporting Carter on some issues like the new Energy Department, proved too resourceful for Carter and his team whose lobbying Long labelled 'sloppy and naive'.[55] The White House tried to use Byrd as a conduit to Long but was unsuccessful, as were attempts to influence both Long and Jackson (whose wife was Georgian) by inviting them and their spouses to dinner at the White House.[56]

The Energy bill that passed the Senate was significantly different from the House version. Most of the revenue raising aspects of the original bill like COET and the standby gasoline tax had been removed by the Senate and replaced by a series of energy tax concessions. These tax changes, if passed, would increase the fiscal deficit during 1978–81 by \$34 bn more than the House bill.[57] The administration used all its resources to influence the outcome of the joint conference when the House and Senate came together to resolve the differences. In establishing strategy for the conference, Carter's staff had two major concerns: firstly, the continued assumption in Congress that the public still did not believe that there was an energy crisis and therefore did not support any 'sacrificial' elements of the legislation; and secondly, that when the pressure of negotiations was applied, the administration (meaning Carter) would compromise too early. For the six-week period between late September and early November 1977, the White House established a task force to manage the lobbying on the bill, employing many members of the administration, including the cabinet and the president.[58] Carter was told not to get involved personally too soon in discussions because 'If we compromise early, the Senate will think we are suckers, and the House will think us unreliable.'[59] In the briefings that Carter had with members of Congress and Lane Kirkland of the AFL-CIO, he emphasized how important the Energy bill was to the prestige not just of the president but of Congress and the Democratic Party.[60] The attempt to move the final bill towards the House version failed because the overwhelming majority of Senate Democrats, including liberals, were opposed to revenue-generating measures like COET.[61]

Despite considerable efforts by the White House and Carter personally, the final passage of the Energy bill did not take place until October 1978. Many elements of the original proposals were defeated by the sheer complexity of the alliances deployed against the administration, often involving Carter's nominal supporters. Congressional liberals watered down gas deregulation proposals and attempts by Carter to reach out to petroleum leaders, arranged by Charles Kirbo, were vetoed by staff concerned about the reaction from environmental groups.[62] Some of the administration's failure was down to decisions made as early as February 1977. The self-imposed deadline to produce the Energy Plan resulted in a limited investigation of alternatives. There were technical flaws in the proposals with errors in some numbers submitted to support the legislation. The initial pre-briefing on the bill was bungled with important material not being ready in time and Carter's brusque style resulted in a failure to explain his policy to members of congress with sufficient clarity.[63] White House effectiveness was hampered by a lack of understanding of the fundamental differences between how the House and the Senate operated.[64] O'Neill's 'one bill' tactics could not be replicated in the Senate and time was wasted by the delayed lobbying of the Senate during the summer recess. Finally, there was the impact of the administration's other legislative initiatives both on the congressional timetable and on relationships with important legislators, who often tried to use their support for the Energy Bill as a bargaining chip for other legislation. Carter remained an active participant in the lobbying, meeting with Long and Jackson as well as intervening, for example, in the Natural Gas conference, to ensure a deal.[65] However not all of his interventions were successful, for instance his talk of oil producers as war profiteers alienated Senate and business leaders.[66] Although there was criticism of the effectiveness of lobbying by inexperienced staffers, Carter was generally exempted from this because of his in-depth knowledge of the subject.[67] However in a rare admission of intellectual weakness, Carter admitted that 'The issues before us are so complicated, it has gotten past me.'[68] He was not successful in persuading the American people of the necessity of his plan. Carter went on TV three times in nine months to try to galvanize support but whilst polls reflected public criticism of oil companies and Congress, only 43 per cent believed that there was an energy crisis.[69] Attempts by Rafshoon to develop a 90–120-day communication strategy to raise awareness failed to increase pressure on Congress to act.[70]

The National Energy Act of 1978 was by any definition a substantial piece of legislation. A new Department of Energy was established. It increased overall energy supply with subsidies for alternative programmes and incentives to utilities to share power. Gas deregulation was deferred until 1984 but controlled prices were increased with future rises established as inflation plus 4 per cent. The legislation set up the Strategic Petroleum Reserve (SPR) with storage capacity of 120 days or 1 billion barrels, which would take seven years to complete and cost $70 bn. Significantly, price incentives for industry and the consumer were rejected by Congress as too costly.[71] Carter's staff quickly recognized that he was not receiving credit for the bill as the press and the public were not so much focused upon what was included in the legislation but what was not and how long it took to pass.[72]

By the end of Carter's second year in office the energy debate had moved onto the issue of oil deregulation. The oil producers and their supporters argued that allowing oil prices to rise to their natural level would provide an incentive for new fields to be explored. Carter believed in deregulation, his policy on the air travel industry being a case in point, but many of his supporters were opposed. Liberal congressmen argued that oil producers would reap huge profits from deregulation which they would not necessarily invest in American oil fields. There was also concern over protecting poorer families who would be hardest hit by the price increase. Environmentalists favoured switching production away from oil to cleaner energy and wanted much more emphasis on conservation. The solution appeared to be linking deregulation with a tax on oil company profits (a Windfall Profits Tax) which could be used to subsidize poorer families and fund cleaner energy. The case for such a tax was by no means clear cut and this argument dominated energy policy for the remainder of Carter's term in office. The administration was 'helped' in this debate by the revolution in Iran as it resulted in OPEC price increases which added $22 bn to the US annual import bill. Although US prices continued to be held below world rates, poor internal oil allocation resulted in local shortages in May 1979. Further attempts to deregulate oil were delayed by the opposition of Carter's own supporters in Congress. Liberals continued to fear the impact on the poor and environmentalists wanted much more emphasis on conservation.[73] Carter tried to make contingency plans in the event of shortages as part of emergency measures, but these were delayed by conflicting messages within his own administration. Schlesinger stated that the energy crisis justified contingency plans for rationing, but his own department argued that US energy stocks were healthy and that even with oil consumption rising, there was no need for contingency plans in the medium term.[74]

The White House worked hard to build a coalition that would support oil deregulation linked to a windfall profits tax. Carter met with senior senators, including Long, and by the end of March 1979 he believed he had enough support to recommend action.[75] However, there remained differences amongst his staff, especially on strategy. His advisors argued that making deregulation contingent on a windfall profits tax would not work because conservatives and liberals would separately oppose each piece of legislation, thus causing deadlock. They recommended using the 1975 Ford Energy Act to phase in deregulation by 1981 and challenge Congress to bring in a tax on excess profits.[76] In the end Carter chose to launch both proposals in his speech on 5 April 1979. In it he continued to remind the public that 'The energy crisis is real. I said so in 1977, and say so again tonight, almost exactly two years later. Time is running out.'[77] He equated the dependence on imported oil as a risk to national security and sought public support to ensure that Congress responded to the crisis. The initial response from the public was favourable[78] but the bill proposed, whilst not as complex as two years earlier, still involved seventeen separate pieces of legislation.[79]

The warning from his staff about the difficulty in passing the Windfall Profits Tax proved prophetic and there was evidence that Carter was becoming increasingly frustrated. Shortages at the pumps prompted a response from Powell which blamed the consumers whose behaviour he characterized as 'Me first, last, and always. Give me mine and to hell with the rest of the country'.[80] This resulted in a push back from Congress with liberal Representative Toby Moffett telling United Automobile Workers (UAW) members that 'The Administration seems to think working people are like spoiled children. Maybe it's the Baptist teacher element.'[81] Speeches Carter made against oil companies were very hard hitting even inflammatory. Eizenstat became concerned that Carter's remarks describing them as 'money-launderers' and receiving 'kickbacks' were not being seen as presidential and had fixed the administration's position when negotiation and flexibility were required in the future.[82] This was not Eizenstat's only concern about Carter's speeches on the administration's new energy proposals. In a speech in Iowa in May 1979, Carter appeared to undermine his carefully worked-out position on deregulation by seeming indifferent to the issue. Eizenstat told Carter how damaging this was to his reputation with Congress and its implications for the future passage of the legislation. Eizenstat was so concerned that he arranged an editorial in the *New York Times* to 'correct' Carter's statement.[83] The continued battle with Congress prompted his team to recommend another nationwide address on energy to mobilize public support for his policies in July 1979 when Carter returned from the Tokyo summit. It was during the summit that a further large OPEC price increase prompted a fresh crisis with petrol queues and a 'riot' of truckers in Levittown, Pennsylvania, on 24–25 June 1979.[84]

Carter's address to the nation a few weeks later on 15 July became known as the 'Malaise' speech but it was supposed to be a speech on 'Energy and National Goals'. Much of the mood of pessimism which pervaded the White House in the run up to the speech was related to the public's frustration with energy policy. As Eizenstat told Carter, 'Nothing else has so frustrated, confused, angered the American people or so targeted their distress at you personally.'[85] Carter's approval rating by this time had sunk to 27 per cent.[86] His speechwriters were equally direct arguing that: 'Gas lines promote anger, not conservation.' 'Hatred for the oil companies is only matched by lack of confidence in the Administration,'[87] but they were struggling to create a draft that would galvanize public opinion. Proposals were to deregulate oil prices over twenty-eight months, and for a Windfall Profits Tax that would be used to build an Energy Security Fund to help the poor and build mass transit systems. In addition, there were to be government initiatives to reduce consumption by 5 per cent including a 55-mph speed limit. However, all of this remained deadlocked in Congress. Draft legislation on creating a Low Energy Assistance Programme for poor families immediately ran into trouble as further OPEC price increases had tripled the cost of decontrol. Pressure from Senate liberals forced Carter to expand this programme of support from $800 m to $2.4 bn.[88]

The agonizing over the energy speech, its postponement and the resulting series of meetings at Camp David moved the debate away from energy. This caused tension between Carter and his advisors. Carter refused to have his energy staff present at Camp David when he met external experts. Eizenstat implied that it was because Carter incorrectly believed his staff had leaked a confidential memorandum to various journalists.[89] This tension was highly unusual in the Carter White House but symptomatic of the atmosphere at the time. Following lobbying from Mondale and Eizenstat the final version of the speech did contain new targets on energy with the aim of inspiring a positive public response. These included the goal of never importing more fuel than the United States had done in 1977, backed by import quotas to ensure that this was achieved. In addition, Carter proposed massive funding from the Energy Security Corporation (ESC) for alternative fuels and mass transit as well as targetting utilities to cut consumption by 50 per cent. Finally, in alluding to the spirit of the Second World War, Carter proposed the creation of an Energy Mobilization Board (EMB) to speed up energy production.[90]

Although initial polling after the speech was positive, Carter yet again failed to inspire the public. *New York Daily News* commented the next day that Carter only had one problem: how 'to wake up the 80 million Americans he put to sleep last night'.[91] Carter's attempt to gain support for a new energy policy was to be made with a new secretary of energy as James Schlesinger had resigned. He had discussed leaving with the president before he left for Tokyo to enable Carter to have someone in post who was 'less scarred by earlier battles'.[92] Schlesinger always claimed have enjoyed a close relationship with Carter but the presidential papers are littered with Carter and his staff expressing concerns to Schlesinger over many issues, particularly over his choice of staff.[93] Carter's advisors had been so concerned that they argued that the resignation was an opportunity for a top to bottom overhaul of the new department.[94] Schlesinger, in later interviews, was highly critical of a number of Carter's decisions. He criticized the limited time he had to develop energy proposals and build a new department. He was equally critical of Carter's leadership style, arguing that his low-key tactics on oil deregulation showed 'the administration and the President of the United States did not understand governing'.[95] Nevertheless Schlesinger did influence Carter in the more interventionist elements of his energy policy, especially in his 15 July speech.[96] His successor, Charles W. Duncan, came from the Department of Defense and lacked energy expertise, but he did have considerable managerial experience and was widely regarded as a more effective operator by White House staff.

The moral elements of Carter's 15 July speech where he asked, 'Why have we not been able to get together as a nation to resolve our serious energy problems?'[97] continued to be debated for the rest of his time in office. But he was determined to implement the specific measures he had proposed. The White House of 1979 was much better organized and it deployed all of its resources to support the new energy goals with an elaborate communication plan.[98] Members of the cabinet and senior staff were co-opted under Anne Wexler's speaker programme to give addresses in support of legislation.[99] Unions like the UAW were engaged in sending postcards to Congress demanding action.[100] Carter himself was heavily involved in meeting with members of congress and lobby groups both face to face and on the phone.[101] Despite these efforts the speech did not change the fundamental politics of Congress. Senator Byrd, due to the support for increased coal production in his home state, tried to take a proactive role but the legislation remained largely in the hands of senators from oil-producing states like Russell Long.[102] There was very little change in the attitude and practice of Congress and so progress remained painfully slow. Pat Caddell, Carter's chief pollster, complained to the president that opinion leaders were not engaging with his programme and that public frustration was being directed at Carter personally.[103] Frank Moore provided Carter with an update in August 1979 which summed up the complexity of the debate in the Senate committees with concerns being expressed on regional, environmental and ideological grounds about the proposed legislation on the ESC and the EMB.[104] Carter's renewed commitment to synthetic fuels and what was felt as a weakening in Carter's backing for environmental safeguards led to the loss of support from environmental groups.[105] These were not the only Carter supporters who were dissatisfied with his July proposals. Liberals in the mid-west and north-eastern states continued to press for more assistance for low-income families hit by the proposed oil price increases. This resulted in the original proposal for a Low-Income Energy Assistance Programme being further increased to $4 bn, much more than Carter had envisaged.[106]

It took nearly a year for Congress to pass the major elements of the president's 1979 proposals. This was mainly due to arguments over the Windfall Profits Tax and the EMB. The Windfall Profits Tax was vital to fund not only support for poorer families but key elements of Carter's energy conservation strategy, such as the development of synthetic fuels and mass transportation systems. His attempt to raise revenue with an oil import levy had been defeated when for the first time in twenty-nine years Congress overturned the veto of a president from the same party.[107] This increased the pressure on the administration to reach a compromise. There was intense lobbying from the White House, but it faced opposition in the Senate where over 100 amendments were submitted from liberals and conservatives who had different views as to how revenue from the tax should be spent.[108] Most of Carter's core supporters in the unions, minorities and the poor had concerns about the impact of deregulation of oil prices and consequently lobbied hard for a bigger slice of the proposed revenues. On the other hand, conservatives representing the oil lobby wanted a greater share of the revenue being allocated to incentives designed to increase local oil production.

These debates persisted until the bill's passage on 2 April 1980. As a result, the legislation was the product of a series of compromises with all the major interest groups. This enabled Carter to claim that the fundamental balance between incentives for production and revenue raised was the same as in his original plan.[109] However, there were major differences. For instance, the revenue generated was far less with $227 bn now agreed compared with $292 bn in the original plan.[110] Given the obstacles in his path Carter had every reason to be satisfied with the final bill. The concept of the EMB, that it would cut through red tape and ensure that energy projects were quickly implemented, had a wide appeal in Congress. But it also raised fundamental concerns over the increased powers of Federal Government in relation to state's rights, and fears, especially from environmental groups, about how and in what circumstances the EMB could overturn ('waive') environmental and regulatory protection. This issue of the 'waiver' was described by House Energy and Commerce Chair, John Dingell of Michigan, as the 'single most important environmental issue this administration has faced'.[111] The usually supportive House split three ways over this with over 200 environmental leaders signing an open letter against the waiver. The White House had failed to win congressional support on this issue by July 1980 when the election was in full swing.[112]

By the first anniversary of the 'malaise' speech Carter could argue that most of the major reforms he had recommended had been passed. He could also point to a substantive list of completed legislation that fulfilled his 1976 campaign promises and addressed the 'energy crisis'. As part of the preparation for running Carter's presidential campaign in 1980, the speechwriter's office was asked to pull together the administration's key achievements on energy. The list was impressive. It included the phased deregulation of oil and gas production, a new Department of Energy, the first integrated Energy Plan, massive investment in alternative energy sources, and a new focus on conservation in government, industry and homes. In addition, there was support for the poor to cushion the effect of price increases, investment in mass transit schemes and an overall 11 per cent reduction in dependence on imported oil.[113] Despite all of this, energy was not regarded as a Carter success story. In all his television addresses, town hall meetings and news conferences Carter failed to persuade the public that a personal sacrifice was required in response to an energy crisis that many believed was not real. In June 1979, 31 per cent of Americans believed energy was the most important problem facing the country but one week before the 1980 election, in a similar poll, only 3 per cent cited energy as the number one concern.[114] Carter himself accepted that his initial use of apocalyptic language, 'moral equivalent of war (MEOW),' was a mistake.[115] The failure to persuade the public resulted in there being insufficient support for those controversial measures that required active personal sacrifice such as tax or price increases. At the same time, by inflating the size of the 'crisis,' Carter created expectations that appeared to be lost in a long-drawn-out battle with Congress. By highlighting the security risk caused by US dependence on imported oil, he also increased the perception of American impotence which reflected badly on him as president. Another problem for the administration was that there were often differences in emphasis in messages from the president and his experts, Carter saying that there was a crisis and the Department of Energy frequently disagreeing. Even in his final year in office there was a major disagreement between members of the DPG and Secretary Duncan on whether to announce an energy emergency in Carter's final State of the Union address.[116]

So why did Carter decide to make energy the priority for his administration? Energy was an archetypal 'Carter issue'. It was a highly technical, complex and long-term problem that affected everyone and therefore required expertise and serious study if a comprehensive solution was to be developed. He believed that solving this problem would be a clear demonstration of presidential and governmental competence. Writers like Charles Jones, Erwin Hargrove and Kenneth Morris,[117] in analysing Carter's failure on energy policy, have acknowledged the moral dimension but have concentrated on his organizational and communication failures. This approach has minimized evidence that Carter saw energy policy in moral terms and was determined to push legislation forward despite the political costs. This was an example of Carter the moral president doing the right thing for the country, but it also highlighted his self-belief, perhaps even arrogance, that he could fix any problem no matter how difficult. These characteristics were more significant than suggested by the later revisionist argument of Alter that paints Carter as an early proponent of green energy, particularly given that his policies in promoting coal and synfuels were bitterly opposed by environmentalists.

This is not to suggest that Carter was totally naive on the complexity of this issue; he realized that he had to mobilize public opinion to overcome resistance from major interest groups. But he underestimated the practical difficulties involved in passing complicated legislation. Although the 1977 Energy Plan's ninety-day deadline and secrecy may have hampered implementation it fundamentally did not affect the outcome. Congressional splits were not on party or even ideological lines but more based on region or geology. As a congressman if oil was in your state your position was fixed whether you were Democrat or GOP or conservative or liberal. Each element of the Carter energy plan created a different type of opposition which often involved strange bedfellows. For example, environmentalist congressmen worked with the conservative oil lobby to oppose the proposed switch to coal. Groups that Carter assumed would be his supporters like the environmental and consumer lobbies were frequently in opposition. The first critic of his 1977 energy plan was consumer lobbyist and supporter Ralph Nader, who complained that Carter's rhetoric was too dark, and the plan needed more emphasis on conservation.[118]

The White House became more effective at lobbying and achieved some well worked compromises on energy policy, for example on the Windfall Profit Tax, but this was not enough to deliver Carter's ambitious goals. Burton and Scott Kaufman argued that Carter's inability to articulate a more positive vision for the country restricted his attempts to implement energy policy.[119] Seeing energy as a moral issue heavily influenced his speeches. In the 'Malaise' speech of 15 July 1979, he argued that 'we are confronted with a moral and spiritual crisis'.[120] It was Carter, the preacher, asking for personal sacrifice for the greater good but such a 'preachy' tone did not motivate the public. Asked in an interview why the American public did not believe that there was an energy crisis, a frustrated Carter commented rather sourly that 'they don't want to face an unpleasant fact'.[121] Carter's decision to frame energy policy in such stark terms was to reduce the chances of establishing a political consensus. Some of Carter's proposals, particularly around conservation, can now be regarded as far-sighted but his rhetoric, as was often the case, failed to present a positive vision for the future. His message did not convince the American people that there was a crisis that justified such a sacrifice. Ultimately it was the failure to energize public support and the consequential inability to outmanoeuvre the powerful interest groups inside and outside Congress that proved decisive.

Carter made energy a major priority throughout his administration. He was more personally involved in policy development than any other domestic issue, including the economy. In addition, he gave television addresses, went to town hall meetings, held briefings for the press and lobbied key congressmen, face-to-face and by phone.[122] Carter recognized that this level of involvement was unsustainable and so it was not repeated for other policies where he delegated extensively. However, this image of micromanagement was to stay with Carter for the rest of his time in office. So, what did energy policy signify about Carter's ideology? It confirmed Carter's belief in the necessity for the government to intervene in the energy market for the benefit of all. The ESC and particularly the EMB were seen as evidence of his liberal beliefs. The *Wall Street Journal,* commenting on his 15 July speech, said, 'The real Jimmy Carter has finally stood up and on the far left of the Democratic Party'.[123] However, the same president deregulated, albeit gradually, oil and gas prices, a key issue for free marketers. These were important changes but were implemented only when Carter felt he had no choice. Unlike his successor, Ronald Reagan, Carter did not believe that the free market could solve all energy problems[124] but other more conservative beliefs were prominent in the battle to pass energy legislation. Carter's fiscal conservatism was often in evidence as he continued to express concern about the cost of energy initiatives, be it coal/gas conversion or the nuclear 'fast breeder' programme.[125] This mix of conservative and liberal actions may suggest a president trying to establish a new 'third way' but there is little evidence to support this. Carter saw energy as a moral and technical challenge for his government to address. Unlike Bill Clinton, who couched his policies within a 'New Democrat' philosophy, Carter attached no ideological framework to the proposals that Schlesinger brought forward. He soon found his programme attacked on all sides ideologically; there was no common ground as with many of his policies and his staff therefore had to build a new coalition of support for each component of his plan.

Carter's energy legacy was substantial, but it all seemed much less than he had promised. Much of his energy programme was dismantled by his successor, including the Windfall Profits Tax, which was repealed in 1988.[126] Ronald Reagan was opposed to Carter's interventionist approach but was helped by more favourable conditions in the global energy market. Reagan benefitted from the fall in OPEC prices in 1983 and the consequential oil glut, so did not have to deal with the immediate challenges that Carter faced. By 1986 oil prices had fallen back to their 1973 levels. However, given the same circumstances of crisis, Reagan would have spoken to the public in a very different way. Whereas Carter emphasized the complexity of the energy problem, Reagan would have simplified the message. He would not have immersed himself in the detail or announced that he was going 'to have an unpleasant talk' with the American people about personal sacrifice.[127] He would have talked about taking the government out of the energy business. An oversimplified even misleading message possibly, but Reagan would always promote a positive vision of America that would leave the audience feeling somehow better, not something Carter was ever able to achieve. The fundamental difference between the two men highlighted by energy policy lay not in their politics but in their character. The optimistic Reagan saw positive outcomes in any scenario whilst Carter, the Baptist engineer, saw the complexity of every problem, the hard road ahead and the need for sacrifice.

Energy was yet another policy area where Carter did not benefit from good fortune. This proved to be a continuing story when his administration sought to solve the long-term problems of welfare, health insurance and social security. Only this time Carter had to meet the expectations of the liberal wing of his party.

5

Health and welfare: Betrayal of the liberals?

Hamilton Jordan did not usually attend in-depth policy discussions at the White House but, in the run up to a decision on welfare reform in April 1977, he attended a Department of Health and Welfare (HEW) briefing with Carter. His honest and insightful note of the meeting to the president demonstrated the closeness of their relationship, the impact of the administration's substantial legislative workload and the nature of Carter's working relationship with HEW's Secretary, Joseph A Califano. Jordan advised Carter against making any immediate decision on welfare reform because he believed that the president did not yet fully grasp the complexities of the subject. He contrasted Carter's understanding of welfare with his involvement in energy policy where he had participated in lengthy discussions with Schlesinger and his team, as well as completing hundreds of hours of reading. Jordan estimated that the time Carter spent on welfare was as low as 5 per cent compared to time spent on energy policy. For Jordan, the questions Carter was asking at that meeting just confirmed his lack of detailed knowledge. He argued that this was not surprising given Carter's other commitments on the Economic Recovery Plan (ERP), the debate over the tax rebate, the Energy bill and the Strategic Arms Limitation Treaty. Jordan believed that the HEW proposals were uncoordinated and flawed but concluded, 'I do not believe that it is humanly possible to have a good welfare reform program ready by 1 May [a self-imposed deadline] that you believe in and are comfortable with.' He also told Carter that he looked exhausted and with his first major international summit in London due in two weeks, he must find time to rest.[1]

Jordan's observations were revealing for several reasons. Firstly, they highlighted that as early as April 1977 Carter and his staff were becoming overloaded with major policy issues. But the view that Carter involved himself in too much of the detail of policy did not apply to welfare, or indeed other domestic priorities. Jordan's memorandum underlined the difficulty for Carter in making decisions on complex issues when he did not fully grasp the detail. This was something that Carter was not used to because, as governor, he was able to be involved in the minutiae of all-important policy issues. Now as president he was already finding the job beyond even his considerable capacity. As Carter delegated it became much more important for his staff to coordinate all viewpoints, both inside and outside the White House, to help him come to a decision. These organizational issues were critical in the development of all the HEW reforms that his administration sought to implement. In addition, welfare reform and National Health Insurance (NHI) were critical issues for the liberal wing of the Democratic Party. This placed major expectations on Carter at a time when the president was facing opposition not just from the GOP and powerful interest groups but from a more conservative electorate who were becoming resistant to what they saw as 'big' government solutions.

As the first successful Democratic presidential candidate in twelve years, Carter faced high expectations, especially from the party's liberal wing. The delivery of welfare and health reforms was seen as an important measure of his 'liberal credentials'. His election campaign and inaugural address gave few indications of his commitment to reform. Reference in speeches to compassionate government and getting people back to work gave little indication that such reforms would be a major priority.[2] The one exception to this was his speech on health to the Student National Medical Association (SNMA) in Washington DC on 16 April 1976. In this speech, Carter's liberal credentials were there for all to see, as he made specific commitments to universal health coverage.[3] His ideas on these reforms, however, had some conservative themes. He acknowledged that the Federal government was inefficient and wasted money and that schemes like welfare were subject to fraud. Carter's focus therefore when dealing with health and welfare reform was as much about establishing an efficient service and clamping down on waste and fraud as on increasing benefits to the poor and sick. In this he was responding to the conservative mood in the country, and this was one of the reasons why Rafshoon wanted Carter in 1978 to make a major national speech on waste and fraud.[4] Another influence on his administration's reform plans was Carter's increasing concern over inflation and his campaign to eliminate the budget deficit. This resulted in pressure from his economic advisors to oppose, or at least water down, any substantial reforms even when campaign commitments were involved. Eizenstat as coordinator of policy found it difficult to bridge the gap between HEW and Carter's economic advisors. These internal policy differences as well as disagreement over legislative priorities amongst White House staff hindered any progress. The prioritization process, managed by Vice President Mondale, pushed both welfare and health reform down the administration's agenda for 1978 and 1979 as difficulties with Congress became more apparent.[5]

Carter's commitment to welfare and health reform would place a heavy workload on HEW and its Secretary Joe Califano. He had been recommended to Carter for the role by Mondale. Two attributes made Califano stand out from most, if not all, of Carter's cabinet appointments. Firstly, his liberal credentials were outstanding as his role in the Johnson administration had helped shape the Great Society reform legislation. Moreover, he had liberal friends in Congress and the media. He was a close friend of Ben Bradlee, editor of the *Washington Post,* and of the Kennedy family. Secondly, his experience of government, particularly of major reorganizations, was invaluable to the new administration. However, he was also regarded as a classic Washington insider, especially by Carter's Georgian staff, and this made him an object of their suspicion. This was exacerbated by the size and nature of the department he ran. HEW was criticized by conservatives for being too large and a source of government waste, especially in relation to welfare benefits. Carter's interest in reducing waste and fiscal restraint often resulted in disputes over its budget.[6] HEW had substantial resources, for example, it had over forty of its own congressional liaison staff,[7] and jealously guarded its lead status on issues. This often resulted in conflicts with the White House on issues such as HEW's anti-smoking policy and its lack of support for Carter's Education bill.[8]

Whilst HEW's anti-smoking stance was in line with Carter's campaign pledges, its active promotion damaged him with southern constituencies, especially in North Carolina. Carter was embarrassed by the announcement of an anti-smoking initiative as Califano gave him no advanced warning and the press had noticed the contradiction between HEW's policy and the administration's backing of price supports for tobacco.[9] Carter understood Califano's position on this issue, as it was a campaign pledge, but he was much less tolerant of Califano's actions on the Education bill. The establishment of a separate Department of Education was also a major campaign commitment, and it was supported by some, if not all, of the unions.[10] It was not surprising that HEW would have reservations about losing a major component of its organization. Nonetheless once the legislation was agreed within the White House, Califano was accused by Carter's staff of continuing to lobby secretly in Congress against the bill.[11] It was cited as one of the major reasons why Califano was eventually fired by Carter in July 1979. Califano's covert actions against the Education bill were not the only source of tension with White House staff. Jordan had made no secret of his deep-rooted suspicion of Califano's liberal background, notably his closeness with the Kennedy family.[12] Califano was criticized for his poor record on recruiting minorities and women and a lack of consultation on hires.[13] He was also condemned for his performance at a Senate sub-committee on Mental Health, Rosalynn Carter's area of personal interest. It was described by a staff member in a memorandum to the First Lady as 'such a discredit to you and to everyone who has worked so hard on the commission and this legislation'. This criticism could not have done anything but damage his standing with the President and his influential wife.[14] Califano in turn had an unfavourable view of White House staff, describing them as naïve and accusing them of leaking negative stories about him to the press.[15]

Carter's attitude to Califano and the role he played in the cabinet were often contradictory. In many ways Califano was only cabinet member carrying out the role in the manner that Carter himself had defined. He wanted his cabinet to be independent, manage their departments efficiently; and Califano had the experience and confidence to do both. Carter, as he was focused on other issues, devolved major responsibilities to HEW to develop important policies on health and welfare. This demonstrated a personal confidence in his secretary. Califano also felt able to comment on a wide range of issues outside his immediate responsibility. For example, he expressed strong views against the position of the Justice Department on the Bakke discrimination case.[16] This flexibility given by Carter to cabinet members became an issue when White House staff became more influential in coordinating policy. It was not just a problem with Califano but given his background and the complexity of the policies he was responsible for, conflict between HEW and White House staff proved inevitable.[17]

Califano's personal relationship with Carter was also not straightforward. On the one hand, White House papers contain numerous hand-written notes of praise from the president[18] who often gave support to Califano in policy disputes with White House staff.[19] They agreed on a number of moral issues, notably abortion on which Califano, as a Catholic, supported Carter who was criticized for this by his own staff. Califano was allowed to be candid with the president about his leadership.[20] But much of the criticism of Califano about not supporting the Education bill and not cooperating with White House staff was passed on to Carter. The Georgians on Carter's staff simply did not trust him.[21] Rafshoon could not understand why Carter and Mondale continued to have faith in Califano even though, Rafshoon believed, he directly lied to them both on several occasions.[22] The HEW Secretary always felt under suspicion because he was part of the 'Washington Cocktail circuit' but to the president it was about being a team player. In the end Carter believed that Califano's position had become untenable with White House staff and cabinet members and so he was eventually dismissed in July 1979.[23] However much of a problem Califano was perceived to be, the fact that he remained Carter's main spokesman for major legislation for over two and a half years suggests that their differences were exaggerated.

If there was an early example of Carter facing up to a moral challenge and 'doing the right thing', it was on resolving America's social security funding deficit. The issue for the new administration was that the social security schemes, delivered principally through Disability Insurance (DI) and Old Age Survivors Insurance (OASI), were due to run out of funding in 1979 and 1983, respectively.[24] In the eventual solution, brokered by the White House with Congress, both parties agreed to tax increases before the 1978 mid-term elections, a risky proposition for many congressmen. Despite this, Congress continued to seek ways to backtrack from that commitment, forcing the White House to develop a more palatable solution to this problem. This, unfortunately for Carter, caused divisions in the White House, leaving him with three competing proposals from the Economic Policy Group (EPG), Domestic Policy Group (DPG) and HEW. This problem was caused by a lack of coordination across the administration and limited presidential engagement.[25] Carter was often criticized for his inordinate attention to detail, but on this, as with other HEW policies, he did not have the time to be involved in policy discussions or study draft proposals in depth. When he was asked by his staff to talk to Senator Herman Talmadge of Georgia about social security, Carter commented that whilst he had done so he did not know if he had helped as 'he knows more about it than I do', an unusual admission for the president.[26] The recognition of the need to plug the gap in funding did not mean a solution could be easily found. The additional money required, Schultze estimated, was $60–80bn over five years.[27] The administration's proposal envisaged increases in payroll tax but also substantial increases in employer contributions. As with other financial legislation, Senator Long was unenthusiastic about any tax increase and Carter's staff worked extremely hard either to secure his acquiescence or at least to mitigate his opposition.[28] The bill was submitted in May 1977 and was passed that December. The law provided long-term funding from 1980 until 2030. It focused on increased payments from the wealthier, lifted restrictions on what retirees could personally earn and still retain benefit, and ended discrimination on the grounds of sex.

The passing of Social Security legislation on 20 December 1977 was a success for Carter but this proved difficult to sustain as pressure from Congress to reduce or remove proposed tax increases soon followed. The DPG argued that part of the problem was how the tax increases were inaccurately portrayed in the press. There was debate within the administration over how Carter should respond. He publicly urged Congress to hold its nerve and not amend the law.[29] The pressure remained so the administration was forced to explore alternatives to the scheduled tax increases. Options included alternative forms of funding and a programme of cost savings.[30] Suggestions to reduce the level of benefits as an option were rejected as this was unlikely to pass Congress. The funding issue continued to be debated right up to the 1980 election with Califano's successor, Patricia Harris, asserting that the administration had to hold the line on the proposals as increases in unemployment and inflation would further deplete scheme funds.[31] Continued disagreement and the forthcoming 1980 election resulted in no further changes to the legislation. The passage of the Social Security bill reflected Carter's idealism but was also a demonstration of his pragmatism, delivering effective legislation across party lines. Social security had been in the past an ideological issue but in this instance all sides, whatever their ideology, recognized that the funding problem was an issue that had to be resolved. This would prove to be a very unusual occurrence and not something the administration could replicate with their other policy initiatives. For Carter it was a question of good government but one with which he had limited personal involvement, given the pressures on his time.

Welfare in the 1970s was delivered through several programmes by Federal and State organizations. These helped the poor, the unemployed, the disabled and their families. Attempts at reform in previous years, like the Nixon administration's radical proposals in the Family Assistance Plan (FAP), had failed because of the complexity of the legislation and an inability to gain cross-party support. However, the pressure for reform had increased, driven by two major factors. Firstly, there was the spiralling cost of these programmes due mainly to increasing numbers of claimants. This was not just a federal problem. Some of the programmes like Aid to Families with Dependent Children (AFDC) were supported by the states and those with large concentrations of urban poor, such as New York, were struggling financially. In California, Governor Ronald Reagan negotiated a deal with his Democratic legislature which made reforms and controlled expenditure.[32] The second incentive for change was increasing public criticism of the welfare system. Reagan and other conservative politicians were arguing that these programmes discouraged employment, were poorly run and subject to fraud. Carter was very sensitive to these arguments. Documents in the Carter White House at the time included a copy of a *US News and World* report headlined 'The Great National Rip Off – How People Cheat and Steal $25,000,000,000 a Year from the Government.'[33] Not all welfare programmes were criticized in this way, but the national mood was stronger than any counter pressure from liberals to improve benefits and increase coverage.

Carter's attitude to welfare had always been sympathetic; his background in rural Georgia meant that he really understood what it was like to be poor.[34] But his approach to reform was as much conservative as liberal. In introducing his ideas for welfare to the nation on 2 February 1977, he balanced the benefits of reform between savings for the tax payer and help for those who 'genuinely' needed it.[35] Carter's insistence on a zero-cost solution was in line with his fiscal outlook but advisors like Schultze and Califano never believed reform could be implemented without at least some initial additional funding.[36] Carter was also conscious of conservative criticism of waste and fraud and constantly sought answers on this from Califano.[37] All of this caused concern among his liberal supporters with Congressman Charles Rangel quoted as saying that 'the poor are not a priority in this administration.'[38]

Welfare reform was a more administratively complex problem to solve than energy policy. Yet there were similarities in how Carter approached each problem. In both cases he opted for a comprehensive solution, and he committed publicly to a fixed deadline; in welfare's case – ninety days. He encouraged his staff to focus on technical rather than political issues and he communicated no overarching theme to guide them. Equally, in both cases, there were powerful groups inside and outside Congress who opposed his plans. However, there were some differences with Energy policy. The first was that the wide range of welfare programmes and the need to create new job programmes required several government departments to be engaged in policy development. The two major departments affected were HEW and Labor but also involved were the departments of Agriculture and Commerce as well as White House staff groups like EPG, DPG and OMB. As a result, the consulting group established to help coordinate this policy had thirty members.[39] Given the nature of the task and the number of interests involved, disputes were inevitable, especially between the two major players HEW and Labor. During the first five months of the administration, there was no organizational mechanism to manage such disputes. The energy policy was developed within a tight group and detailed proposals were not seen outside the group until much later. Also, Carter could resolve any policy issues as he was heavily involved in the detailed discussions. This was not possible to achieve with welfare reform due to its complexity and, unlike energy, outside consultation which was encouraged by Carter resulted in more issues being raised.[40] He tried to resolve the bureaucratic infighting by using Schultze to adjudicate, albeit without success.[41] Finally, a major difference with energy was Carter's own involvement. From the start he immersed himself in the detail of energy policy, but with welfare he stepped back and left responsibility to Califano and his team.[42] This was partly a response to his heavy workload. Hence, he was only able to give broad direction to Califano which was to cause, at least initially, confusion in critical areas of policy.[43]

Carter imposed two specific restrictions on welfare reform that impacted on policy development. He established an arbitrary deadline of 1 May 1977 to bring forward proposals and specified that any plan would be at zero additional cost. Califano, whilst not challenging the deadline, wanted a further sixty days for 'consideration of programme and budgetary alternatives and political feasibility'.[44] Carter agreed to wide consultation but would not move the date. Califano also could not envisage any comprehensive reform without incurring cost, at least initially.[45] The issue of zero cost continued to be a source of friction between Carter and not just Califano but other members of his administration.[46] For example, Califano and his team were shocked when he presented options that required additional funds to ensure that more claimants gained from the reform than lost, that Carter rejected those proposals. Carter's response, reported in the *New York Times*, was 'Are you telling me that there is no way to improve the present welfare system except by spending billions of dollars? ... In that case, to hell with it, we're wasting our time.'[47]

The principles of welfare reform were agreed by Carter on 12 April 1977. This included simplifying administration, redirection of CETA (Community and Employment Training Act) to the poorest, a freeze on the state supplement for AFDC and the provision of universal minimum benefit. The principle was also established that non-working families would not have higher benefit than working families, and incentives would be provided for recipients to work and keep families together.[48] There were major disagreements between Labor and HEW over how the job creation programme would integrate with the structure of HEW benefits. These issues were not finally resolved until 20 May 1977, after Carter's self-imposed deadline.[49] There was also scepticism over whether the Department of Labor could deliver the promised number of up to 1.4 million new jobs and so it was decided that no jobs target would be discussed at Carter's initial press briefing.[50]

This was not the only issue that required resolution in May. The HEW proposal to fund claimants through negative income tax was administratively simple but ran the risk of being seen by Congress as providing cash handouts and therefore being a disincentive to work.[51] There was also recognition that not all welfare programmes could be covered initially so the plan focused on AFDC, Supplementary Security Income (SSI) and Food Stamp programmes. However, as late as 29 April 1977 Califano was expressing concern over the negative reaction from Congress to the White House's Food Stamp proposals and so suggested a delay in their implementation.[52] As the issues were debated in the run up to Carter's announcement, domestic policy staff were still recommending an alternative phased approach[53] and the OMB expressed concerns about the accuracy of HEW's costing for the programme.[54] The White House therefore started discussions with Congress with many issues unresolved and increasing concern that important legislators would be in active opposition.[55]

Carter's announcement of his proposals emphasized his commitment to reform but he confirmed to Congress that his first priorities were the Energy bill, Tax Reform and Social Security.[56] Califano was concerned about the timing because he feared that the cost of Carter's Tax Reform bill would eat into funding for welfare and, later, health reform.[57] Whilst there was little controversy over HEW's welfare principles, the *LA Times* called them 'about as controversial as the Boy Scout oath',[58] there were major objections from across the political spectrum to the detailed proposals. Liberals argued that the benefits were too low and thirty-eight states, mainly in the north, would have to supplement payments. They also argued that not enough jobs or training were being offered and the payment of minimum wages would undercut the employment market. Conservatives, on the other hand, opposed the reform because they believed that the guaranteed income plan discouraged work, the jobs programme was too expensive, and the proposals would increase welfare rolls.[59] In addition individual congressmen and lobby groups had specific concerns. AFL-CIO favoured a permanent government job creation programme.[60] Several legislators like Al Ullman, Chair of the House Ways and Means Committee, recommended a phased implementation which Carter rejected. The zero-cost option had resulted in more welfare recipients being worse off than better. Califano, as late as 25 July 1977, was requesting additional funds from Carter to address this.[61] At the same time the president received a memorandum from Lance suggesting that even without additional funds, HEW's 'zero cost' budget was $3.3bn in deficit.[62] The political analysis from his domestic policy team was, if anything, more pessimistic. They told Carter that the programme would be attacked by both wings of the Democratic Party and that Long and Ullman, as committee chairmen in the Senate and House respectively, wanted more conservative options presented. They further suggested that there were three constituencies for welfare reform: one that sought savings for the taxpayer, another increased benefits and the states that sought fiscal relief for their own benefits bill. The DPG analysis of these groups was that the latest proposals did not bring any reduction in the size of the welfare bill and the modest fiscal relief was only provided by making 6.5 million AFDC recipients worse off by an average of $400 annually. Suggested changes to the proposals were rejected by Carter as unlikely to receive Long's support.[63] Despite these major reservations, some amendments were agreed, and the legislation was formally submitted to Congress on 6 August 1977.[64]

In the ensuing legislative battle, the White House failed to get its proposals out of committee onto the floor of the House. Ullman, whose concerns were well known, in the end proposed his own version of the bill which also failed to pass his committee. In addition general concerns over the cost of the legislation caused Congress to seek an independent review of HEW's budget which found flaws in its cost assumptions.[65] Administration efforts continued to push for legislation with Speaker O'Neill's support,[66] but by the end of 1977 welfare had ceased to be a priority and was not mentioned by Carter in the following January's State of the Union address.[67] Whilst Carter had by no means given up on welfare reform, his already limited personal involvement declined after 1977. The initiative for reform passed to Califano and Congress. Ullman, Long, Moynihan, James Corman and other legislators introduced bills at various stages during 1978 and 1979, each representing a different approach to reform. Califano initiated a further attempt at legislation in March 1978.[68] This did not receive enthusiastic support from the White House with Eizenstat expressing scepticism over its chances of passage, but he nevertheless recommended Carter's support, claiming it would prevent him from being accused of giving up on a campaign commitment.[69] This still did not get full backing from White House staff with McIntyre at the OMB not only continuing to oppose such legislation but unusually submitting OMB's own counter proposals.[70] Carter supported the Califano initiative and a later incremental and more limited proposal in early 1979,[71] but both failed at the committee stage after facing criticism from conservatives and liberals. White House staff continued discussions with Congress up until March 1980 before Carter cancelled the last attempt at reform due to budgetary pressures.[72]

Historians Laurence E. Lynn and David de F. Whitman have argued that the failure of Carter's welfare reform was a result of poor management and ineffective communication.[73] The policy development process without Carter's direct and sustained involvement had no mechanism to bring together the different views in his administration or evaluate the political consequences. This role would be taken in future by Eizenstat and his team, but this function was not in place during the first part of 1977. Consequently, no consensus was reached on legislation submitted in August 1977. The focus placed on policy development resulted in no thought being given as to how reform was to be supported in Congress. As a result, the legislation produced was so complicated that it would prove impossible to pass, even in the House where there was a clear Democratic majority.

There were issues outside the administration's control which would hamper any efforts at reform, not the least the hostile attitude of the public to taxation and to the payment of benefits to the 'undeserving poor'. Sensing this trend, Carter continued to seek a wide-ranging solution but at zero cost. But his commitment to deliver jobs, a campaign promise, to extend coverage and his promise not to consolidate programmes, all at zero cost, could be delivered only by making many of the current beneficiaries worse off.[74] To liberals in his administration, including those in HEW, his apparent willingness to accept this was incomprehensible. It was a continuing source of tension between Carter and Califano, who went back to him with additional options to improve the terms. To those intimately involved in the crafting of the reforms, what Carter was asking of them was impossible and to those in HEW it just confirmed the president's natural conservatism. However, Carter may well have not seen this as an ideological issue but a question of delivering what he viewed as a practical solution given the circumstances. He was already facing defeat at the hands of conservative Democrats on tax reform and key elements of his energy policy. He feared the same outcome with any measure that was not fiscally conservative, whatever his personal views. Equally he was not likely to be convinced by technical arguments in favour of more generous benefits because he lacked the detailed knowledge that he had in other policy areas like energy.

Although Carter was not engaged in the detail of welfare reform this did not necessarily mean his personal involvement would have changed the outcome for his legislation. Nixon's welfare policy initiative, the Family Assistance Programme, failed in 1970 and again in 1972 despite active support from a president about to win a landslide election victory. Carter took on a highly complicated policy issue. He was unable to manage his administration in a way that delivered legislation that could pass Congress. It would be misleading, however, to imagine that a fully engaged president supported by a united, well organized administration could have been more successful. A Labor Department policy paper said, 'The politics of Welfare are treacherous under any circumstances.'[75] Whilst admitting that the complexity of welfare surprised him, Carter was sufficiently attuned to the public mood to understand that any increase in spending and government bureaucracy would meet strong resistance in Congress. It would be difficult to envisage that any government could have created legislation that would satisfy liberal and conservative viewpoints. The outcome for the president was clear: a major plank of Carter's campaign in 1976, welfare reform, had failed to gain congressional approval.

Whilst Carter can be criticized for his inability to prioritize and plan his legislative programme, the administration's approach on health policy was more measured. The decision to concentrate on controlling hospital costs, made in January 1977, was consistent with the president's economic policy and was seen as a necessary first step in achieving in 1978 the liberal 'holy grail' of comprehensive NHI.[76] The White House recognized that controlling spiralling health costs, projected to rise to $200 billion by 1979,[77] would align with Carter's anti-inflation policy. This message would be used by the administration as the main argument in selling the legislation after 1977. Carter believed that the case for mandatory cost controls was overwhelming and would receive support inside and outside Congress. Yet there were major obstacles to overcome if his proposals were to become law. The bill needed to pass four health sub-committees and five full committees, as well as the floor of both Houses.[78] This process would take time which helped medical interest groups like the American Medical Association (AMA) and American Hospital Association (AHA) to develop their opposition. These groups proved to be highly effective at influencing members of congress. The White House's improved capability to mount outreach campaigns in support of legislation, in place by 1978, was unable to work effectively on the Hospital Cost Containment (HCC) bill. Anne Wexler, responsible for outreach, argued that this was because opposition to the bill was well entrenched, and that the public were not directly affected by its benefits as personal medical costs were incurred by insurers not the individual.[79]

The legislative strategy followed by the White House was to work with Herman Talmadge who chaired the Senate Health Sub-committee.[80] By April 1977 Califano was already reporting on the depth of the opposition from the AHA. He informed Carter those hospitals employed one in thirty of all US workers and that pressure against the bill would be applied to congressmen even before proposals were published. He concluded, 'In short, the hospital cost containment legislation will not be enacted unless the Administration is willing to expend significant political energy.'[81] Carter launched the HCC bill on 25 April 1977[82] and continued to work with Congress for the next eighteen months. The bill that eventually passed the Senate, based on the Nelson amendment, was a compromise in which voluntary cost controls were to be initially trialled and, if unsuccessful, would be replaced by mandatory rules. This success was due to effective congressional lobbying and the willingness of Carter to compromise, not something that he regularly achieved elsewhere in his legislative programme. The bill still had to pass the House. Carter's continued commitment to HCC was confirmed in his 1979 State of the Union address: 'There will be no clearer test of the commitment of this Congress to the anti-inflation fight than the legislation that I will submit again this year to hold down inflation in hospital care.'[83] He followed this up by establishing a legislative task force to support passage of the bill.[84] In his announcement of legislation in March 1979 he argued, 'The American people want me, and they want other elected representatives, to take action, action that is strong, prompt and effective.'[85] For the remainder of the year, the White House worked hard for the bill to pass the House and Carter was involved in personal lobbying and made speeches.[86] Despite this intense effort, House members rejected the bill. Carter's staff continued to argue that HCC was still worth pursuing and that projected savings alone were worth $1.1bn in the 1981 budget.[87] However, no further attempts were made with Congress even though there remained a bill in the Senate. A proposal was made to use Carter's executive powers to control hospital spending, but this was abandoned on legal advice.[88] For the remainder of the administration hospital costs were managed as part of Carter's overall anti-inflation policy which focused on monitoring and voluntary cost restraint.

Carter saw the battle over HCC as one between his administration and the medical lobby. He believed that his loss was down to the AMA's huge financial contributions to three or four Illinois congressmen.[89] This is perhaps an oversimplification but unlike some other policies submitted by Carter, HCC did have more proponents in Congress and the White House made fewer mistakes in managing that support for the bill. Effective compromises and alliances were built in the Senate, particularly with liberals. Ted Kennedy's support was achieved by the promise of future cooperation on NHI. However, the AMA and AHA proved more effective in the House in equating mandatory controls with increased government involvement, an important issue for the public. The power of these medical interest groups would be critical when Carter sought to advance healthcare reform.

Carter did not focus on healthcare policy until November 1977, but his commitment to reform had been established nineteen months earlier. His speech on national health policy to the SNMA in Washington DC was passionate and specific.[90] He talked about Medicaid being 'a national scandal' and criticized the bureaucracy of programmes that were spread over fifteen departments and were ripe for reorganization. He pledged reform, stating, 'Coverage must be universal and mandatory. Every citizen must be entitled to the same level of comprehensive benefits.'[91] This speech was important because its content had been negotiated with the unions by Eizenstat, at the time a key advisor in Carter's campaign team. The outlined policy was very close to union proposals on health and fell just short of the Kennedy-Corman Health Security bill drafted in 1975. This bill, with its 'cradle to grave' entitlements, was at the time stalled in Congress.[92] Carter's speech would frame the expectations of the unions, congressional liberals and their standard bearer on health policy, Senator Kennedy.

Although politically damaged by his involvement in the death of one of Bobby Kennedy's female staff at Chappaquiddick in 1969, Kennedy remained a powerful figure in the Senate and the Democratic Party. He was regarded as the champion for universal health care and used his chairmanship of the Human Resources sub-committee as a platform for health reform. There would be questions from the Carter White House about the motivation for his actions on this legislation but Kennedy's commitment to health reform was genuine and longstanding. He first submitted proposals in 1973 and saw health reform as a moral issue, like civil rights, not something that could wait until the economy could afford it.[93] He was to remain influential on this issue right up until his death in 2009, being one of the sponsors of the Affordable Care Act of 2010. To the Carter White House, he was a major player in Congress with a good voting record in support of the administration, but he was not regarded as the most important Senator on this issue; they were the Chairs of the Finance and Health sub-committees, Senators Long and Talmadge. Both men were conservative Democrats and critical to the success of any health legislation. Outside Congress Kennedy had developed a close relationship with the unions, particularly Doug Fraser of the United Automobile Workers (UAW), who were staunch supporters of Carter and universal healthcare. Consequently, the White House worked very hard to keep Kennedy involved in the policy development process, often using Peter Bourne, Special Assistant to the President on health issues, as an additional channel of communication.

Health policy was developed in a similar way to welfare reform and HCC. Carter devolved responsibility to Califano and did not involve himself in the detail. However, he did not impose a rigid deadline as was done with welfare nor did he exclude other policy makers from the process as he had done with his energy plan. This was to be in contrast with his Democratic successor, Bill Clinton, who in 1993 imposed secrecy and time restraints on the development of his ultimately unsuccessful Health Reform bill. The White House had to manage conflicting views in Congress and an overcrowded legislative schedule to make progress on any proposals. Finally, like welfare and HCC, the administration faced strong and effective opposition from interest groups. Carter found himself caught between, on the one hand, his social conscience and a campaign commitment and, on the other, his concern for fiscal restraint and his commitment to achieve a balanced budget. His economic advisors, especially the OMB, applied consistent pressure to restrict the scope of any HEW proposals on the grounds of cost. The planning of health reform was discussed by his staff throughout 1977. Carter's economic advisors wanted to postpone proposals indefinitely but he was anxious to maintain union support and so wanted to proceed.[94] Peter Bourne continued to feedback Kennedy's concerns, stating that Kennedy had hinted that lack of action from Califano could prompt him to go public with his criticism.[95] Jordan, in response, defended Califano and the White House strategy but also expressed concern about promoting Kennedy over other congressmen like Rostenkowski, Long and Talmadge who were in his view equally, if not more, important to the success of any health legislation.[96] It was agreed that a White House decision on the draft proposals would be made by 15 December 1977 with legislation to be sent to Congress in April 1978.[97]

It quickly became evident that whilst HEW officials were developing a comprehensive scheme broadly in line with the Kennedy-Corman bill and Carter's health policy speech of April 1976, there were major obstacles to passing such legislation. Califano believed that consultation on reform would take several congressional sessions and not enough time was being allowed for this.[98] In a briefing from his domestic policy team for a meeting with Kennedy, Carter was told that there was wide disagreement amongst his advisors and in Congress. His economic team continued to express concern about the cost of reform. Many in Congress were opposed to significant Federal involvement in the scheme as part of general antipathy to big government initiatives. This coupled with a restricted congressional timetable indicated that the chances of passage of a reform bill were limited and it would be better to wait until after the mid-term elections in 1978. Bourne, a liberal on health policy, presented a more positive picture on progress. He argued that HEW's policy was mainly settled and that any delay had been due to the need to 'educate' Califano. He believed the impact of the 1978 mid-term elections would be marginal and that so far Kennedy had been very restrained in not criticizing the administration.[99] But

Bourne's view within the administration was a minority one. At the same time, Fraser, as leader of the UAW, was querying why Carter would not just support the Kennedy-Corman bill as its content broadly aligned with Carter's SNMA speech.[100] Despite his staff's reservations, Carter decided that he would present legislation in 1978, accepting only the necessity to delay its introduction until July of that year.[101] But there was no specific commitment on the sort of policy that would be presented. Although Carter vehemently denied this, the unions continued to believe that he was committed to draft legislation on the lines of the Kennedy-Corman bill.[102]

Throughout 1978, Carter was under continued pressure from many of his advisors to postpone his legislative proposals until after the mid-term election. Califano believed much more time was required to gain support whilst Carter's economic advisors objected to the cost of a comprehensive scheme. In a series of meetings with the unions, UAW and AFL-CIO, Carter and his staff attempted to persuade them to change key elements of their proposals. Carter was worried about their scheme being federally funded with no patient contribution, as this would drive up the cost and reinforce congressional opposition to government involvement.[103] In March 1978 Kennedy and the unions produced what they believed was a compromise. This accepted in principle that healthcare could be administered by the private sector, but their proposals were still largely based on the Kennedy-Corman bill with comprehensive benefits and universal coverage. Carter's advisors viewed the revised proposal as too costly both politically and economically. Joseph Onek, from Carter's domestic policy team and a former Kennedy aide, warned that most unions provided good health cover, so could take a tough line without risk to their membership. In addition, although NHI was a popular measure with the public, many people already had the cover it provided, so there was no direct benefit to them in the legislation. Without this personal stake many would oppose NHI if it were seen as too expensive.[104] Discussions with Kennedy and the unions throughout April failed to reduce the cost of their proposal because the White House could not get agreement on reduced coverage, limited patient contribution and more effective cost control.[105] By mid-May consultations had been extended to include key members of congress, only to find more conflicting opinions. Califano found in his round robin congressional discussions that Ullman opposed the Kennedy-Corman proposals in principle and did not want any NHI bill as he believed it contradicted anti-inflation policy. Senators Long, Talmadge and Ribicoff only favoured their own limited health bill which federalized Medicaid and provided cover for catastrophic injury. All congressional leaders opposed sending forward a bill in 1978, whilst Long went as far as to say that his bill would be the only one to pass his Finance Committee. Only Kennedy and Corman favoured putting a comprehensive NHI bill forward but even Corman had raised objections about the proposal by the unions to use private insurers.[106]

Despite these difficulties Carter wanted to honour his campaign commitment and in this he was supported by Califano. The HEW secretary opposed Carter's economic advisors who were arguing on cost grounds for a phased scheme as the only realistic option that had support in Congress. Califano maintained that the phased option would fail, Carter could not continue to 'string Kennedy along', and that it would be better to fulfil his campaign promise by submitting a comprehensive scheme even if it eventually failed.[107] Eizenstat in principle supported Califano but wanted to delay submitting a bill until after the mid-term elections. He did, however, acknowledge the validity of the concerns over cost articulated by the Chief Economic Advisor (CEA), Treasury, Commerce and OMB.[108] These disagreements hindered Carter's commitment to Kennedy and labour to publish his proposals by July 1978. Carter's economic advisors delayed attempts to finalize the administration's NHI principles by refusing to sign them off. They submitted their own version of NHI based on affordability that would be implemented in phases over future years.[109] Carter met Kennedy in June 1978 and warned him that while he still supported a comprehensive scheme, all his economic advisors opposed this and wanted a phased solution.[110] The agreed compromise on the principles between liberal and conservatives in the administration left undecided the issue of how the scheme was to be implemented. Whilst it set out a path to comprehensive insurance, the financial triggers required in the proposal made the long-term goals problematic for Kennedy.[111] In the final critical meeting on 28 July 1978 Carter argued, 'It will doom healthcare if we split … I have no other place to turn if I can't turn to you … I must emphasise fiscal responsibility if we are to have any chance.'[112] But Carter was unable to convince Kennedy or the unions that a phased approach would guarantee comprehensive legislation. Kennedy withdrew his active support fearing that the White House plan 'would perpetuate two separate but unequal systems of care'.[113] This decision ultimately, as Carter predicted, doomed any hope of successful legislation.

The initial response from the National Insurance Association of America to Carter's plan was positive: they characterized it as a 'good start'.[114] But there were divisions both inside and outside the White House. There were three proposals before Congress. A Senate bill sponsored by Long, Talmadge and Ribicoff, which provided cover against catastrophic illness and federalized Medicaid, would cost

$13bn. The Kennedy–union comprehensive plan would cost $59bn. Finally, the cost of the Carter plan, which was phase one of a comprehensive solution, was initially estimated at $25bn.[115] In addition there were continued disagreements within the White House over legislative tactics. Mondale favoured, in August 1978, going for a quick deal on the Long bill as he viewed this as the most realistic option. This was rejected at the time because of reservations about the limited scope of Long's proposals as well as an underlying concern about whether Long could be trusted.[116] There were also disagreements with Califano who believed that a phase one bill would not pass, and that the Long plan was fundamentally wrong. He therefore wanted HEW to demonstrate the administration's long-term commitment by presenting a comprehensive plan.[117] Eizenstat led the opposition to this, arguing that in the increasingly conservative climate the mere highlighting of the expensive comprehensive plan would damage any chances that Carter's bill had of passing Congress. This dispute between the DPG and HEW was eventually resolved in February with limited involvement of the president in the discussions.[118] To have any chance of success in 1979, the administration had to move quickly and gain the support of the liberals in Congress. Meetings were organized with Kennedy and the unions in February. The proposal was to gain support for phase one in return for an agreement on the content of the final comprehensive scheme. Eizenstat recognized that this would be difficult to achieve but believed that Kennedy would make concessions.[119] Carter, however, was unable to persuade either Kennedy or the unions to accept a phase one approach and/or that his proposal was more generous than the Long bill. The liberals remained wedded to a comprehensive policy even though the chances of gaining congressional approval were slim.

The administration continued to try and pass a bill that met the requirements of both wings of the party – a tough task made even more difficult by objections from Carter's economic advisors about the cost of even the phase one element of his plan. McIntyre wrote to Carter wanting a meeting to discuss a cheaper OMB alternative whilst Schultze also raised concerns.[120] There was intense debate during May 1979 that focused on a plan to provide increased help for the poor whilst controlling costs. The objective was to occupy the centre ground and force conservatives like Long to support Carter or form an alliance with the medical lobby to vote down the bill.[121] As for the liberal supporters, by June 1979 differences between Carter on the one hand and Kennedy and the unions on the other had become unbridgeable. Financially the gap between the White House and the Kennedy plans was nearly $40bn, which Carter deemed simply unaffordable.[122] As a result of compromises White House staff managed to form a coalition of potential supporters across the party to be present at Carter's public announcement of the proposed legislation on 12 June 1979. The inclusion of James Corman, co-sponsor of the Kennedy-Corman Health Security bill, was a major coup due to compromises Carter felt able to make.[123] Whilst Carter was prepared to see congressmen Long, Rangel and Ullman prior to the announcement, he left the unions to Mondale. He also rejected the opportunity to make a full speech explaining his proposals, opting instead for a short statement. This was perhaps a measure of Carter's scepticism of the chances of the proposal's success. The press conference merely highlighted the differences with Congress, with a less than enthusiastic endorsement from Long.[124] This was followed by a statement released by Kennedy which, whilst emphasizing that he would continue to work with Carter, criticized his plan as fundamentally unfair and ineffective in reducing costs.[125] When Kennedy launched his presidential bid in November 1979, NHI became a political issue but even before then his public criticism ensured that Carter's bill would be attacked by liberals as well as conservatives in Congress. In addition, attempts by the White House to get any health bill passed by the Senate Finance Committee were delayed by other administrative priorities on the Windfall Profits Tax and Hospital Cost Containment.[126] The conservative political climate and approaching 1980 election, as well as the existence of three different congressional proposals on health, made a successful outcome very unlikely. The most positive conclusion that the White House could present going into the 1980 election was that they had submitted a bill and the intention remained to pass NHI legislation should Carter be re-elected.

The creation of a comprehensive national health scheme was an article of faith for the liberal wing of the Democratic Party and the union movement. Following his speech to the SNMA in April 1976, they believed that they had a president who was committed to pass such legislation. Whilst Carter accepted the need for a comprehensive health scheme, unlike his Democratic successors, Presidents Clinton and Barack H Obama, he did not make this his number one legislative priority. In contrast to Clinton, he chose to prioritize welfare policy over health and was prepared to compromise over the final legislation. But like both his successors he found that critics characterized his legislative proposals as imposing 'big government', a damaging message when both he and later Clinton had been elected to change the way the government operated.[127] Carter did not immerse himself in health policy and he was, therefore, dependent on his advisors. To his chagrin, health insurance became an issue that split the Democratic Party and caused fundamental disagreements amongst his White House staff. The coordinating role of Eizenstat's domestic policy team was on more than one occasion bypassed by McIntyre's OMB, who not only disagreed with the fragile consensus of the policy teams but presented their own counter proposals. This hindered the ability of HEW and White House staff to formulate a consistent policy during 1978–9. Califano, who cut a frustrated figure during this period, believed that Carter recognized that he was caught between his campaign commitment and a lack of money.[128] Ultimately Kennedy and the unions believed it was right to submit a comprehensive health bill even if, given the conservative make up of Congress, there was no possibility of its passage. It was Carter who took the pragmatic view and supported a phased proposal because he believed that had the best chance of success. This involved lobbying Ullman and Long, as they had powerful positions in Congress, and not Kennedy who simply did not have such legislative influence.

In the end it was ideological disagreement as well as highly effective lobbying from the medical industry that ensured that no health legislation was passed before the 1980 election. Carter believed that Kennedy's constant criticism of his health policy was a product of an early decision to run against him in 1980.[129] This view was held by several of his staff and may explain Jordan's unusual level of involvement in health policy. Yet whilst health did become an issue in the primaries and at the Democratic Convention, there is little evidence to support this view prior to the summer of 1979. For Kennedy, health policy was, and would continue to be for the rest of his political life, a question of principle. Carter did make every effort to pass health legislation, but he seemed to lack the passion, commitment and even the evangelical fervour of Kennedy who saw health as a moral issue.

In his speech on health policy to the SNMA, Carter quoted his favourite philosopher Reinhold Niebuhr by saying 'the sad duty of politics is to establish justice in a sinful world'.[130] The reforms he sought in health and welfare brought together his religious faith and his belief in government to achieve social change for the greater good. This might indicate that Carter was acting as a social liberal in carrying out these policies. If this was the case, it raises the question of why Carter was not more proactive. Why for example did he not use his office more to persuade the American public of the need for reform? The concept of the 'bully pulpit' came naturally to Carter as a lay preacher and he had used it regularly during his administration on subjects like energy and inflation. It was before his trip to Japan in April 1979 though that he began to express doubts about the effectiveness of his many speeches in support of energy reform.[131] This period of reflection could well explain Carter's reluctance to speak out on health reform thereafter. His perceived failure to match Kennedy's commitment to healthcare was seen as both a failure of leadership and a betrayal of liberal principles.

Carter's handling of health and welfare policies during this time contrasted with the way that many historians have characterized his working style. He did not immerse himself in the detail as he did on energy policy but delegated the work to policy experts. Whilst he did impose arbitrary deadlines, he did not exclude key members of his administration from the policy-making process. He displayed a much more pragmatic approach, trying to negotiate an agreed plan with members of congress opposed to his legislation. This contrasts with the image of Carter in the media as a leader who was involved in the detailed workings of his administration and who would not make deals. These changes were partly driven by the pressure on his time. He was much less personally engaged in these policy debates than he was on energy or even the economy. The legislation left over from Carter's first year in office adversely affected the HEW-sponsored bills being put forward in 1978. His congressional liaison team made it clear that bills on Energy and Tax Reform would take priority during 1978 and even beyond. So, if a log jam hampered Carter's Health and Welfare bills, it was one of his own making. The deteriorating economic conditions strengthened the position of conservatives in the White House and on Capitol Hill as Carter sought to achieve change at minimal or even zero cost: a near impossible task. The role of the OMB after 1977 became more influential in challenging the cost of HEW programmes, reminding Carter of the potential impact on his anti-inflation strategy and his commitment to a balanced budget. He did not have the more favourable political climate in the legislature enjoyed initially by both of his Democratic successors, Clinton and Obama. He was also not helped by the unrealistic expectations of liberal supporters whose position on reform became more entrenched at a time when such views were in decline in the country.

Carter's commitment to social reform was genuine. He grew up with poverty and cared about solving the problems of health and welfare, but he lacked the passion of the liberals in his party. There were few major speeches calling for sacrifice to help the poor and the sick. Kennedy ultimately regarded health reform as fulfilling a deep human need for protection against the cost of illness whilst 'Carter saw a broken inefficient healthcare system to be re-engineered'.[132] Liberals in Congress had been his most consistent supporters, but he never regarded himself as one of them. They were an important constituency whose programmes needed to be accommodated if possible. His approach to solving such problems lacked Kennedy's moral certainty and at no point did his proposals veer away from the practicalities of fiscal restraint. His response was pragmatic in trying to establish a middle ground between conservative and liberal positions. His speeches on health and welfare issues placed much more emphasis on cost savings and reducing waste and fraud than the social benefits of the reforms being proposed. This may well have been a realistic assessment of the country's mood but there was no natural constituency on Capitol Hill and beyond for this approach and hence it was ultimately doomed to failure. He did not give up easily on these policies, sustaining the fight through most of his remaining time in office, but he continued to refuse to give them legislative priority.

Carter's track record on delivering HEW's social legislation was poor. Only his attempt to save the social security system from bankruptcy was a notable success but even that suffered from attempts by conservatives to claw back the agreed tax increases. The policies on health and welfare were fundamental to the Democratic Party and many liberals felt that Carter had failed to deliver on his campaign promises. This was an accurate if not fair assessment given the political environment, but it would lead to an increasingly frosty relationship with some of his core liberal constituencies in the Democratic Party and would ultimately lead to a liberal challenge to his leadership in 1980.

The changing base: Carter and the unions

In December 1980 following Jimmy Carter's defeat in the presidential election, White House staff were writing memoranda on the administration's achievements for his final State of the Union address. Deputy Chief of Staff Landon Butler wrote the brief on the relationship with organized labour. Butler had been Carter's liaison with the unions, principally the American Federation of Labor and Congress of Industrial Organizations (AFL-CIO), during the 1976 election campaign and then throughout Carter's term of office. His report, at least initially, presented a balanced picture of White House–union relations but Butler ended by saying that 'it is no exaggeration to conclude that no political leader in the country enjoys more loyalty and support from labour leaders than yourself'. He justified his argument with a description of union resources, believed to be in the region of $12–15 million, deployed to support the president in the 1980 campaign.[1] Butler's argument that Carter secured greater backing from the unions than he had done in the 1976 election was misplaced. Whilst the White House was able to build a good relationship with union leaders, it ultimately proved to be a flawed strategy in that the Democrats in the 1980 election were unable to convert this support into votes from either union or non-union workers. The success of Ronald Reagan in persuading millions of the American working class to vote for him signified a failure not just for Carter and for those union leaders who supported him, but the continued decline in the Democratic New Deal coalition.

Historians in writing of this period have focused on the long-term decline of union influence but have written very little on Carter's policy towards labour. Carter's relationship with the unions, an interest group with strong ties to the Democratic Party, highlights misconceptions of his leadership style and his attitude towards organized labour. His perceived predilection to immerse himself in the detail of policy and his hostility to interest groups were not evident in his administration's labour policy. Jimmy Carter, in running for president in 1976 as an outsider initially, made few specific policy commitments but as his race with President Ford became closer, he was forced to rely on the more traditional elements of the New Deal coalition of which the unions were a major component. The eventual narrowness of the victory would restrict his freedom of manoeuvre with Congress on his domestic programme. The implication of this was that his administration would continue to need the support of traditional democratic constituencies such as the unions.

Carter's attempts to deliver an effective labour strategy were shaped by the decline in labour influence in the economy and the political process. Since the inception of the New Deal the unions had been a key component in the electoral alliance that had helped keep the Democratic Party in power. The economic boom after 1945 had brought full employment, high wages and substantial increases in real income but it also saw the end of the unions' active involvement in the Federal government. The economic growth of the 1950s ensured a continuation of labour's economic influence but the rise of the new defence and technology industries in the Sunbelt states (the American south-west) signified a direct challenge to union power. To incentivize the transfer of industries and their skilled workforce from their traditional base in the north and north-east, southern states created attractive tax incentives and passed 'Right to Work' legislation which banned not only closed shops but in some cases unions altogether. By 1955 seventeen states had passed 'Right to Work' laws.[2] This trend contributed to a decline in union membership and was one of the major factors in the AFL-CIO seeking to reform the Taft-Hartley Act of 1946. The transfer of jobs to the Sunbelt also signalled the decline in traditional industry in the north and north-east where the blue-collar workforce was unionized. This threat to the union's economic power was mirrored by the decline in its powerbase in the Democratic Party.

Reforms initiated in 1971 by the Democratic Party to increase grassroots membership weakened the influence of union bosses on the nomination of delegates to the party convention. The unions faced competition for influence from emerging social movements representing women, minorities and environmental groups who had different political and economic goals and were often critical of older national institutions like the unions.[3] This resulted in the labour leadership having less influence over the nomination and election of members of congress, and by 1976 the number of traditional labour constituencies had declined.[4] In addition the unions faced major demographic changes in the workforce with a decline in unionized blue-collar jobs, counterbalanced by a rise in the white-collar employment which tended not to be unionized.[5] This trend, often stimulated by reforms like the introduction of the minimum wage, would continue until there were more white-collar jobs than blue collar by 1982.[6] Butler suggested that the AFL-CIO had struggled to meet these challenges due to what he characterized as 'institutional disarray'. He argued that the AFL-CIO split with liberal unions like the United Automobile Workers (UAW) and uncertainty over a successor to the ageing AFL-CIO president George Meany made collective decision-making difficult. In addition the decrease in union influence nationally resulted in the leadership being, in Butler's view, 'intimidated by minority views'. He quoted, as an example, the UAW's success in persuading the AFL-CIO to oppose Carter's proposals to remove controls on energy prices. Butler believed that often the easiest way for the AFL-CIO to mollify minority union opponents was to be seen to criticize the president directly.[7]

Given this uncertainty it was not surprising that the AFL-CIO in 1976 did not commit to any Democratic Party presidential candidate until after the convention. Its electoral steering committee concentrated its resources on the encouragement of voter registration.[8] However, several major unions chose to ignore this and formed their own 'Labour Coalition' which endorsed individual candidates during the primary campaign. Rather than commit himself to deals with the 'old institutions', like the AFL-CIO, Carter found his natural support with those more liberal unions such as the UAW and the National Education Association (NEA). Carter had little if any experience of unions in his home state Georgia and he said very little about them during the campaign. Whilst they viewed themselves as legitimate representatives of the working class and part of the New Deal coalition, Carter saw them as just another interest group albeit one that supported his party. In office he had to be reminded by Butler that referring to labour as special interests in speeches was counter-productive and using the term 'great institutions' was suggested as an alternative.[9] The unions had a historically privileged position in the New Deal coalition, but Carter rarely referred to this in his campaign rhetoric. He neither framed himself as a successor to FDR nor did he choose him as a role model. Instead, he suggested, somewhat unconvincingly, that Truman was the president he most admired.[10] The absence of AFL-CIO support during the primaries encouraged Carter to make common cause with individual unions over specific policy issues like health insurance (UAW) and education (NEA). He also promoted issues such as deregulation and government reform that did not have union backing. However, he was not 'anti-union' and would, as the 1976 race became closer, tailor his rhetoric to ensure their support.

As president, Carter relied upon experienced members of his team in developing labour policy and in handling day-to-day relations with the unions. He often used Mondale and his contacts within the Democratic Party to maintain dialogue with labour, but his key appointment was Ray Marshall as Secretary of Labor. Meany had made it clear to Carter that he wanted President Ford's Secretary of Labor, John Dunlop, to get the job. Meany, whilst respecting his pro-labour credentials, feared that Marshall would focus too much on non-union labour and discrimination issues. At their respective interviews Carter got on with Marshall, a fellow southerner with whom he had worked before, but not with the Republican, Dunlop. In the end on the key labour appointment where Carter had a free hand, he chose to ignore the advice of the President of the AFL-CIO. Perhaps this was a sign of Carter's attitude to what he regarded as labour's biggest interest group. The union leadership's limited influence on Carter's decisions even applied to his supporters. Jerry Wurf, leader of the American Federation of State, County and Municipal Employees (AFSMCE), ruefully commented, 'I didn't get much out of Carter but one thing I did get is that Dunlop did not become Secretary of Labor.'[11] Marshall, as with other cabinet members, was given the freedom to make his own appointments and he regarded himself as enjoying an advantage of being the only person in the cabinet who knew about the unions.[12] He was also not without allies in the administration on labour issues, often enjoying the support of Mondale and Carter's chief domestic policy advisor Stuart Eizenstat. At staff level Butler's responsibilities as deputy chief of staff included labour liaison whilst Bert Carp of the DPG established regular information sessions that kept business and unions informed of government policy, with the occasional if reluctant presence of the president.[13]

From Carter's viewpoint, union support through most of the 1976 campaign was sporadic at best. He had only been able to get direct backing from the unions on a state-by-state basis in the primaries. At the convention he was endorsed with Mondale's help by the AFL-CIO, but he was widely regarded by them as the least bad option. Carter continued to campaign in 1976 as an outsider, separate from the big organizations, like the unions, which he viewed as part of the system. His relationship with Meany would be pivotal to a successful labour strategy. Meany had been a reformer within the union, a strong campaigner against discrimination on the grounds of race or religion.[14] He was also a conservative on foreign policy issues, backing President Richard Nixon against his liberal Democratic challenger George McGovern over Vietnam in the 1972 election. He was eighty-two when Carter took office and had been president since 1955.

His organization was facing serious economic and political challenges, and he was looking to a Democratic president to help meet them.

Carter's major legislative priorities were not driven by concern over labour, but some policies had a close association with specific unions. The UAW influenced administration proposals for National Health Insurance whilst the NEA were staunch supporters of the formation of the new Department of Education. But Carter could not afford to ignore the AFL-CIO. In a memorandum to Carter his closest advisor Hamilton Jordan warned that they were the 'single most formidable force on the Hill'. Many Democratic congressmen in the north and north-east had run ahead of the national ticket in 1976 due to their support.[15] The AFL-CIO submitted their own 'shopping list' to the White House following their Miami conference in February 1977. They were determined to reinstate the four labour bills that had been passed by Congress but vetoed by President Ford. They wanted an increase in the minimum wage to $3 per hour as well as amendments to the Taft-Hartley Act which, they argued, would restore the intended balance between employers and workers.[16] Carter did not accept or reject these proposals but discussions facilitated by Eizenstat with Marshall, Mondale and Butler established the administration's position which was confirmed at a meeting with Meany and his deputy, Lane Kirkland, on 4 March 1977.[17] Although the unions wanted White House support for their agenda, they did not believe that they would need it to pass the legislation that Ford had vetoed.[18] They had developed a formidable lobby organization over the years and expected the loyalty of members of congress that they had supported during the election campaign. This confidence proved to be misplaced. Changes in the congressional committee structure and the increasing influence of both left- and right-wing pressure groups on Democratic members had reduced union influence. Meany complained that it was not just the AFL-CIO which was suffering; Democratic Party leaders found that 'quite a few new House members are not paying attention to their instructions'.[19] In response to these difficulties labour formed a progressive alliance to fight the conservative trend in Congress and the Democratic Party.[20] However, the unions soon found that they were to become more reliant on the administration for practical support to pass legislation.

The first test of Carter's labour strategy was the passage of the Common Situs Picketing bill. The bill, one of those vetoed by Ford, applied mainly to the construction industry and allowed picketing of all workers on a site even if they were not directly involved in the dispute. Although this legislation's impact was negligible nationally, the business lobby argued that it was a denial of rights and an abuse of power. The bill was part of the Democratic Party platform in 1976 and so Carter agreed that if passed he would sign it. He did express concern about the impact on small businesses and the union's decision to remove a clause from the original bill which imposed a thirty-day cooling off period in disputes. Eizenstat urged Carter to demand that this latter clause be replaced but also reminded the president of his need for AFL-CIO support on other issues.[21] Carter chose not to insist on the clause's reinstatement, partly because he had made no commitment to support the bill actively, just to sign it if it passed. The union's refusal to compromise with the opposition in Congress demonstrated their confidence that their legislation would pass the House, but this judgement proved incorrect. Their discussions with new Democratic members failed to detect reservations about the bill and as a result thirty-seven out of the sixty-eight freshmen voted against it, ensuring the vote in the House was lost.[22] This defeat was a major surprise to the unions and it encouraged the business lobby and conservatives in Congress to ramp up its opposition to the unions' next objective, the Labor Law Reform Bill (LLRB).

Following the defeat of Common Situs, the proposed LLRB was seen by the AFL-CIO as a major test of its political strength and, by implication, a measure of Carter's labour credentials. The administration accepted that the original Taft-Hartley Act had not been working as intended. The new bill was promoted by its supporters as a series of sensible measures to strengthen the powers of the National Labour Relations Board (NRLB). It increased penalties for breaches of the law, accelerated the process of union recognition and closed loopholes used by employers to disregard the act. The most controversial element of the bill was the proposal that employers who were found guilty were to be denied Federal contracts.[23] From April to early July 1977 administration officials worked with the unions to shape the draft bill. White House reservations over certain aspects of the bill, such as union insistence on repealing the 'Right to Work' law, were resolved in the administration's favour. In briefing Carter, his staff acknowledged that the unions had been realistic in their demands.[24] His senior advisors, Marshall, Mondale and Eizenstat, recommended that Carter endorse the revised bill. In support of this Jordan also emphasized that the legislation was backed by those liberal unions such as UAW, the Machinists and Communication Workers of America (CWA) which were strong Carter supporters. Whilst indicating some minor reservations, Carter accepted his staff recommendations and put the full resources of his administration behind the legislation.[25]

The Labor Law Reform Bill was submitted to Congress on 17 July 1977 and passed the House in October of that year. Its final passage was dependent upon the government getting the sixty votes in the Senate to overturn any filibuster by the opposition. Carter's congressional liaison team were confident of getting the necessary votes. There was an option that an early move to a vote in the Senate after October 1977 might have garnered enough votes to succeed but the legislation was delayed because Carter prioritized passage of the Panama Canal Treaty. The subsequent delay of four months enabled the business lobby, marshalled by a National Action Committee, to send out 8 million leaflets which painted the bill as a radical measure designed to increase union power. In addition, several senators who had backed Carter on Panama did not want to be seen voting for two 'liberal' measures consecutively.[26] Carter's staff were confident of the support of fifty-nine Senators and initiated heavy lobbying of a further seven to get the extra vote. The administration used every resource, including Carter personally, to persuade these legislators to vote for the bill but this was to no avail; they could not overturn the filibuster.[27] Subsequent proposals to pass a weaker bill were rejected by the unions.[28] Plans to reintroduce the bill in 1979 were also rejected on the grounds that the 1978 mid-term elections had resulted in the loss of eight senators who had previously supported this legislation, thus making it impossible to pass anything other than a watered-down version.[29]

Carter was subsequently blamed for the failure but at the time Meany gave him high marks for his support.[30] The AFL-CIO president put the bill's failure down to 'a heavily financed, well-orchestrated coalition between big business and right-wing extremists'.[31] Despite a well-financed lobbying effort by the unions, the conservative mood in the country and the new committee structures in Congress proved too difficult to manage, even with Carter's full backing. As an indicator of the difficulties the administration faced, sixteen Democrats voted against the bill, most of them from the south, despite heavy lobbying by a Secretary of Labor and a president from the same region.[32] From Carter's perspective he was comfortable with this labour reform as it had no major budgetary implications.[33] The same could not be said of labour expectations of his economic policy.

The unions broadly endorsed Carter's Economic Recovery Plan (ERP) which was designed to address the recession he inherited from the Ford administration. The plan contained two policies that aligned with union conference resolutions: measures to address unemployment and an increase in the minimum wage. Carter was able to reach agreement with the unions on these issues as part of the 1977 budget, but this stimulus package was the last traditional Democratic budget he was able to submit. He was the first Democratic president since the war to face an economy that was not growing substantially, so many policies recommended by the unions would have to involve a redistribution of the economic cake or an increase in taxation.[34] The unions wanted Carter to prioritize a stimulus package that addressed unemployment over tax cuts which were advocated by conservatives. They hoped that the passage of the Humphrey-Hawkins Full Employment Act, signed into law by Carter on 27 October 1978, would compel future governments to focus on growth and unemployment. This proved to be a false hope as many of the act's more proscriptive provisions, such as the prohibition of Right to Work laws, had to be removed to enable its passage. Carter continued to back programmes to help the unemployed, principally through the Comprehensive Employment and Training Act (CETA),[35] but he did not accept that the government should prioritize full employment over problems like inflation.[36] In terms of fiscal policy during 1977–8, the AFL-CIO had reason to be fairly satisfied with Carter. However, they expressed concern over the conservative nature of his tax reform proposals which had kept many of the loopholes that favoured the rich without significantly reducing the tax burden on poorer families.[37] Despite this disappointment they continued to try to influence the administration's spending priorities in the later budgets.[38]

As the economy deteriorated, the administration gave priority to controlling inflation. This created various issues for the unions. Firstly, whilst labour leaders would always support liberal interventionist policies to help employment and growth, they were fundamentally opposed to any government intervention in wage bargaining. There was also concern that as Carter's inflation policy took centre stage less attention would be given to achieving full employment. The president was also opposed to statutory wage controls and reassured the CWA at their convention that 'My own belief is that the system of free enterprise, the great union organizations can best handle their affairs through equal authority at the bargaining table.'[39] But the support of labour along with business was critical to the success of any voluntary anti-inflation policy.

Another consequence of the shift in economic policy was the increase in influence of economic advisors such as Charles Schultze, Fred Kahn and Jim McIntyre, all of whom had less sympathy with the union view on the economy.[40] The administration went through a series of phases in its anti-inflation programme but managed to keep union support through most of 1978. In direct discussions with Meany, Marshall persuaded the labour leader that inflation was a direct threat to AFL-CIO members' standard of living. He also played on Meany's fear that if the unions did not co-operate, the public would blame them for the policy's failure. Meetings with labour leaders highlighted their absolute opposition to mandatory controls, their deep mistrust of business leaders and concern that they would not be able to persuade their membership to support government policy in their pay settlements.[41] In May 1978 the White House was able to gain union support for its policy provided there were no fixed-figure targets for pay settlements.[42] This was a major achievement for the government and ensured that the unions were locked into the policy by their membership of tripartite committees with business and the government. However, even with full cooperation there was no guarantee that a voluntary policy would work, and as the inflation rate continued to rise, the pressure on the government to toughen penalties for non-compliance increased. This would lead at the end of 1978 to a very public disagreement with Meany.

By September 1978, the White House was seeking to further tighten wage controls. The unions were concerned that as the wage-price guidelines were policed by the employers, business could adjust its prices to inflation regularly whilst the unions were usually committed to three-year wage deals.[43] The AFL-CIO became publicly critical of Carter's inflation policy and refused to support the proposed September 1978 guidelines which were based around 7 per cent wage settlements. Meany's action was as much about his inability to control his own members on wage settlements as it was a disagreement with the White House.[44] The public dispute with Meany was resolved by early 1979 but disagreements persisted over wage settlements and wider economic policy for the remainder of Carter's term in office. Labour continued to argue that Carter's anti-inflation policy was fundamentally unfair because, unlike wages, the controls being applied to prices were so flexible as to be almost non-existent. There was also a suggestion that Marshall had lost credibility with labour leaders by continuing to defend Carter's economic programme.[45]

Despite the ultimate failure of Carter's inflation policy, his administration continued to receive the union's reluctant support until he left office. The AFL-CIO, however, found it increasingly difficult to restrain its members in their settlements. In addition, the powerful independent Teamsters union blatantly ignored the guidelines in 1979.[46] The agreement between the government and union leaders announced on 28 September 1979, known as the National Accord, enabled the unions to have continued participation in the bodies that monitored inflation in return for their involvement in government decisions. This ensured labour support for the annual agreement of the wage-price strategy, but it can also be seen as a wider strategy to keep the union leadership engaged.[47] The wage settlements made during this period were broadly in line with the guidelines set and so were, to a limited extent, an economic success. However, the overall anti-inflation policy was a major failure which brought no great benefit to the unions, its members or the working population as a whole. After the passage of the ERP in 1977, the unions could point to few if any economic policy successes. The Carter White House could and did argue that the battle with inflation was in part for the benefit of union members but after the administration's first year in office, little priority was given to labour's twin goals of increased growth and full employment. The National Accord gave Meany's successor, Lane Kirkland, a seat at the table in discussions on the draft 1981 budget but he could not stop attempts to reduce public spending and the increased expenditure on defence.[48]

Some policy initiatives from Carter could be linked to the unions which had supported him in the 1976 campaign. The National Education Association (NEA) was a staunch supporter of the creation of a separate Department of Education. Whilst Carter was unable to increase funding for education significantly during his term of office due to economic constraints, he was determined to deliver on his campaign promise to create a Department of Education. He was faced with internal opposition from Health, Education and Welfare Secretary Joseph Califano, the American Federation of Teachers (AFT), the AFL-CIO and conservatives in Congress. He was forced to intervene with Califano to stop him stalling and lobbying against the bill.[49] But he had strong support within his administration from Mondale and Jordan who recognized the importance of keeping the backing of the NEA's two million membership.[50] The new Department of Education was finally signed into law on 17 October 1979, and despite subsequent campaign promises and threats of closure from Carter's GOP successors, the department has remained in place to this day. Another union which supported Carter in 1976 was the United Automobile Workers under the leadership of Douglas Fraser. This partnership proved less sustainable as Carter was unable to deliver on his campaign commitment to pass a National Health Insurance bill. He kept Fraser informed of the bill's development even though the UAW leader supported Kennedy's more liberal plan. Fraser was critical of the conservative nature of Carter's tax reform plans,[51] but he was able to maintain his influence on the White House on various issues, including the enforcement emission standards under the Clean Air Act.[52]

Marshall argued strongly in favour of Carter's labour legislative record, stating that the president had defended protective labour laws, strengthened occupational safety, created job growth in the private sector and expanded youth and minority training.[53] But some of the bills sent to Congress by the administration that had strong union support failed, notably Labor Law and Health Insurance reforms. The AFL-CIO News described the result of the first

Congress in ten years under a Democratic president as 'not a monument to forward looking legislation but a tombstone'.[54] This was an unfair criticism of Carter. Whilst not heavily engaged in supporting labour legislation, he did try to honour his campaign commitments and ensured his staff co-operated with the union lobby. The reason for failure lay not with the president but the makeup of Congress and the decline in union influence nationally. The new committee structure and 'sunshine rules' hampered the 'closed door deals' on which union lobbyists thrived. The increase in the number of conservative interest groups also resulted in a countervailing pressure on individual members of congress. Andrew Biemiller, AFL-CIO legislative director, noted in 1979 that 'more than ever before you have to see practically every member of congress if you are to have any hope of success'.[55] Carter's liaison team had quickly found out that this was now the normal practice but for the union lobbyists this was something totally new.

Labour's difficulties with Congress were also reflected in a poor public image. A Harris poll in 1977 found that 64 per cent of the public believed that union leaders were connected to criminal elements.[56] Perhaps even more worrying for the union leadership was their declining influence over the working-class vote. An early example of this was the union campaign in June 1978 against California's Proposition 13 which sought to restrict increases in property taxes. The unions campaigned fiercely that a yes vote would have severe implications for state services, particularly in education. Yet despite this not only did the vote pass easily but subsequent polling found that most teachers had supported the proposition.[57] This proved to be a sign of the effectiveness of conservative messaging on both union and non-union audiences and would have profound consequences for the 1980 election.

Although labour's political influence was declining, it had become important to their leaders, particularly Meany, that they were seen to have regular access to power, especially as there was a Democrat in the White House. Meany felt threatened by the independent actions of the more liberal unions which had backed Carter earlier in the 1976 campaign and he tried to persuade the White House that the AFL-CIO should be the first point of contact for all unions.[58] This was not accepted by Carter who continued to invite union leaders like Jerry Wurf and Doug Fraser to meetings when he sought a range of views on policy matters.[59] Meany expected access to Carter not only on economic and labour issues but on foreign policy matters that concerned him.[60] When he thought he was being ignored he reverted to a confrontational style which often took the form of personal attacks.[61] Carter ensured that Meany was given considerable access and sent him personal notes,[62] but there was no rapport between them. Carter was once upset over a draft letter due to go to the AFL-CIO President that addressed him as 'President George Meany'. Carter told his staff, 'I don't call him George.'[63] For Carter, although he regarded the unions as another interest group, they were major supporters whose views had to be considered when formulating policy. He recognized that it was important that he kept all members of the Democratic coalition together on issues, particularly where there was potential conflict, but there was no meeting of minds.[64]

In early meetings White House staff acknowledged the practical help that the AFL-CIO had provided during the election and transition. They scheduled specific briefings on the administration's ERP and Civil Service Reform.[65] Although Carter's legislative record did not deliver on key union priorities, the White House continued regular dialogue with labour leaders on matters of mutual interest. These meetings denoted a degree of 'embedding' of the unions in the administration's consultation process, which was to increase when the National Accord was established.[66] Dialogue also continued outside the domestic policy sphere, with Carter seeking AFL-CIO support for the Panama Canal Treaty whilst Meany argued for greater congressional control of the Federal Reserve.[67] After six months, Carter's staff provided him with a list of 'significant actions' that the administration had taken since coming to office. The section on labour covered a wide range of issues, including the minimum wage, trade quotas, the Teamster union pension fund support, health and safety reforms, unemployment benefits, as well as draft labour legislation.[68] However, there remained tensions as neither party felt that their efforts were being reciprocated. Carter was irritated when Meany's criticisms of him appeared in the press. In response to an article in which Meany highlighted Carter's alleged indecisive handling of the miner's strike, bemoaned his lack of consultation and even hinted that he might switch his support to California Governor Jerry Brown, Carter commented, 'I'm getting tired of this.'[69] Butler's attempt to reassure Carter that this was just Meany responding to negative comments from his mid-level union officials did not diminish the president's disquiet.[70] Two months later, Jordan encouraged Carter to voice his annoyance at a meeting with Meany about the union's failure to acknowledge or promote to their members Carter's efforts to support policies that helped them.[71] There were efforts made by the White House to improve relations. In early 1978 Butler recommended to Jordan that the president should allocate more time to meet with the unions by attending international labour conferences taking place in Washington.[72] Carter's speech at the steelworkers' convention that autumn was an attempt to promote the administration's track record.[73] Staff also reviewed labour-related actions taken by the White House in the previous eighteen months, which covered events for and invitations to union leaders. This included the practice of Carter calling two or three union leaders a week.[74]

The breakdown in relations in September 1978 was due to tension between the administration on the one hand and labour and business on the other over wage-price controls. Union anger at business leaders who blamed them for wage inflation came to a head in July 1978 when Fraser resigned from the Labour-Management group stating that he believed that 'leaders in the business community .... have chosen to wage a one-sided class war in this country'.[75] The AFL-CIO's increasing concern over Carter's policy on wage-price controls was evident when Meany demanded a meeting with Carter the day before the September announcement of the new inflation policy. Carter's alleged refusal to meet prompted three months of non-cooperation from the AFL-CIO leader.[76] This failed to cause any major crisis for the White House because Carter's staff, supported by the vice president, worked assiduously to maintain contact with the individual union presidents who were AFL-CIO members. These contacts included invitations to White House dinners and briefings from Marshall and the Office of Management and Budget.[77] Cooperation was formally resumed in January 1979 following a meeting between Carter, Mondale and the president's advisors with Meany, Kirkland and six union presidents. Consultation arrangements were agreed with monthly meetings between the AFL-CIO and Mondale.[78] The continued failure of the administration's inflation policy increased pressure for strong counter measures and therefore tension with the unions. The White House wanted greater flexibility from labour if a new tougher anti-inflation policy was to be successful. The circumstances for a deal were helped by the declining health of Meany who handed over day-to-day control to Lane Kirkland in April 1979 and formally stepped down later that November. Kirkland, an intellectual southerner, was to be more amenable to a deal but only at a price of greater union involvement in policymaking.[79]

The signing of the National Accord was regarded by the White House and the unions as a major contribution to improved relations. It was modelled on the European Social Contract and was principally negotiated by Kirkland and the newly appointed Secretary of the Treasury, William Miller.[80] The Accord's aim was, 'To provide for American Labour's involvement and cooperation with the Administration on important national issues.'[81] For the administration the Accord locked the unions into the anti-inflation plank of its economic policy at the price of increased consultation on a wide range of issues, including some on foreign policy. For the unions it presented an opportunity to influence and to be seen to influence government policy. They also hoped that the tripartite board involving government and business would help ensure that the price of austerity was more equitably distributed.[82] Carter's staff established a series of formal meetings with Mondale and Marshall to keep the AFL-CIO leadership informed and undertook to consult them on major policy decisions at a preliminary stage. This would give the AFL-CIO leadership the opportunity to influence important government policies in advance of a final decision.[83]

Despite the initial fanfare, the Accord had no meaningful sanctions on dealing with inflation and concern was expressed by Carter and some of his staff about its effectiveness. In June 1980, Eizenstat and Democratic Party Chair, Jon White, complained that the deal was a one-way street after the unions were perceived to have 'ambushed' the administration in Congress over the renewal of the Council on Wage and Price Stability. Butler defended the unions, highlighting that they had largely complied with the wage guidelines and had tacitly supported Carter's position on oil and gas deregulation. In addition, he argued that Kirkland had not promoted Edward Kennedy's election campaign and the Accord had helped bring in union support during the primaries.[84] Butler remained a convinced advocate of the Accord, stating that whilst it was at times on 'very thin ice. .... unless some development occurs, I don't expect it to break'.[85] Eizenstat was more realistic about its limitations but nonetheless urged Carter to back the Accord claiming it was a price worth paying to get union support. He also argued that it would be a signal that the administration was equitable to labour and help gain their backing for the 1980 election.[86] The Accord did provide an effective vehicle for the administration to engage with union leaders in the final year of Carter's term in office. It was noticeable, however, that the work to establish the Accord, as with all the administration's labour policies, was conducted by his labour advisors with little direct input from the president. The Accord, Butler's rather overblown defence notwithstanding, did help with the president's election campaign by ensuring the union leadership's financial support.

The decision of Senator Kennedy to run against Carter in the Democratic primaries created a dilemma for the unions as Kennedy had been a long-standing friend of labour. Although the AFL-CIO maintained formal neutrality, many unions took sides. The more liberal unions such as the UAW, AFSCME and AFT backed Kennedy whilst Carter received the support of most unions, many of which had benefitted from his policies.[87] This support was not necessarily reflected on the ground during the primary campaigns as the Kennedy unions were often better organized in getting out their vote.[88] During this phase of the campaign Carter maintained regular contact with Kirkland. White House staff believed that Carter's sensitive response to Meany's death in January 1980 with his public statement, the lowering of the flag at the White House and the issue of a commemorative stamp had been appreciated by the unions. Whilst officially neutral Kirkland had continued to speak in favour of Carter's foreign policy and had refused to invite Kennedy to speak at the AFL-CIO conference.[89] A series of early Carter primary victories resulted in White House staff seeking to build bridges with Kennedy unions in the summer of 1980. Butler reported that he was optimistic about the level of labour support and that only a few unions would not support Carter in the coming presidential election. In the end only the air traffic controllers (PATCO) and the Teamsters union endorsed Reagan during the 1980 campaign although the backing of some liberal union leaders was less than wholehearted. This still constituted a major success for Carter; however, the ability of union leaders to turn this support into votes was now the critical question.

In contrast to his negative attitude to interest groups in general, Carter was personally involved in a series of meetings with the unions in the run up to the 1980 presidential campaign against the GOP candidate Ronald Reagan.[90] This would be part of a pivot strategy that was to focus his campaign resources on Reagan's anti-union policies.[91] The Carter team remained confident throughout the campaign of strong union support. Writing to Jordan, Butler argued that the administration had better knowledge of the unions after nearly four years in power and had more union support at state level following the primary campaign.[92] However, this was at the price of increased union influence over Carter's policies. Labour representation at the 1980 Democratic National Convention had increased from 20 to 29 per cent. Kirkland played a key role in the dialogue between the Carter and Kennedy camps to ensure the final agreement of the Democratic platform.[93] This resulted in Carter accepting, against the wishes of his economic advisors, a commitment to spend $12bn on job creation.[94] Kirkland continued to meet Carter under the umbrella of the Accord and sought to persuade the administration to increase spending on his proposal for a Re-industrialisation Finance Corporation (RFC) which became a major plank of the Carter campaign. Kirkland also tried, less successfully, to make the Carter message more positive as he felt uncomfortable with the tone of anti-Reagan message.[95] In return the unions contributed substantial resources to the campaign, but with limited results as this support did not translate into votes for Carter from their members. Union membership represented a third of the electorate in six key states such as Ohio and Pennsylvania, but in 1980 they were all lost to Reagan. In comparison to 1976, Carter's share of the union vote dropped 17 points to 46 per cent and for non-union workers it dropped 8 points to 35 per cent.[96] The administration's success in winning the support of union leaders simply did not translate into votes at the ballot box.

Carter's approach to dealing with labour in office highlighted some differences from the way he was perceived in the media. His deep suspicion of interest groups could have caused difficulties with labour's expectation of special treatment, but it did not result in any serious breach in their relationship. One of the reasons for this was that despite Carter's reputation for micro-management he delegated the union relationship almost entirely to Marshall, Mondale and his White House advisors. This was even the case when there was a crisis, for example during the miners' strike in early 1978. This dispute affected large areas of the country and there was concern over the impact on energy supplies. Marshall worked hard to deliver a compromise acceptable to both parties and Carter was kept informed of his progress. It was Carter who made the final decision based on Marshall's recommendation to invoke the Taft-Hartley Act that forced the miners back to work which eventually resulted in a settlement.[97] On labour policy Carter did not involve himself at all in the detail – contrary to his presidential image and reputation – and in nearly all instances he accepted his advisors' recommendations. This enabled his administration to meet most of its campaign commitments to the unions. Where union-supported legislation failed in Congress it was not from a lack of effort by the White House, and his staff could point to policies that were passed due to Carter's direct intervention to quell internal opposition; the transfer of Mining Enforcement and Safety Administration (MESA) from Interior to Labor being a case in point.[98] Where he was less successful, as in the case of the Labor Law Reform Bill, union criticism of Carter was notably muted. There was recognition from labour leaders that the decline in their influence was not a result of lack of interest or effort from the White House. Meany admitted that by the mid-1960s workers, who had prospered in the 1950s and began owning homes in the suburbs, had become more middle class in attitude and were less interested in labour issues.[99] The unions also became more focused on being seen to have the trappings of power. Leaders like Meany and Kirkland wanted both the government and business to acknowledge that the labour movement was a positive force in the economy.[100] The National Accord was the administration's attempt to accommodate that need in return for labour's support for Carter's anti-inflation policy. Carter was comfortable enough with this strategy as he had to give up very little in the negotiation.

There was a strong theme in press coverage at the time and in the historic literature of painting Carter as a president who was obsessed with the minutiae of government. His handling of labour policy was more typical of Carter's managerial style. He delegated to Marshall on all labour issues and the debates on strategy usually took place without his participation. He invariably accepted the recommendations of his advisors, and this included when to meet with union leaders and key members of congress on labour issues. Carter's labour policy also demonstrated that his natural antipathy to interest groups, another leadership trait highlighted by historians, was more nuanced than previously suggested. Where an election was involved, either in fulfilling a campaign commitment or during the run up to the election itself, Carter worked diligently to accommodate labour's views. Interest group or not, the politician in Carter recognized the importance of key stakeholders and did everything he could to retain their support. In fact, these interventions signified the actions of Carter the flexible politician rather than the influence of any ideological or moral viewpoint. Eizenstat observed how 'a president who was so consciously apolitical in his governance … could turn on a dime when campaign season began'.[101] Early support from more liberal unions was a product of co-interest on specific policies, which soon dissipated if the policy failed. Labour may have been regarded as a liberal cause but to Carter his interest was not based on ideology but political expediency and the need for electoral support.

Carter's overall labour strategy of cultivating union leadership to gain labour support in the country was in many ways well executed but it was based on a premise which was no longer valid and therefore doomed to failure. National union leaders no longer had the influence at the ballot box they once enjoyed, and workers (whether unionized or not) were listening to different, often conflicting, messages from other sources. These were not just from conservative organizations but also from other more liberal groups who opposed the more traditional labour views on issues such as the environment, urban renewal, gay and women's rights. This was one of the many shifts in American society that influenced the political scene in the 1970s and framed the atmosphere in which Carter sought to govern. To succeed in this environment Carter had to appeal directly to all blue- and white-collar workers on the issues that mattered to them. Unfortunately, unlike Reagan, Carter lacked both the understanding and rhetorical skills to appeal to such groups even if his advisors had argued that such an approach was necessary. It was this failure to recognize the changes affecting unions and the working population that ultimately doomed Carter's labour policy to failure.

Fighting the culture wars

Historian Bruce Schulman stated, 'In race relations, family life, politics, and popular culture, the 1970s marked the most significant watershed of modern American History. The beginning of our time.'[1] One of the consequences of this was the rise of alternative views of how society should develop. These differing opinions often prompted fierce debate which commentators such as James Hunter in the 1990s were to call the 'Culture Wars'.[2] The roots of this conflict lay in the 1970s with the rise of interest groups on social issues such as religion, race, women and the environment. Whilst national in scope they represented distinct and often conflicting views on society. Given President Carter's deep suspicion of the Washington lobby in general, he was expected to be wary of their influence. However, in the case of these groups, he had not only received their full support during the 1976 election campaign but had espoused their views in one form or another. They were Carter's natural supporters, but they represented radical change. Yet they in turn faced a serious challenge from conservative groups which reflected 'the widespread feeling America had taken a wrong turn in the 1970s'.[3] These conflicting views both for and against further change appeared to be answered by Carter who stood as an 'outsider' from Washington. His track record as president in these areas of policy was in some ways impressive but could never match the expectations created by his election victory. For these movements who argued for sweeping change, Carter's record in office was never enough but for those conservatives who like the Religious Right opposed even the status quo, his policies constituted nothing less than a betrayal. How Carter dealt with these challenges would affect his chances of a second term in the White House.

The 1970s saw the politicization of religion, mainly through conservative evangelicalism. For Carter, as a man of faith, this related directly to how he used the issue of his character in the 1976 election. When he presented himself to the American people, he put his character front and centre of his campaign by describing the roles he had played: a scientist, a farmer, a businessman and a governor, but he always ended by saying that he was a Christian. His faith influenced his behaviour as a both politician and president. Having become a 'born again' Christian in 1966, he played an active part in church life, holding minor office, teaching Sunday School and going on outreach missions to Massachusetts and Pennsylvania. He continued to affirm his faith in his speeches despite any potential political disadvantages and concerns from liberal advisors who believed that highlighting his 'born again' or evangelical credentials (Carter preferred the former term) would alienate many voters. Carter did not accept this argument. His faith was an integral part of who he was, and it was politically relevant as he was standing on the issue of his character. He believed that being an active Christian helped his campaign, particularly in the south. He stood as someone who could be trusted; hence, his campaign line, 'I will never lie to you.' Carter believed his character and faith tapped into the electorate's desire for moral leadership following Watergate and Vietnam.[4] His faith was reflected in many of his speeches, not least his successful 1976 Democratic Convention address, which was described as the 'language of the pulpit, not the podium'.[5]

Carter came from a progressive strain of evangelicalism that supported social improvement of the poor, Civil Rights and an enhanced role for women. He articulated this view in his Law Day Speech at the University of Georgia on 4 May 1974, in which he highlighted the inequalities of the justice system and argued that as 'the powerful and the influential in our society shape the laws' an unsatisfactory status quo had been maintained.[6] He was unusual in that during the 1960s evangelicals did not generally participate in politics. But Carter believed, having studied the Christian writer Reinhold Niebuhr, that it was possible to be a politician without compromising one's beliefs.[7] He believed that by emphasizing his moral character, he could earn the trust of the American people. There was a part of the electorate to whom Carter's faith was of great interest: his fellow evangelicals. To an evangelical movement that was beginning to develop a conservative political agenda, Carter seemed to be the ideal candidate. But as was soon to become apparent, there were fundamental differences between his approach to faith and political power and their own.

During the 1960s and 1970s the revival in interest in religion had resulted in a tripling of Americans who talked of the growing role of faith in their lives. In addition, 1976 was declared by *Time* magazine as the 'Year of the Evangelical'. Leaders like Pat Robertson, James Robison, Jim Bakker and Jerry Falwell had an estimated 100 million followers. Pat Robertson set up the Christian Broadcasting Network (CBN) which focused on fundamentalist issues and had

5 million viewers.[8] It was Falwell who established the 'Moral Majority', a lobby group that grew to 2 million supporters and campaigned for pro-God and family policies. Despite these developments, evangelicals were at first reluctant to become involved in politics. In the 1960s Falwell spoke out against evangelicals campaigning[9] but this started to change in the 1970s with progressives such as Carter campaigning for social justice whilst conservatives responded to what they saw as the challenge to their fundamental values by the state.[10] This fear was triggered by Supreme Court decisions on prayer in school (1962) and abortion (1973).[11] As a political force, they joined conservatives within the Republican Party who campaigned in 1974 against President Gerald Ford's choice as vice president, Nelson Rockefeller, a liberal and divorcee. They subsequently formed with business an effective pressure group to defeat pro-labour legislation and campaigned against the ratification of the Equal Rights Amendment (ERA), abortion and school busing. They were also prominent in the conservative right's targeting of Senator Dick Clark of Iowa in the 1978 mid-term elections. It was the campaigning of religious groups on the issue of abortion that contributed to Clark's surprise defeat.[12] Despite this move to the right, the evangelical movement had political expectations of their fellow believer. Carter seemed to be 'one of their own' with impeccable 'born again' credentials and they voted for him in large numbers in 1976, helping to secure the south for the Democrats. They were to be disappointed by the end of Carter's term of office but the clues to their differences were to be found in the 1976 campaign.

Carter emphasized moral leadership during that campaign. He spoke simply and frankly about his religious faith. This was appealing to the Religious Right and in the south, but Carter recognized that his 'born again' beliefs could be regarded as strange in some quarters. His attempt to address this and other questions about himself, including his perceived vagueness on policy issues, resulted in his decision to grant an interview in September 1976 to *Playboy* magazine. It was also a misguided attempt to emphasize that he was 'normal' and appeal to a younger, more liberal audience. This objective lay behind his choice of *Playboy* for the interview – Californian Governor Jerry Brown had used this magazine successfully – and his professed admiration for Bob Dylan, his sons' obsession not really his. Conservative Christians were clearly upset by some of the language and the choice of the medium to publicize his views but what they should have been more concerned about was what he said in the main interview. He made it clear that whatever his personal faith, he would neither propose nor be influenced by an evangelical political agenda.[13] John Kennedy took a strikingly similar position as a presidential candidate when he gave a speech to protestant ministers in Houston in September 1960 in order to reassure the public about his Catholicism.[14] Carter's campaign reinforced this point when he promised few if any changes to the liberal social legislation already in place. Nevertheless, this ultimately did not erode the widespread support of evangelicals that he received across the south, and this factor enabled him to win the election.

In January 1977 Jimmy Carter became America's third Baptist president after Warren Harding and Harry Truman. There were many visible signs of his religious background during his presidency from the careful choice of biblical quotes in his inaugural address, his secret service code name, Deacon, his regular attendance at his new church in Washington and his insistence on teaching Sunday school there. There were also more subtle signs of the influence of his Baptist background. He attempted to take the ceremony out of the presidency by walking with his wife and daughter to the White House after his inauguration, reducing the use of 'Hail to the Chief' when he arrived at events, and even carrying his own bags onto Air Force One. But his faith did not translate into concrete policies in his new administration. As he explained at a press conference in November 1978, 'I have been very careful not to inter-relate my Christian beliefs with my responsibilities as President. But it is a great personal gratification for me to have that religious faith'.[15] Whilst reinforcing the importance of faith to him *personally*, he carefully drew a line between his beliefs and his responsibility to the office. He argued that he had a rational approach to the presidency unaffected by faith or for that matter ideology. In effect he was arguing in personal terms for the separation of Church and State. This would prove to be a lot more difficult to achieve than he had imagined.

Carter may have wanted to downplay the influence of the Religious Right on his presidency, but it was a matter of supreme irony that it was the actions of his administration that did most to politicize that movement. This was caused by a policy which one conservative strategist described as having the effect of kicking 'a sleeping dog'.[16] The issue was the Inland Revenue Service (IRS) decision to enforce the *Green v Connally* court ruling of 30 June 1971 that allowed the IRS to withdraw tax allowances on segregated schools.[17] The ruling was designed to penalize schools that had been established in the south to avoid desegregation legislation and put the onus on these schools to prove non-discrimination. Carter's new IRS commissioner, Jerome Kurtz, believed enforcement would prevent education establishments like Bob Jones University in South Carolina from blatantly refusing to accept black students. This was consistent with administration policy of enforcing Civil Rights laws. It was an administrative decision that required no political authorization from the White House. However, many of the affected schools had been set up in response to genuine concerns about children's education such as the court judgements on banning prayer in school and the Federal government's decisions on sex education. These parents felt under attack for their beliefs and bitterly resented the implication of racism.[18] As a result of its decision the IRS was inundated with protests. Kurtz received 126,000 letters of complaint and was forced to request secret service protection.[19] Activists such as the Moral Majority co-founder Paul Weyrich and Director of National Christian Action Bob Billings Sr. were able to frame IRS action as an attack on religious freedom and mobilized support across the country. They were also able to utilize this activism for wider political action against the administration on other conservative issues. Billings was quoted as saying that 'Jerome Kurtz has done more to bring Christians together than any man since St Paul'.[20] Although the IRS produced modified guidelines in 1979, the protests continued. Carter himself was personally criticized. Republican Congressman John Ashbrook of Ohio symbolized evangelical incredulity by finishing a letter of protest to him by saying, 'You must not desert your religious followers by inaction'.[21] But Carter did not respond, leaving the issue to the IRS despite reservations from some of his advisors. Carter's reticence 'galvanised the Religious Right. It was the spark that ignited their involvement in real politics'.[22]

Carter's decision can be explained by his attitude to his faith and politics. His desire to separate his personal beliefs from political decisions meant he often saw religious groups just as fellow believers, not as political actors. On taking office he declined invitations to speak to and requests for meetings with evangelical groups. He did meet some moderate religious leaders at the White House but in his diaries expressed concern about evangelists using television to politicize Christianity.[23] He was advised during the transition in the winter of 1976–7 to appoint someone 'religious enough to understand religious mind-sets and political enough to understand issues'.[24] But Carter declined, and his administration's early outreach activity focused on liberal groups. By the end of his second year in office the White House had developed a sophisticated outreach programme targeting all the key interest groups. But Carter did not appoint a special assistant for religious affairs until May 1979. Bob Maddox had known Carter since the 1960s and had applied for a religious liaison role in the White House but had been turned down twice, once by Carter himself. This was despite White House staff acknowledging that they needed Maddox's contacts in the evangelical movement.[25] This showed that Carter continued to be reluctant to acknowledge the Religious Right as a political force.

On appointment to his role Maddox spent the remaining eighteen months of the administration trying to rebuild Carter's support among religious groups. He travelled widely in meeting evangelicals but persuaded Carter to see them only in January 1980. That meeting appeared to go well but in a press conference afterwards Falwell distorted what Carter had told them about his attitude to gay rights.[26] Despite this and his comment that they had sounded 'really right wing', Carter still believed that these leaders were fundamentally supportive of his presidency.[27] Whilst some present remained loyal to Carter, many reflected Tim LaHaye's view who in a prayer after the meeting stated, 'God, we have to get this man out of the White House and get someone who will be aggressive about bringing back traditional moral values.'[28] This meeting demonstrated Carter's basic misunderstanding of their position on political issues. The Religious Right now had a political agenda and like any other interest group they expected Carter, as a fellow believer, to deliver on it. For example, when Robertson interviewed him for CBN, Carter agreed to consider evangelical candidates for jobs in his administration but none of the twenty CVs Robertson sent over were ever considered.[29] They also became frustrated by the way Carter limited their political access. His suspicion of interest groups was well known but other groups, particularly those who were supporters, received serious consideration of their priorities. To Carter religion was essentially a private not a political matter. This approach was reflected throughout his presidency.

On no other issue was this attitude more controversial than on abortion. The evangelical movement had started to move away in the early 1970s from a previously sympathetic position on abortion and to form an alliance with Roman Catholics on the issue. The landmark Supreme Court decision, *Roe v Wade*, established in January 1973 the legality of abortion in certain circumstances. Although women's groups sought to widen the criteria, conservatives wanted the ruling overturned. In an increasingly volatile climate, Carter maintained his position of refusing to overturn *Roe v Wade* whilst expressing his personal opposition to abortion. He supported the Hyde amendment which restricted the use of Federal funds for abortion except when the life of the mother was threatened. Fellow evangelicals challenged Carter's attempt to separate his personal beliefs from his public position. Maddox believed that Carter was blindsided by how emotive the abortion issue had become because as governor of Georgia it had not been a major problem.[30] But it was just one of many issues on which evangelicals felt let down by Carter. Much of the Religious Right's critique of Carter was rooted in a fear of communism both at home and abroad. This extended into criticism of his policies on the SALT II agreement with Russia, Rhodesia, the Panama Canal Treaty and defence spending. Carter's refusal to legislate for prayer in school and his support for gay rights through his opposition to California's Proposition 6, which sought to ban gays teaching, was linked by evangelicals to failure to stand up to atheistic communism.[31] Their forgiveness of his presidential opponent Ronald Reagan on Proposition 6, even though he had campaigned against this proposal, was perhaps due to his very strong anti-communist credentials. To the Religious Right these were not just policies but matters of conscience and they could not accept that a president who was 'born again' would not act on them.

Sensing an opportunity, the Republican Party shifted its position on ERA and the IRS rulings on religious schools to align with the Religious Right's agenda. In addition, as presidential candidate, Reagan promised to appoint 'Godly men' into his administration.[32] He was rewarded with staunch support during the 1980 campaign. Evangelical groups sent out 840,000 leaflets. The Christian Voice raised $500,000 whilst the Moral Majority Political Action Committee (PAC) supported twelve Republican congressional challengers, eleven of whom were elected. Their impact went beyond the south and the evangelical movement as their support ensured the victory of Catholic candidates in Alabama and Oklahoma.[33] The politicization of religious groups was symbolized by Bob Billings Sr. who had led the fight against the IRS, became the Moral Majority's first Executive Director and later President Reagan's religious affairs advisor.[34] Maddox believed that despite his efforts on Carter's behalf to engage with evangelicals, the tide had turned against him as early as 1979 with some groups even questioning whether the president was a Christian.[35] There were personal attacks against Carter which extended to his family with a particularly vicious campaign against his evangelical sister, Ruth Carter Stapleton.[36] In the 1980 election Reagan picked up more of the evangelical vote than did Carter and in the ninety-six most Baptist counties, Carter ran 18 per cent down on his performance in 1976.[37] This contributed heavily to Reagan's gains in the south.

Carter's religious beliefs were reflected throughout his political career in his behaviour and approach to government. His speeches were often delivered in the style of a preacher and laced with moral themes. His marked reluctance to strike political bargains was largely a Baptist trait.[38] His beliefs gave him a sense of inner calm and detachment from the pressures he faced as president. In the 1980 election, however, he was unable to convert his public profession of faith into political support from the growing influence of conservative Christians. He failed to recognize the change in religious mood in the country and their evolution into an interest group. He was always happy to discuss matters of faith, but he was not prepared to change his policies. His anger at a press photograph of him attending church showed his belief that faith was a private matter.[39] When it came to his faith Carter was admirably consistent in his approach, but in campaigning in 1976, he did use his personal piety for political advantage. Whilst sticking to his principles as president he failed to grasp an important consequence of the Culture Wars: the politicization of religion. Other interest groups were treated flexibly nearer campaign time but not his co-religionists. This cost him politically. The separation of faith and politics was incomprehensible to many of his fellow believers who felt under attack by changes in society. They expected as a matter of conscience for Carter to act on their core issues. His lack of action on issues like abortion and the IRS rules on religious schools was viewed as nothing less than an act of betrayal. Carter had built his image in 1976 around his faith as a key element in his message of trust, but by 1980 his personal piety was not enough for his fellow believers. They had lost faith in him. It was unsurprising therefore that in the 1980 election they swung their support behind Reagan who offered them the promise of what they wanted, although they were to be disappointed by his policies in office.

Since President Kennedy had defined the Civil Rights question as a moral one in his landmark speech on 11 June 1963,[40] this issue had become a question of character for all presidents, a test of their moral compass. It was an issue on which Carter was seen to be on the right side, despite his 'southernness'. He came to the attention of northern Democrats in January 1971 when he announced in his inaugural speech as governor of Georgia that 'the time for discrimination was over' and by hanging a portrait of Martin Luther King in his office.[41] This marked him out as one of a new breed of southern Democratic politicians who were determined to accept desegregation and strive for equality. His was a dual message not just for southern conservatives to accept the new reality but for the north to recognize that the south was no longer backward and racist. His primary campaign for governor in 1970 against the liberal former governor, Carl Sanders, had been a calculated attempt to win the pro-segregation vote,[42] but there were several examples from his early life when Carter had taken a personal stand against racial prejudice. His refusal in 1962 to join the White Citizens Council was widely noted but less so was his standing up for a Black naval classmate, Wesley Brown, at Annapolis, for which he was accused of being 'a God dammed nigger lover'.[43] He also argued strongly against the exclusion of Blacks from his church.[44] By 1976 the great moral legislative battles over Civil Rights had been fought and won. The remaining issues of social and economic inequality were by their nature more complex. Carter's belief in equality of opportunity did not equate to support for radical change. He was not so much a liberal on race but more someone who wanted to expand opportunity within the confines of the current law. The declaration at his inauguration in 1971 was not a call for sweeping change but a confirmation that change had occurred; it was time for this to be recognized and the law to be enforced. Carter's commitment to social justice was genuine but he wanted to help all groups to improve their social and economic status, not just African Americans.[45]

Only a handful of Black leaders had campaigned for Carter in 1976. These included Andrew Young from Atlanta, Mayor Coleman Young from Detroit and Martin Luther King's father, 'Daddy' King. Nevertheless, Black interest groups believed that they had been essential to Carter's election victory and expected the first Democratic president since Lyndon Johnson to deliver on their agenda. Carter's campaign as a Washington 'outsider' implied criticism of the very government welfare programmes that poor Blacks were dependent upon.[46] He accepted that he needed the support of 'Civil Rights Heroes' to overcome the 'stigma' of being a southerner.[47] The irony of this situation was not lost on the *New York Times* which commented on a 'South Georgian white man with a mint julep drawl being sent to the White House by the grandchildren of slaves'.[48] Equally there was pressure from northern conservative groups concerned about having to bus their children to Black schools to achieve desegregation and the level of taxation required to support welfare. In addition, whilst Black groups continued to lobby Carter for fairer income distribution through measures like the Humphrey-Hawkins bill, they faced competition for government funding in a restricted economy from groups like women, the disabled and environmentalists.[49] If the age of discrimination was over, so was the age of major Civil Rights legislation. Attempts to improve the circumstances of poor Blacks would have to be addressed as part of a wider economic agenda that included welfare reform, urban renewal and job training. This did not preclude the use of symbolic actions by the White House to reinforce support for equality, such as 'Daddy' King's presence at Carter's inauguration and sending his daughter Amy to a local, mainly Black school in Washington.[50] Such actions became matters of debate early in the administration when 'Roots', a television programme about slavery based on a book by Alex Haley, was broadcast to huge audiences nationwide. Eizenstat saw the political value of Carter presenting an inaugural book to the author, commenting that 'such action would have powerful symbolism and yet would not offend virtually anyone in the south'.[51]

Whilst attuned to the symbolism of Black issues in general, the administration was slow to notice the implications of a university selection case under review by the Justice Department. Alan Bakke had applied in 1973 to the University of California (UCLA) medical school but although he was, at thirty-three, above the usual age for a new student, he scored highly in his application and was recommended to the school. He was turned down for a place both initially and on appeal. Bakke took the Regents of UCLA to court, arguing that the school's policy of affirmative action, which reserved 16 per cent of its places for minority (and by implication less qualified) students, denied him as a white man equal protection under the law.[52] The case had been working its way, almost unnoticed, through the minor courts but in 1977 had reached the Supreme Court for a final ruling. The issue, as seen by Carter's Justice Department, was whether to submit an Amicus Curiae brief to the court giving the government its view as an interested party. It was reluctant to do so as UCLA had mismanaged the selection process and therefore Bakke would not make a good test case. When Attorney General Griffin Bell did decide to proceed, he dismissed any concerns about the political implications for affirmative action programmes and delegated the work to Wade McCree, whom Bell described as 'the best black lawyer in America'. However, McCree, only recently appointed, delegated the brief to a holdover from the Nixon administration.[53] Whilst happy to show the draft brief to Carter, Bell did not want any involvement from liberals in the White House but that was exactly what happened.[54] Concerns had been raised with Eizenstat in February 1977 on the potential impact on schools of a negative decision on the Bakke case that would set back 'affirmative action programmes 3–5 years'.[55] Eizenstat responded by turning to Walter Mondale in what became the first test of the Vice President's role in the White House. Mondale assessed the impact of a negative decision on other universities and, following advice from Hamilton Jordan, persuaded Carter that the draft Amicus brief required wider consultation.[56]

The Domestic Policy team received the draft brief at the end of August.[57] Once circulated it drew major criticism not only from White House staff but from cabinet members Joe Califano (HEW) and Patricia Harris (HUD). Califano's written objections, which he sent to Carter, ran to sixteen pages.[58] There was concern that a weak or neutral brief would result in a decision that damaged current affirmative action programmes and as a consequence weaken the administration's relationship with liberal and minority groups.[59] Liberals within the administration such as Eizenstat argued that the Justice Department was focused far too much on defending Bakke, and not enough on supporting affirmative action.[60] Carter had similar concerns about the draft brief. He wanted it to reflect his views on affirmative action which he insisted must not include the use of quotas as they were likely to be declared unconstitutional by the courts. This meant that Justice had to present a nuanced argument in favour of a solution that distinguished between evaluating the potential of disadvantaged groups and selection based on that criterion; unlike quotas this would not be a rigid process.[61] The other issue Carter was concerned about was Bakke himself. He wanted to ensure that whatever the result Bakke would not lose out and could be accepted by UCLA medical school without compromising affirmative action programmes.[62] During this process Carter was apprised of the wider risks involved. Jordan warned him that even though he was not involved in the detail, the case was important as a symbol of Carter's personal commitment to equality. Jordan implied that Bell did not grasp the case's importance and was inordinately comforted by the fact that the detail was in the hands of two Black lawyers, McCree and Solicitor General Drew Days III. Jordan argued that even they would be discredited by their community if the message was poorly formulated.[63] Concern expressed by the National Association for the Advancement of Colored People (NAACP) confirmed Jordan's point.[64] The Justice department was able to submit a revised brief. The subsequent judgement which found in Bakke's favour did confirm the validity of taking race and ethnicity into account when making decisions. This encouraged the use of affirmative action to increase diversity, whilst confirming the unconstitutionality of quotas.[65] The administration was therefore able to reflect positively on the result in the press and maintain the momentum of affirmative action programmes.[66]

In policy terms Carter had made only limited promises on Civil Rights issues in the 1976 election. In his view the Civil Rights battles of the 1960s and early 1970s were over, and the emphasis should be on the interpretation of the law and increased regulation to enforce it. So, whilst there was to be no new Civil Rights bill, the enforcement unit of the Department of Justice was reorganized and its budget substantially increased from $74.2m to $124m in order to increase the pressure on employers.[67] An early example of this was the enforcement of Title VI of the Civil Rights Act, which prohibited discrimination in any programme receiving Federal aid.[68] Another major effort to consolidate African-American support was Carter's plan to appoint more Black officials. His Q & A at the National Black Network in July 1977 highlighted this, as did the appointment of Drew Days III and Eleanor Holmes Norton to the posts of Solicitor General and Chair of the Equal Opportunities Commission.[69] Carter reinforced this approach in a series of personal notes to the cabinet and heads of agencies reminding them of their responsibility to appoint more people who were women and/or from ethnic groups.[70] The administration did try to accommodate the views of Black interest groups in the development of policy but the Bakke case highlighted a weakness in Carter's White House organization: a lack of staff who dealt with the Black lobby on a regular basis. Although this was resolved in August 1978 with the appointment of the Georgian Louis Martin as special assistant, Carter continued to rely upon the liberals in his cabinet and his staff for support on Black issues. Martin was able to establish links and set up meetings with Black groups, including the congressional caucus, that Carter attended. These were often successful but frequently Carter delegated such meetings to Mondale or Eizenstat.[71] The president, however, was always conscious of the image of the administration with the Black and minority communities. In an early meeting with his staff, Press Secretary Jody Powell organized a photographer from *Time* magazine to take a team picture, but Carter ordered the photographer out when he realized that there was only one Black person in the group and the only woman was his wife.[72] He was also aware of the need to ensure that the Black viewpoint was considered by the cabinet in day-to-day policy decisions.[73]

As part of the programme of enforcement, Carter continued the policy of desegregating schools despite increased opposition from local white communities. In the early 1970s it was possible to find solutions locally, often with the support of black churches, as was the case in Atlanta.[74] But by 1977 any attempt to enforce desegregation entailed complex negotiations and a joint task force involving at the very least HEW and Justice Departments. The issue became politically sensitive in the north where cities like Chicago, at the time the third largest public-school system in America, refused to submit any plans to desegregate. Despite strong resistance from local Democratic politicians, the administration took Chicago to court and a desegregation plan was eventually implemented in the summer of 1981.[75] The Public Works Employment Act was the main piece of legislation from the administration that supported minorities. Passed on 13 May 1977, it allocated 10 per cent or up to $4bn of the government's procurement budget for minority employers.[76] Carter wanted to incentivize minority businesses and continued to keep track of the act's implementation after its passage.[77] The main concern of Black interest groups, not least the Black caucus, was to influence the administration on the economy. Congressman Parren Mitchell of Maryland requested access on economic matters in February 1977, but though wanting to help, Carter offered only cabinet member Harris as a liaison.[78]

As Carter's economic policy concentrated more on austerity and fighting inflation, there were increased Black concerns, particularly as African-American youth unemployment had reached 35.5 per cent by March 1979.[79] These concerns were to continue right up to the 1980 election. Harris and

Martin were at pains to remind Carter of the importance of the Black electorate. Harris highlighted the Black vote in the 1976 election (Carter had won 85–90 per cent of it) to stress the importance of a high turn-out through effective urban policies.[80] Although the administration spoke with pride of its record on minority appointments, support for minority businesses and enforcement on Civil Rights, Carter's main emphasis was on his track record on the economy and promises of future investment.[81] Despite what was a comprehensive defeat to Ronald Reagan in 1980, the Carter-Mondale ticket still managed to receive 83 per cent of the Black vote.[82] This result alone suggests that Carter's policy was successful in maintaining Black support, although he was helped by what was regarded by most Blacks as an unsympathetic GOP candidate.

In what was a valedictory address at a Black leader's luncheon on 5 January 1981, Carter enumerated his successes.[83] His appointment of 12 per cent Black officials during his term in office, particularly to judgeships, compared favourably with that of his predecessors and his successor, as was his support for minority businesses.[84] The administration's policy was to use affirmative action and regulation in federal appointments to reflect the demographics of society. Such an approach, as indicated by the Bakke case, did not prove easy to enforce. The Justice Department found that this was also the case with the enforcement of minority contracts as white companies often used small Black companies as 'fronts' to circumvent the regulations.[85] Carter's policies, though perfectly in keeping with his vision of an efficient government, did not fulfil the dreams of Black leaders for structural economic reform. It was not just Carter's anti-inflation policies that threatened the social programmes on which minority groups were dependent but also the growing tax revolt that increased resentment over Federal expenditure on welfare which was seen to favour Blacks. Despite his mistrust of interest groups, Carter recognized the importance of the Black lobby and he worked hard to accommodate their views and give them access to his administration.[86] But he did not change his policies. Carter may not have wanted radical change, but his scope for even minor reform was severely limited by the state of the economy. Given these constraints his record of achievement in Civil Rights was solid, if not spectacular.

One lesser-known aspect of the 1964 Civil Rights Act was that discrimination was made illegal on the grounds of not just race but also gender. The formation in 1966 of the National Organization for Women (NOW) was just one example of a wider women's movement that sought to encourage the role of women in all aspects of American life and to widen and deepen that influence economically and politically. By 1970 women made up 43 per cent of the paid work force and this would grow to 52 per cent by 1980.[87] NOW was successful at increasing its representation at the 1976 Democratic Convention. However, the growth of the women's movement was faced in the 1970s with a conservative backlash from women who felt threatened, not emancipated, by this new-found independence. Leaders like Phyllis Schlafly of the Eagle Forum often brought strong emotional arguments against what they saw as pro-feminist proposals. She testified at a congressional hearing against establishing domestic abuse centres because they would become places of 'feminist indoctrination'.[88] Even at what was regarded as the high-water mark of the women's movement, the National Women's Conference in November 1977, conservative groups under Schlafly were sufficiently organized to control one-fifth of the seats. The majority at the conference, under the Chair of Bella Abzug, laid out an agenda for 1977 that assumed a major role for the Federal government in promoting women's rights, but conservative opposition ensured that this would be challenged.[89]

Nothing symbolized the Carter administration's commitment to women's issues more than the role of Rosalynn Carter in the White House. After the resignation of his friend Bert Lance in August 1977, Carter's wife became his closest political confidant. Eizenstat argued that she was the most influential First Lady since Eleanor Roosevelt and that she laid the groundwork for future First Ladies such as Hillary Clinton.[90] She attended cabinet meetings, and her political campaigning – according to Carter's pollster Pat Caddell – gave her 'a much better sense of what was going on outside the White House bubble than the president'.[91] Aides such as Caddell, Jordan and Rafshoon used her as a sounding board before taking their ideas to the president. She was present at many of the major decisions of the administration. Most notably, her support of Caddell was largely responsible for persuading Carter to accept the key themes of what was to become his famous 'malaise' speech of July 1979. Carter's faith in her was exemplified by his decision early in his administration to send her on an official visit to seven Latin American countries on his behalf. She was also the first First Lady since Eleanor Roosevelt to testify to Congress in her capacity as honorary chair of the Presidential Commission on Mental Health.

It was not surprising therefore that Carter and his wife were staunch supporters of women's issues, particularly on Federal appointments and the Equal Rights Amendment (ERA). Unlike White House dealings with other interest groups, Carter appointed staff early in his administration to consult with the women's movement. The main contact in the White House was Public Liaison Assistant Midge Constanza, who was later replaced by Sarah Weddington. This role could not always be regarded as an indication of Carter's personal commitment to all women's issues. He did regard Constanza as essential but only because, as he said, 'she takes a tremendous burden off me from nut groups that would insist on seeing me if they could not see her'.[92] Whilst Carter argued that he was, through his appointments strategy, a supporter of equality, his backing for the ratification of the ERA was seen by the women's movement as the authentic indicator of his equality credentials.

Republicans and Democrats supported the constitutional amendment on women's equality when it passed both Houses of Congress in 1972. It had to be ratified by thirty-eight states before the 1979 deadline to become law. The proposed amendment established gender equality before the law which would be enforced by Congress if required. It had bipartisan support when introduced under President Richard Nixon and was endorsed by his successor Gerald Ford. By the time of Carter's election thirty-four states had ratified the amendment and therefore only four more were required. This outwardly positive situation hid what had become a largely negative trend. Since 1975 seventeen states had had the opportunity to ratify the amendment but only one, North Dakota, had done so. In addition, during the same period two states, Tennessee and Nebraska, had rescinded their original decision of support. The impact of this would have to be tested later in the courts.[93] Most of the remaining states were in the South or the Sunbelt where there were fewer groups who were prepared to campaign for ERA.[94] The more negative political climate was linked to the growing concern articulated by Schlafly and others. Schlafly appealed to conservative men by arguing that ERA was nothing more than a Federal power grab, but she gained even more support from married women who were worried that the amendment would remove their traditional protections. Whilst both sides were concerned about women's economic vulnerability, the fear that ERA would weaken the commitment of men to family life and force women out of their 'normal lives' was gaining support by the time Carter was elected.[95] This was particularly the view of religious groups, with 98 per cent of opponents of ERA being churchgoers.[96] Carter's ongoing support for ratification linked him in their eyes with the 'anti-family, pro-lesbian ERA'.[97]

Carter was not discouraged by the unfavourable political climate on ERA that he inherited in 1977. Early narrow defeats in North Carolina and Nevada, partly offset by victory in Indiana in March, were followed by a pessimistic assessment of ERA chances in a further five states.[98] Yet Carter remained committed to the cause. He made numerous speeches which equated ERA to Human Rights in his foreign policy and the Civil Rights legislation of another era. He was also supported by the active involvement of his wife and daughter-in-law Judy Carter in the movement.[99] The overall campaign was coordinated by ERAmerica under Mary (Liz) Carpenter and Mildred Jeffrey but was assisted by White House officials, particularly Sarah Weddington who organized help from the president and his cabinet in states like Illinois.[100] Ultimately the many phone calls from Carter and his colleagues proved ineffective. The vital Illinois vote failed to pass because local Democratic politicians believed ERA would lose them votes in national elections and the damaging impact of a court action brought by Schlafly based on erroneous charges that the administration had sought to bribe one of the legislators.[101] Carter and his wife continued to support local campaigns by attending events, making calls and even complaining when they felt they were not being used enough.[102] If he was unable to affect events locally, Carter did persuade Congress to extend the ERA deadline until 30 June 1982. He remained committed to the amendment throughout his time in office, in terms of direct intervention with both state politicians and speeches across the country. Fundamentally, however, ERA's success or failure was dependent on local campaigns. The states that were yet to endorse ERA in 1977 lacked the infrastructure of support that was available in the earlier ratification campaigns. These states were generally much more conservative. The extension of the deadline to 1982 proved no more than a gesture as no other state ratified the amendment. In his White House diaries, Carter blamed church groups for its failure.[103] Whilst there was much misinformation propagated by conservatives, the end of gender segregation of prisons if ERA passed being just one,[104] the proposed amendment created genuine fears that conservatives were able to exploit successfully.

Other than ERA, Carter's focus on women's issues was on using his office to appoint more women to key roles. As with minorities, Carter encouraged cabinet members and White House staff to appoint more women and engaged with women's groups to establish a pool of well-qualified candidates.[105] He focused on appointing women to Federal Judgeships but bemoaned difficulties with Congress on such appointments.[106] The White House also hosted a Women's National History Day and established a cabinet-level interdepartmental task force on women.[107] There were bills in Congress against discrimination on pregnancy in the work place and on establishing domestic abuse centres, which the administration supported, albeit unsuccessfully.[108] The White House continued to encourage women's groups to organize and establish an agenda for the future, the 1980 White House Conference on the Family being a case in point. Many women's issues became entwined with the government's economic policy but one that stood out and continued to be divisive for Carter personally was abortion.

Whilst the President projected a liberal image on women's issues in general, he remained personally opposed to abortion except when the health of the mother was at risk or pregnancy was due to rape or incest. To Carter this was a matter of personal faith and as with all such matters, he did not hide his views. He continued to comply with the Supreme Court decision, *Roe v Wade*, which conservatives and religious groups wanted to overturn. He supported sex education for teenagers, better adoption arrangements, and established women and infant children support programmes. But he opposed Federal support for abortion.[109] Carter's attempt to distinguish his own views from public policy did not prevent major criticism from women's groups and even his own staff. Califano, who as a Catholic had similar beliefs to Carter's, highlighted that Constanza had organized a petition in the White House in protest at Carter's views on abortion, which was supported by cabinet members Patricia Harris and Juanita Kreps.[110]

This opposition was also evident in Carter's own National Advisory Committee on Women (NCAW). Its co-chair was New York Democrat Bella Abzug whose views were those of a Culture Wars warrior. She was quoted as saying that 'I spend all day figuring out how to beat the machine and knock the crap out of the political power structure'.[111] A view unlikely to endear her to Carter. Her opposition to Carter's 1979 budget proposals with its increased defence spending and cuts in social programmes resulted in her abrupt sacking in January 1979.[112] Concern about limited access to Carter perceived lack of support on ERA and abortion, and the removal of Abzug and Constanza caused groups such as NOW to back Kennedy in the Democratic primaries of 1980.[113] Carter's attempts to regain the initiative with the White House Conference on the Family backfired as damaging splits between liberal women's groups and the conservative Eagle Forum disrupted the event. Despite attempts by Carter to maintain a middle ground, an inability to agree on ERA, the abortion rights controversy and arguments about what constituted the family forced the White House to divide the conference into three separate events. This still failed to produce any sort of consensus and sparked walkouts from conservative groups.[114]

Carter's personal commitment to support women's equality was sustained beyond his presidency even when it touched on his faith. He and Rosalyn left the Southern Baptist Convention in 2000 over the issue and he spoke out again in 2009 in a speech entitled 'Losing my Religion for Equality'[115] when he criticized all the major religions for their treatment of women. Decades earlier during his presidency his track record on appointments had been impressive. The forty new Federal judgeships quadrupled the number of women on the Federal bench.[116] A symbol of this success was the appointment of Ruth Bader Ginsburg, a future Supreme Court Justice, to the Federal bench. When asked later if she always wanted to be a judge, she replied, 'It wasn't in the realm of the possible until Jimmy Carter became president and was determined to draw on talent of all the people not just some of them.'[117] However, the rise of feminism was never a natural part of the New Deal coalition and faced major opposition from both parties in Congress. Carter's personal support did raise expectations in the Women's movement that he was unable or, in the case of abortion, unwilling to fulfil. In addition, his fiscal policies were heavily criticized as they often weakened programmes that helped women, for example his refusal to endorse equal pay due to the risk of inflation.[118] It was also the case that he did not feel comfortable with the militancy of some feminist groups, often characterizing them in private as 'crazy', and he was not sympathetic to what he felt were the radical women's policies in the 1980 Democratic Party Platform.[119] Yet despite some unfair criticism of his performance on women's issues, more women than men voted for Carter in the 1980 election and women's rights was the only policy issue in the polls on which Carter led Reagan.[120] Carter's administration had a credible record on women's issues but the more radical changes sought by many in the movement were not a realistic option given the rising tide of conservative opposition and the administration's fiscal constraints.

The environmental movement was a relatively new phenomenon when Carter was elected. It grew out of concern over the impact of the economic expansion of the 1960s. The celebration of the First Earth Day on 22 April 1970 triggered a reaction from politicians who responded with a series of environmental laws.[121] Carter cared deeply about the Planet. In his inaugural address as governor in 1971 he warned that the environment was 'threatened by avarice, greed, procrastination and neglect'.[122] His books and diaries included many such comments, and his 1976 campaign biography, *Why Not the Best,* contained a chapter on his love for the Georgia outdoors.[123] As governor, with the support of environmental groups, he prevented the building of the Sprewell Bluff Dam on the Flint River even though it was to be fully funded by the Federal government and reclaimed the Chattahoochee River for recreation.[124] Carter therefore entered office with genuine environmental credentials and high expectations from that lobby. He seemed determined to make a difference as president. Carter wrote in the afterword of his White House diaries that one of the three key themes of his presidency was the environment (including energy conservation). In an early entry as president on a potential dispute on air pollution with auto manufacturers, he said that 'my inclination when there's a direct conflict is to stick with environmental quality'.[125] Carter would find it difficult to adopt this approach in practice.

On environmental issues he appeared to enjoy public support as well as the backing of the environmental lobby. This enabled him to appoint specialists to important positions and gave him the opportunity to secure congressional backing for new legislation. Unfortunately, the first battles Carter chose to fight on water projects and energy created major difficulties with Congress and damaged his environmental credentials. The proposed reduction in the number of water projects across the country was environmentally and fiscally sensible. It also reflected Carter's deep mistrust of the Corps of Engineers based on his experience as governor. Not only did Carter think that these projects were economically or environmentally inadvisable but, according to one aide, he believed that the 'people who were supporting pork-barrel projects were corrupt people'.[126] Carter sought to impose more stringent financial controls and, for the first time, an environmental assessment of each project that was submitted to Congress. He failed to recognize that these projects brought financial and political benefits to the states and the congressmen concerned. These politicians were of both parties and held key positions of influence within Congress. So, despite the support of the Water Resources Council, the Council for Environmental Quality and seventy-four congressmen, Carter's political defeat and eventual retreat on this issue damaged his reputation.[127] He was unable to recover his position politically, even when he made concessions over the Tellico dam in September 1979 that gave priority to economic and political concerns over environmental issues.

The complexity of Carter's energy proposals, sent to Congress on 29 April 1977, caused major splits within the environmental movement. Some groups wanted the elimination of fossil fuels, some the ending of nuclear energy, others promoted solar power, whilst some groups prioritized conservation. Carter's proposals included many of these ideas but not to the satisfaction of any faction within the movement. The economics of energy policy caused the fragmentation of the political coalition that supported Carter. He was forced to choose between allies such as environmentalists who championed conservation and labour unions determined to protect jobs in automobile manufacturing, coal mining and other industries. Whereas he indicated initially that he would concentrate on protecting the environment, this position became politically less tenable as the economy deteriorated.

Although he had made no major speech on the environment during the 1976 campaign, Carter did make his intention clear early in his administration that he was going to prioritize the issue. His environmental message sent to Congress on 23 May 1977 was comprehensive.[128] In his legislative programme he was able to pass improved Clean Air and Water Acts which Ford had previously vetoed. He increased the responsibilities of the Environmental Protection Agency (EPA), made improvements to National Parks, established the National Heritage Trust, regulated strip-mining through the passage of the Surface Mining Control and Reclamation Act of 1977 and expanded coverage under previous legislation on National Trails and Wild and Scenic Rivers.[129] Another major piece of legislation was the Comprehensive Environmental Response and Compensation Liability Act, signed into law by Carter in late 1980. It established a superfund worth $1.6bn to protect the public against the damage from toxic waste.[130] Not all this legislation was straightforward. The Clean Air Act required the EPA, with Carter's support, to steer a careful political path between the auto manufacturers and the United Automobile Workers on the impact of tougher emission standards on fuel efficiency.[131] Similarly the establishment of the Redwoods National Park was achieved only by compromise over land usage in order to gain the support of the lumber industry.[132] In both cases Carter delegated legislative strategy to his staff and accepted their advice to enable the bills to pass.

Despite having a credible legislative programme, the administration's relationship with environmental groups was far from smooth. Part of the problem for the White House was logistical. Gus Speth, Carter's Chairman of the Council on Environmental Quality, reported that there were over fifty nationally based environmental groups and between 2,500 and 5,000 local groups, which totalled some 4 million members. Speth stated that such groups were largely middle class, cohesive and politically active. Carter's energy policies alienated many of them as they opposed his recommendations on synthetic fuels, coal and the creation of the Energy Mobilisation Board.[133] A sense of anger created by Carter's energy policies caused many groups to campaign against them, and some supported Ted Kennedy in the Democratic primaries in 1980.

The environmental lobby also had some reservations about Carter's signature legislation, the Alaska National Interest Lands Conservation Act (ANILCA), which was eventually passed on 12 November 1980. ANICLA provided, to varying degrees, special protection to over 157 million acres of land, including national monuments, parks, wildlife refuges, rivers, recreational areas, forests and conservation areas. It was the most sweeping proposal of its type ever to pass Congress. It doubled the size of land designated as national parks and almost tripled the amount allocated to wilderness. It also, consequently, prevented exploitation by oil, gas and lumber companies as well as the state government.

Carter called it 'one of his most gratifying achievements'.[134] It was a demonstration of his personal commitment and tenacity. He had continued to push for this legislation from his first environmental message in early 1977 until his eventual success at the end of his presidency. He faced some robust opposition, principally from Alaskan Senators Ted Stevens (GOP) and Mike Gravel (Democrat). Under the provisions of the Alaskan Native Claims Settlement Act of 1971, Congress had until the end of 1978 to agree on which lands could be withdrawn from development for conservation purposes. Carter's Secretary of the Interior, Cecil Andrus, shaped the administration's proposals that sought to limit access to developers. Internal debate within the administration saw the OMB lobbying for more flexibility for developers but Carter supported Andrus.[135] However, by the end of 1978 it had become clear that no legislation would be passed in time and so Carter acted on the advice of his cabinet and staff to use his executive powers under the Antiquities Act, and for Andrus to use his powers under the Land Policy Management Act to withdraw nearly 100 million acres in total pending legislation.[136] This was to give the administration breathing space but it prompted wide protests across Alaska, which included Carter being burnt in effigy and a serious civil disobedience campaign known as the Great Denali Trespass.[137]

Carter maintained a high profile on the issue, supporting legislation by visiting Alaska and quoting in press briefings that he regarded the bill as 'the top environmental priority of my administration, perhaps of my life'.[138] He continued to press Congress for legislation and worked with Mo Udall, Chair of the House Interior Committee, to pass a bill in May 1979, and with the Senate to pass its own bill in the following year. But as the Senate debated the measure, allies in Congress, principally Udall and Senator Paul Tsongas, guided Carter; often their advice was for him to stay quiet.[139] He made calls to senators when requested, which were usually successful,[140] and balanced the demands of the pro-environmental Alaska Coalition with the need to keep the support of Senator Stevens who, although Republican, was prepared to back a compromise. Unable to pass the bill before the presidential election, the imminent arrival of the Reagan administration, with its threats of rolling back environmental protection, ensured that potential objections to a compromise from liberals both in and outside Congress did not materialize. Carter may have had a poor track record of persuading Congress to back many of his proposals, but in late 1980 he was able to see the landmark bill passed. This was arguably the most important piece of legislation achieved by his administration. It succeeded because Carter delegated, accepted his staff's advice in working closely with his allies in Congress and was prepared to compromise.

Eizenstat argued that Carter's track record on the environment was impressive.[141] He built on the trend of environmental reform established by his Republican and Democratic predecessors. Yet this still failed to win him the wholehearted support of those in the environmental lobby who were opposed to his energy policy. Bert Carp and other advisors were highly critical of these groups, calling them 'impossible to deal with'.[142] This opposition did not last when faced with a potential Reagan presidency, and despite the initial support of some groups for Kennedy in the primaries, environmentalists rallied behind Carter in the 1980 campaign. Carter's personal commitment to the environment was matched by a legislative record that not even the Reagan administration could totally eradicate. ANICLA doubled the size of the National Park system and protected huge areas of wilderness from being despoiled for mining and drilling for oil and gas. His presidency built on and surpassed the record of Lyndon Johnson's administration and no subsequent president until Barack Obama could claim a more substantial record on the environment.[143]

The conflict inherent in the Culture Wars of the 1970s presented all politicians with stark choices on major social issues. The nature of the debates on issues like abortion, the ERA, conservation and prayer in school left little room for manoeuvre between these groups. They represented movements that campaigned for profound social change. Although they were Carter's natural constituency and voted for him in large numbers in 1976, they also represented a major challenge for his administration. His perceived espousal of their causes created immense expectations for his presidency. While he agreed with many of their views, he took a moderate rather than radical line on reform. Faced with the ideological divide between liberals and conservatives on policy, Carter invariably stood on the middle ground and so ended up being attacked from both sides. As a moderate he sought to build on previous legislation by enforcement and using increased government oversight to ensure that such views were represented more fully in his administration. Carter was not an initiator of radical change; every action reinforced or supplemented measures that had gone before. His famous quote that 'the time for discrimination was over'[144] was typical of this approach. Civil Rights has long been regarded as a moral issue on which presidents were expected to demonstrate leadership. Carter's nuanced stance, focusing on incremental change, did not fulfil such expectations. This moderate response was deemed inadequate by minority groups who saw their cause as a moral necessity.

While Carter endorsed the broad aims of these movements, his support was neither impassioned nor unqualified. He did not have the luxury of backing wholeheartedly any one cause as other political factors had to be considered. He did not feel comfortable dealing with activists whose views he found to be rigid and extreme. His character and beliefs influenced his relationships with these groups. His decision to proceed with cutting the water projects budget in 1977, for example, may have been economically and environmentally driven but he also opposed these projects on moral grounds.[145] His fraught relationship with fellow evangelicals was due in part to Carter's belief in the separation of his faith from his role as president. Such a belief was never understood by these groups who often saw issues in one-dimensional terms. They misread the degree of Carter's support for their cause. This resulted in reactions from activists that ranged from disappointment to even a sense of betrayal. Much of this disenchantment came from liberals who expected a Democratic president to follow an agenda based on progressive social values. Carter may not have been a liberal in the broadest sense of the term, but he made sincere attempts to implement many of these reforms. His own fiscal conservatism, however, restricted these efforts. These programmes required increased government expenditure, and this conflicted with Carter's anti-inflation strategy. Finally, all these groups faced growing opposition from a conservative movement that was gaining popular support. Conservatives were leading protests against tax increases, affirmative action, ERA and government regulation in general. This backlash was effective in blocking reform, even more so when their ideas were taken up by the Republican Party by the end of 1978.

Carter was in many ways a victim of the Culture Wars. He found himself in the middle of warring interest groups on almost every issue with little room for manoeuvre. Despite these inherent difficulties, the administration could claim some major successes, especially in environmental protection. Carter's handling of these issues revealed little evidence of his alleged antipathy to working with interest groups. They were natural Carter supporters and he generally approved of their goals. In the case of ethnic minorities, women and environmental groups, he was happy to delegate to members of staff who understood and sympathized with their objectives and consulted closely with them. In these circumstances there was no indication of Carter micro-managing policy, as is widely believed by scholars and the public – in fact quite the opposite. It was his advisors who guided Carter. Despite a sense of disappointment with his lack of radical action on their behalf and a brief dalliance by some with Kennedy, he was able to retain the support of activists in the 1980 presidential campaign. The exception to this was the evangelical movement. Despite their common faith, Carter did not collaborate with them politically as he did not recognize them as a political force, despite evidence to the contrary. It was paradoxical that he lost the support of the one interest group with whom he had the most in common personally. The Religious Right moved to support Reagan but much of their social programme, including the repeal of *Roe v Wade*, was not implemented during Reagan's time in office. The other liberal groups were to have reason to mourn Carter's electoral passing as under Reagan many of his administration's achievements in energy and the environment were reversed. Some changes survived, such as the appointment of minorities to the federal bench. The most notable exception was the Alaska National Interest Lands Conservation Act which proved to be the greatest long-lasting domestic policy achievement of Carter's presidency.

1980 election: The battle against Kennedy and Reagan

On 15 July 1979 Carter gave a television address about America's latest energy crisis but he mainly talked about what he saw as a much deeper problem. He described it as 'deeper than gasoline lines or energy shortages even than inflation or recession'. He went on to argue that 'the erosion of our confidence in the future is threatening to destroy the social and the political fabric of America'.[1] This pessimistic assessment was followed by the expression of confidence that a solution was possible, and he outlined his plans on how this could be achieved. The 'Malaise speech', which many regarded as one of Carter's finest, was intended by the White House to be a watershed moment for the administration. It was designed to signal a new approach on how Carter was going to govern in the run-up to the 1980 presidential election, which was only sixteen months away. As part of this reset to his presidency, he made a series of organizational changes designed to make his administration more effective in addressing policy failures on the economy and energy. The roots of this speech related back to research conducted by pollster Pat Caddell, which explored the public mood. Carter's response to the survey was to have a major impact on his prospects for re-election.

In October 1978 Carter's newly appointed religious liaison, Bob Maddox, wrote to him about his discussions with religious leaders. He reported that all of them had highlighted the need for the president's moral leadership because they believed that the country was 'at a crisis point in our spirits'.[2] This view was reinforced in Carter's mind by Caddell's 'State of the Nation' survey conducted from the end of 1978 to January 1979 which made for gloomy reading for the administration. It described a pervading sense of pessimism in the country. The number of voters who were pessimistic about the future had doubled since January 1977 and now outnumbered the optimists 48 to 16 per cent. This trend was accelerating and represented the worst figures since Watergate.[3] Carter was seen to lack relevance, the public had 'tuned out' of his messages and, most troubling, whilst his personal qualities continued to be appreciated, the majority did not believe that he was a competent president.[4] It was these findings that Caddell used in April 1979 to produce his report 'Of Crisis and Opportunity'[5] which heavily influenced both the tone and content of Carter's energy speech in July of that year. Caddell argued that there was an underlying pessimism in the country that Carter needed to address before trying to solve the energy crisis. Not everyone in the White House agreed with this analysis, particularly its inherent pessimism; some staff dubbed Caddell's paper 'Apocalypse Now'. However, from April 1979 onwards, few in the White House would disagree that the administration was in serious trouble.

The latest fuel crisis sparked by the revolution in Iran had resulted in the doubling of the price of oil in twelve months. Increases in petrol prices triggered a trucker's strike and widespread queues at gas stations. Between April and early July 1979, the White House was focused on drafting what would be the president's fifth speech on energy. Carter's advisors were split on the approach he should take. His speechwriters were worried, noting that the mood in the country was 'grim' and that 'hatred for the oil companies is only matched by the lack of confidence in the administration'. For his latest speech they warned of the dangers of Carter's preachy style and argued for 'no more berating the American people for waste and selfishness'.[6] Eizenstat and other liberals in his administration were more optimistic that a focused energy speech could work. During the 1976 election and his early years as president, Carter prided himself on his connection with the American people but there were signs in April 1979, before he left for an economic summit in Japan, that he was increasingly frustrated by his inability to convince the public on energy policy. He described the draft speech he received before he left as the worst he had ever seen.[7] His uncertainty persisted when he returned to Washington. He called Lance and said, 'I came back from my meeting in Tokyo, and it all seemed to be falling down around me in the White House. I don't know what to do about it.'[8] These were uncharacteristic signs that Carter was suffering from his own personal 'crisis of confidence'.

His solution was to cancel the speech and invite a wide range of prominent Democratic Party figures, members of congress, governors, labour leaders, academics and clergy to Camp David from 9–12 July 1979 to confer on the state of the nation. The feedback received from the participants reflected the internal debate within the White House. They told him that he had to convince the American public that the administration had credible solutions to solve its energy problems whilst addressing the underlying 'crisis of confidence'. This debate was reflected in the drafting of the speech after Camp David. Eizenstat, Mondale and other liberals argued for a practical energy programme matched by a speech to the public that was not 'too much like an old scold and grouch' and 'instead … play [ed] to their better instincts'.[9] Eizenstat was highly critical of Caddell's ideas, describing him as 'Rasputin like', whilst Mondale was 'visibly angry' with Caddell and Carter. He told the president at a meeting that 'you're very tired and this is affecting your thinking'.[10] Caddell argued that addressing the underlying pessimism was the only way to regain the public's attention and gain their active support. The final speech was a compromise which reflected both perspectives. Carter delivered his speech to a television audience of 65 million, twice the number compared with recent speeches. The initial response from the public was positive. Carter's approval rating went up 11 per cent.[11] Letters into the White House ran 85 per cent in favour with a positive reaction to his call to rebuild the American spirit.[12] The press was generally supportive, some praising it as his best speech, but conservative media remained critical. The most devastating attack came in the *New Republic* which said, 'The past two weeks will be remembered as the period when President Carter packed it in, put the finishing touches on a failed administration.'[13]

The ultimate success of the speech was dependent upon the administration's ability to pass meaningful energy legislation after the congressional summer recess, but the initial goodwill had largely dissipated before then. Carter's aggressive energy speech in Kansas the following day[14] and the sudden removal of five members of his cabinet appeared to contradict his message of unity. The problem for Carter was as well as attempting to address the country's crisis of confidence; he was trying to deal with the second negative element in the Caddell polls, his leadership. The public wanted strong leadership from their president which they did not believe Carter was providing.[15] The administration response to this was to refresh the cabinet and reorganize the White House. The intention was not only to improve the administration's effectiveness but also to demonstrate Carter's strength as a leader. The manner and timing of the cabinet departures of Griffin Bell, Michael Blumenthal, Joe Califano, James Schlesinger and Brock Adams (Transport Secretary) were heavily criticized in the press.[16] The decision to request pro-forma resignations was originally supposed to include undersecretaries and White House staff but the targeting of the cabinet so soon after his keynote speech created the impression of a crisis.[17] Some of this criticism was unfair as Bell and Schlesinger had already indicated their intention to leave and Adams' indecisiveness on whether he would stay forced Carter to remove him. The only substantive dismissals therefore were those of Califano and Blumenthal, both of whose poor relations with White House staff had made their long-term future untenable. The new additions to the cabinet, particularly Bill Miller at the Treasury and Charles Duncan at Energy, did improve the relationships within the administration. There was one other appointment that did have a profound impact on not only the presidency of Carter but also his successor. Paul Volcker's arrival at the Federal Reserve, and his subsequent policies, eventually resulted in the defeat of inflation. But unfortunately for Carter, the initial impact of Volcker's policies of high interest rates triggered a recession that would last beyond Carter's term in office and contributed to his defeat in 1980.

The staff changes within the White House, which established a streamlined structure, did improve efficiency. The appointment of Jordan to the role of chief of staff caused some initial problems, particularly as he remained unpopular with members of congress, but he left the detailed work to his deputy Alonzo McDonald.[18] McDonald was one of three experienced advisors brought into the White House after the 15 July speech. Lloyd Cutler became Counsel to the President and Hedley Donovan a senior advisor. All three improved the administration's efficiency, but it was McDonald who had the greatest impact, streamlining White House operations from issue management to speechwriting.[19] This improvement would continue until the end of Carter's term in office with Jack Watson replacing Jordan as chief of staff in June 1980 when he left to join Carter's campaign team.

For White House staff like Jordan, the 15 July speech was an opportunity for Carter to reassert his leadership, supported by a streamlined organization and a more effective cabinet. Although these personnel changes were acknowledged as successful by staff,[20] the envisaged 'relaunch' of Carter's presidency did not materialize. The 'post-malaise' mood continued into August. Adding to the sombre atmosphere was the departure of Carter's United Nations Ambassador Andrew Young who was forced to resign for meeting secretly with representatives of the Palestinian Liberation Organization. In addition, Jordan was investigated by the FBI for taking cocaine. Although this charge was false, the speculation was damaging to the administration.[21] Symbolic of this sense of disappointment was the 'thank you lunch' held by the White House at the end of July for the 150 people who participated in the Camp David Summit. Barely half attended as many did not want to be associated with what was now perceived to be a failure.[22] Carter began his speech on 15 July with, 'This is not a message of happiness or reassurance', but by 1979 this was not what the public wanted to hear. Conservatives such as Ronald Reagan refused to accept that there was a crisis of confidence in America. They believed the pessimism was caused by a failure of presidential leadership and Republicans would fight the 1980 election on that basis.[23]

Carter also soon realized that the speech had failed to reassure the liberal wing of his party, and hence he would be dealing with an internal challenge before he could face the Republicans. Ted Kennedy, in launching his campaign in Boston on 7 November 1979, focused on the need for new leadership and touched on Carter's July speech. He said, 'Before the last election, we were told that Americans were honest, loving, good, decent, and compassionate. Now the people are blamed for every national ill and scolded as greedy, wasteful, and mired in malaise.'[24] Kennedy's analysis of Carter's speech from a liberal perspective was to be the same as Reagan, although their solutions to the country's problems were to be markedly different. Carter would therefore be faced with a political war on two ideological fronts.

Carter's relationship with the Democratic Party had always been problematic. Historian Douglas Brinkley went as far as calling Carter the 'Partyless President'.[25] His campaign in 1976 had mainly bypassed national and state organizations using local volunteers to reach the state electorate. Carter said in an interview in 1982, 'Very few of the members of congress or members of major lobbying groups or distinguished former Democratic leaders had played much of a role in my election.'[26] This view was not entirely accurate as many Democratic groups at state and national level provided invaluable support. His attempts to shape the party after 1976 were at best sporadic and not always successful. His wish to make fellow Georgian Philip Wise national chair was unsuccessful and he often supported local opposition to key party leaders like Mayor Richard Daley in Chicago.[27] Alonzo McDonald argued that from the party viewpoint, Carter appeared unreliable because he was so independent. In addition, being non-ideological in a party where philosophy mattered made him vulnerable to attack by both conservative and liberal members.[28] It was the liberals, oddly Carter's most consistent supporters in Congress, who felt the most disappointment with his presidency. Liberal uncertainty over Carter's ideology went back as far as the 1976 primary campaign when the entry of the liberal, Jerry Brown, resulted in five primary victories for the Governor of California.[29] But it was Carter's perceived failure to deliver on key liberal policies like labour law reform, healthcare, ERA and especially on the economy that caused the most anger. Some of this criticism was unfair because with the country becoming more conservative, much of the proposed liberal legislation did not have congressional or even public support.

The liberals, however, remained in the majority in the party and they used the mid-term party convention in December 1978 to criticize the president publicly. The appointment of Anne Wexler as Special Assistant for Public Outreach in September 1978 did improve the level of engagement between the party and his administration. But Carter reflected in his diary after the 1980 election that due to his nervousness about interest groups, he paid too little attention to his party and did not do enough to prevent liberal defections during the election.[30] Carter had worked hard, however, to court the party's liberal standard bearer, Ted Kennedy.

Carter and Kennedy had always been seen as rivals who aspired to lead the party. Carter's speech at Georgia University's Law Day in May 1974 was arguably designed not only to enhance his growing reputation nationally but also to upstage Kennedy, his fellow speaker on the day.[31] Kennedy had decided not to run in 1976, largely due to the illness of his son Teddy, but he left open the option to run in 1980 or 1984. An Atlanta reporter alleged that Carter had said on winning the nomination in 1976 that he was pleased to have won the nomination without 'having to kiss Ted Kennedy's ass to get it'.[32] There was a view in the White House, especially amongst the Georgians, that Kennedy would not wait until 1984 and would use policy issues such as healthcare as a means of differentiating himself from the administration. This rivalry contributed to the White House staff's suspicion of Secretary Califano because of his close relationship with the Kennedy family. Califano's dismissal in July 1979, following White House advisor Peter Bourne's departure the previous year, deprived Carter of the only informal channels he had to the Kennedy camp. Despite this, during Carter's presidency, Kennedy's voting record, at 84 per cent in favour of the administration's legislation, was exemplary.[33] Kennedy was also fulsome in his praise of Carter's support for his initiative on Northern Ireland.[34]

It was disagreements over healthcare policy that finally brought about Kennedy's split from Carter. Kennedy believed that comprehensive healthcare was a fundamental right and not something that should be dependent upon the state of the economy. In June 1979 Carter's long-awaited reform plan recommended only a phased implementation of comprehensive healthcare which depended upon the prevailing economic conditions. His fiscal conservatism and fear of inflation prevented him from giving a guarantee of automatic implementation. Kennedy could not accept this, and he argued that 'health care and health insurance were the issues that damaged our relations beyond repair'.[35] The inference that this was the reason Kennedy decided to enter the Democratic primaries was supported by Eizenstat. He believed that

Kennedy could not accept the Carter proposal on healthcare as it would lose him the support of the unions which represented his natural constituency.[36] But even Kennedy was not definitive about the source of the rift. In his autobiography he highlighted Carter's failure to appoint his friend Archibald Cox to a Federal judgeship, despite a personal appeal, and his negative reaction to Carter's 'malaise speech'.[37] Carey Parker, Kennedy's policy director, argued that conflict between the two men was inevitable once Kennedy realized Carter's agenda was conservative in its nature. Kennedy's speech at the mid-term convention in December 1978 which talked about liberals 'sailing against the wind' was the first signal to the party of an alternative to Carter in 1980.[38] To Jordan, the reason Kennedy stood was much more straightforward. He argued that healthcare had nothing to do with Kennedy's decision to run. It was just the simple belief that he could beat not only Carter but the likely GOP candidate, Ronald Reagan. Jordan said, 'He thinks we're weak, and he has reason to believe from the polls that he would win. That's why he's going to run.'[39] Kennedy formally launched his campaign on 7 November 1979 following discussions with his family that summer. His decision to run ensured that Carter was committed to campaign for the next year against two formidable opponents at a time when his approval ratings were declining.

In the twelve months before the election, Carter had to deal with two foreign policy crises that would have a major impact on his campaign: the taking of US embassy hostages in Tehran and the Soviet Union's invasion of Afghanistan. Two days before Kennedy declared his candidacy, the deterioration in relations between Iran and America following the overthrow of the Shah culminated in students storming the US embassy in Tehran and the taking of fifty-two American hostages. Despite the administration's best diplomatic efforts, as well as an attempted military rescue authorized by Carter in April 1980, the hostages were not released until after Reagan's inauguration on 20 January 1981. The hostage crisis affected the Carter campaign in several ways. Whilst his opponents did not make direct political capital out of the crisis, it became a wider symbol of Carter's perceived ineffectiveness and lack of leadership beyond just his foreign policy. The complex diplomatic situation hampered Carter's attempts to resolve the crisis and there was as a result several alleged breakthroughs which raised false hopes. It would also prove a distraction not only for Carter personally but for Jordan, his chief campaign strategist, whom the president used during the crisis as an unofficial envoy.[40] The absence of Jordan, in many ways the architect of Carter's victory in 1976, until much later in the campaign was to have a detrimental effect. The hostages further impacted on the nature of presidential campaigning as Carter and his advisors decided that he would not campaign in person but remain in the White House to deal with the crisis. Dubbed the 'Rose Garden' strategy, previous presidents had successfully used this when standing for re-election but in Carter's case, with him languishing in the polls, this did not prove to be an effective approach. This was eventually abandoned at a press conference on 30 April 1980 where Carter rather lamely suggested he could start personal campaigning as the challenges the country faced were 'manageable enough'.[41]

The Soviet invasion of Afghanistan on Christmas Day 1979 was a major blow to Carter's policy of détente. It killed all hope of Congress passing the second Strategic Arms Limitation Treaty, a key political objective for Carter. The invasion was not only a gift to conservative Republicans like Reagan who had always demanded a much harder line with the Soviet Union but caused Carter to reverse his policy on defence spending. His request to increase military expenditure by 6 per cent in the proposed 1981 budget had major implications for the administration's economic policy. The increased expenditure all but removed any hope of Carter fulfilling his commitment to a balanced budget without a dramatic reduction in social spending. Any such cuts would be opposed by Kennedy and other liberals in the party. These two crises did not have an entirely negative effect on the Carter re-election bid as public support, at least initially, for a president in a time of crisis did help him in the primary campaigns. Whilst in presidential elections foreign policy issues do not always become major factors, Republicans used the hostage crisis and Soviet invasion of Afghanistan to highlight their general view of Carter as a weak and ineffective leader.

The public maintained its support for his handling of the hostages and Afghanistan crises well into the summer of 1980. His policies at home on the other hand were to receive much more criticism. For Carter, the effectiveness of his administration's domestic policies was always going to be the critical issue in the upcoming election. This was particularly the case as Carter had stood in the previous election on the issue of his competence. This claim would bring all of his domestic policies under scrutiny during the campaign. In particular his handling of a deteriorating economy and pressure on his commitment to balance the 1981 budget was brought into sharp focus. The initial White House forecast for the 1981 budget became unsustainable with pressure from the unions to help the poor and unemployed against recession, and the impact of Carter's decision to increase defence spending. In January 1980 inflation rose to 19.2 per cent which caused a panic on Wall Street. Eizenstat admitted that the White House was 'proposing a budget program which is unachievable as well as undesirable in the present recessionary climate'. As a result, Carter recalled the budget from Congress and tried to impose further spending cuts, but these would still result in a deficit of $16.5bn. Even so Congress humiliatingly rejected this revised budget.[42] It was against this unfavourable economic background that Carter prepared his campaign.

Despite these difficulties the White House remained confident of defeating Kennedy in the primaries. The president's leaked comment to congressmen on 25 June 1979 about 'whipping his [Kennedy's] ass' if he ran was stage-managed, according to Mondale, to make Carter seem tough.[43] Carter's campaign tactics for the primaries were in line with his 'Rose Garden' strategy. This involved not actively campaigning but instead using surrogates like Vice President Mondale, other senior Democratic Party figures and Rosalynn Carter, by now a formidable campaigner in her own right, to visit the states concerned. Carter's position within the party started to improve. Wexler reported on a poll of party chairmen in December 1979 that showed an improvement in the president's standing.[44] Carter sought to build campaign momentum by bringing forward the dates of primaries in the southern states which were his natural constituency.[45] This tactic was largely successful in that Kennedy had no significant primary victories until two wins in New York and Connecticut in late March 1980. Carter was helped by some lacklustre electioneering from Kennedy. His campaign launch in Boston, just three days after the taking of the hostages in Tehran, was viewed as insensitive. More damaging to his electoral image was a televised interview with Roger Mudd of CBS, broadcast on 4 November 1979. In this Kennedy seemed unable to answer a basic question about why he wanted to be president.[46] Kennedy's policy director admitted that his staff were simply not prepared for the campaign in November and were not properly organized until the following February.[47] Unfortunately, by then Kennedy had slid further in the polls as the public rallied round the president following the Soviet invasion of Afghanistan. Initially at least, Kennedy found it difficult to attack Carter's leadership at a time of national crisis. He sought to maintain the support of business by downplaying his liberal agenda.[48] However, in a campaign that was to bear some striking similarities to Reagan's primary battle with President Ford in 1976, Kennedy started to win primaries by breaking free of such constraints to focus more on a liberal agenda. Victories in Connecticut, New York, Pennsylvania, California and New Jersey, all critical states for the presidential election, prolonged the race up to the Democratic Convention in August. Kennedy believed that this new momentum, where he was gaining support not only from liberals but from blue-collar and minority groups, could be enough to snatch victory at the convention.

He was appealing to blue-collar voters in key states, those who would later become known as Reagan Democrats. There was also polling which suggested that Kennedy was not only leading Reagan but was also more trusted to defeat inflation, a major policy issue for the electorate.[49]

Nevertheless, by late May 1980, confident of victory, the White House had drawn up detailed plans to 'reintegrate' Kennedy backers, particularly his labour supporters, into the Carter camp.[50] But at a meeting with Carter that June, not only did Kennedy refuse to step down but his supporters began lobbying for a free vote at the convention. Kennedy believed he had momentum and that Carter delegates from earlier primaries would switch sides and throw the convention to him. In addition, Kennedy asked for a public debate with Carter. Neither of these options were realistic propositions but the president was unable to persuade Kennedy to step aside.[51] The White House position was further complicated by indications that Senate leader Byrd was involved in an attempt with other Democratic Senators to persuade Carter to step down. This may have been influenced by Byrd's anger with the president who had not told him in advance of the hostage rescue attempt, but it was more likely prompted by Byrd's fear of congressional losses in November.[52] So, despite having a clear lead in delegates, Carter was faced with uncertainty in the run-up to the Convention in August 1980.

For a sitting president, the party convention in an election year was used as both a 'coronation' and launch pad for the forthcoming campaign. This was not the case for the Democratic Convention in 1980 because most of the delegate and media attention was on Ted Kennedy. Attempts to unite the party were blocked by Kennedy's team even after it was certain that the delegate vote would be lost. The convention, held in New York, became a bitter battle over the party platform. To try and end a public split the White House agreed prior to the convention to many elements of the liberal agenda, including commitments on labour law reform, ERA, education funding, full employment and tax reform. Attempts to include policies on wage-price regulation and control of energy prices were successfully resisted by Carter's supporters. However, Carter was forced to concede a platform commitment to spend $12bn on a jobs programme. This would undermine his own policy of achieving a balanced budget and damaged his credibility on fiscal restraint.[53] When Kennedy did finally concede defeat, he did it in such a way that hurt Carter politically. Kennedy's convention speech on 12 August 1980 'electrified the delegates with a rousing New Deal, New Frontier style speech'[54] which was indirectly critical of the administration's policies. He said, 'Let us pledge that we will never misuse unemployment, high interest rates and human misery as false weapons against inflation' and 'Let us pledge that unemployment will be the priority of our economic policy.'[55] Jordan was in no doubt of the impact of the speech, he stated that 'We may have won the nomination but Ted Kennedy had won their hearts.'[56] A second and perhaps more damaging incident was Kennedy's late and unenthusiastic appearance on stage after Carter's acceptance speech at the end of the convention. Such stage-managed events were meant to signify party unity but Kennedy's late appearance, if anything, symbolized quite the opposite. White House staff, including Powell, were convinced that the slight was deliberate[57] whilst Carter alluded to Kennedy having had 'a few drinks.'[58] Kennedy's own version of these events some years later was at best confusing and certainly unconvincing.[59] His insistence on staying at a nearby hotel and the subsequent delay in arriving on stage could have been better managed by both parties. But his refusal to raise hands in a victory salute with Carter was a deliberate snub. The overall image was described by Lance as 'people saw supposedly the most powerful man on the face of the earth cooling his heels up there waiting for a fellow he's just whipped'. The press was much harsher. Mary McCrory described Carter 'as looking like an airline pilot whose passengers have just defected to the hijacker.'[60] What was clear was that Carter left his party's convention weakened not strengthened by the Kennedy challenge and having failed to reunite his party.

Carter's ability to bounce back from unfavourable poll numbers in July 1979 to beat Kennedy in the following year demonstrated his resilience but damaged his political credibility. Reagan shared Kennedy's critique of the Carter White House. Like Kennedy, Reagan did not accept that there was a 'malaise' in the country and argued that the fault lay in Carter's weak leadership. Kennedy's later success in the primaries was largely based on his promotion of liberal policies; he offered 'a choice not an echo'.[61] Kennedy's nine primary victories represented 164 electoral college votes which Carter needed if he was going to win the election. He had to win back liberal voters. In a memorandum early in the campaign, Secretary of Labor Marshall described Kennedy supporters as more intense and committed than Carter's but early polling at the convention suggested only 23 per cent of Kennedy delegates intended to vote for the president in November.[62] The Democratic platform was designed to attract liberal support but doubts about Carter's commitment to this persisted. This was particularly true of how the platform commitment to spend $12bn on job creation squared with Carter's own fiscal conservatism. The president's challenge in winning back liberal support was further complicated when John B. Anderson decided to stand as a new third-party candidate. Anderson, a maverick liberal Republican congressman from Illinois, had run against Reagan in the primaries but he had been encouraged to run again by positive national polling. Carter's main opponent, though, was the formidable Republican nominee, Ronald Reagan, who unlike Carter had a largely united party behind him and had built an early lead in the polls.

In announcing his candidacy on 13 November 1979, Reagan chose to highlight the roles he had played in his life. He stated that he had seen America as 'a sports caster, as an actor, officer of my labour union, soldier, officeholder and as both a Democrat and a Republican'.[63] He explained his life in this way, as Carter had done in 1976, to emphasize the range of his previous responsibilities and the rich experience he brought to his candidacy. He was especially keen to highlight his tough upbringing in small-town Illinois during the Depression. This was important to Reagan because for many of the electorate he was remembered just as a Hollywood actor. He was always underestimated by his opponents throughout his political career. Clark Clifford famously called him 'an amiable dunce'.[64] But his time as an actor gave him important skills for a politician; he could follow a script, handle the public, and his producers and directors were his advisors. His move from a New Deal Democrat to a conservative Republican started with his involvement as a leader of the actor's union during the anti-communist period of the 1940s. His work giving speeches to the employees of General Electric in the 1950s helped him develop a conservative philosophy that became the bedrock of his political career. Reagan's optimistic view of America was supported by a belief in small government, low taxes, increased defence spending and strident anti-communism. One of Carter's aides said of Reagan's philosophy, he 'sees the world, I think, very simply. His great success as a politician and public figure is that his entire world is testable against four or five sentences', with the result that he 'knows what he believes in and he believes it, and every time you ask him a question or decision, he tests it against that'.[65] A historian described Reagan's beliefs 'as inerasable as grooves in an LP'.[66]

He rose to national prominence during the 1964 Presidential election as a supporter of the conservative Barry Goldwater. His recorded speech 'A Time for Choosing' raised not only his profile but also $8m for his cash-strapped party that year. He gained his first major electoral victory in 1966 by defeating the liberal incumbent, Pat Brown, for Governor of California. He served two terms and proved to be a successful, pragmatic politician who made deals with local Democratic leaders to pass legislation on taxes and welfare reform.[67] In 1976 he ran unsuccessfully against President Ford, but he gained enough support to damage the incumbent president in his failed campaign against Carter. In his 1980 campaign he was riding a rising tide of conservative support funded by contributions from business leaders worried about stagflation, high taxes and regulation. Reagan's mantra of less government interference and lower taxation met their needs whilst his successful courting of the Religious Right on social policy ensured that he quickly became the only viable conservative candidate.[68] Reagan's acceptance speech in Detroit on 17 July 1980 set the tone for his campaign. He was optimistic about America's ability to succeed, rejecting Carter's rather gloomy analysis of the country's troubles. He saw no malaise other than that of the president's 'mediocre leadership which was eroding our national will and purpose'.[69] Unlike Carter, Reagan left his convention on a high.

The 1980 election has been characterized as not only a watershed but a meeting of diametrically opposed politicians in terms of policy, ideology and personality, but this was not entirely the case. Both candidates had a similar perspective on the effectiveness of government in that they saw its inefficiencies and waste and agreed on the need for radical reform. Carter even talked at a Democratic Party gala of getting 'the government nose out of the private enterprise of this country'.[70] But whilst Carter argued that a reformed bureaucracy could and should be an agent for good, Reagan famously stated that government itself was the problem and needed to be dramatically cut back. There were also striking similarities between their economic policies. Carter's policies of long-term commitment to deregulation, controlling government spending and making fighting inflation his main economic priority were very similar to Reagan's views. Carter's late espousal of monetary policy and increased defence spending in response to Soviet aggression would also become major policies of the Reagan administration.[71] In addition, some of their supposed political differences did not play out in practice. Reagan's social conservatism turned out to be a lot less extreme than the Democrats predicted, as his new-found supporters on the Religious Right were to find out. The major distinction between the candidates was not so much about ideology or even policy but was related to personality and political skill.

Reagan was an optimist who saw things in simple terms both personally and politically. His belief in the greatness of America was total and so he refused to accept Carter's view of any limit on American power, let alone the presence of a 'malaise'. This was reflected in all his speeches. Whereas Reagan saw life in simple terms, Carter saw its complexity and nuances. He studied issues carefully, reaching conclusions based on logic. To him complicated problems generally did not have simple solutions. He accepted that US power had its limits and that there were restrictions on what could be achieved both at home and abroad.[72]

Both men had different political strengths which were to be highlighted on the campaign trail. Yet Carter's intellect and capacity for hard work did not prove to be a major advantage over Reagan. As Bill Moyers said about Reagan, 'we didn't elect this guy because he knows how many barrels of oil there are in Alaska. We elected him because we want to feel good'.[73] Reagan was known as the 'Great Communicator', but this was largely based on his ability to project a positive image on television. In face-to-face situations like answering questions for the press or the public he was much less comfortable. Paradoxically, Carter, known as a poor communicator, was highly effective in interactive environments like town hall meetings and phone-ins. However, the main communication channel that would be used in 1980 was television, and Reagan, both as a former actor and TV performer, was a master technician. His clear, simple messages matched by his relaxed style and self-deprecatory humour helped him win over audiences. Reagan acted as if he was 'born for TV'. Carter's preachy and convoluted speaking style was not regarded as inspiring, and his television image, in contrast to Reagan's, was rather unappealing. This was to prove a major disadvantage for the president who faced a charismatic, likeable, oratorically adept candidate who by the early summer of 1980 was leading in the polls.

As president, Carter faced a different type of campaign in 1980 compared to four years earlier. As a virtually unknown candidate he had run an 'insurgent' campaign in 1976 which was four years in the planning. He and his team worked with volunteer activists not state party structures. In 1980 he was president and his skill in meeting people 'on the stump' would be negated by limits on his time and the security restrictions that were imposed on an incumbent. In addition, he had a record in office to defend and, like Ford in 1976, he had already fought a dangerous opponent in the primaries. This all took place in the middle of the hostage crisis which resulted in his main campaign strategist Jordan being initially unavailable.[74] Kennedy's delay in withdrawing from the campaign and the often-bitter battle over the Democratic platform at the convention contributed to the disaffection of liberals. Such divisions encouraged the third-party candidacy of John Anderson, who benefitted from electoral discontent with both candidates. On the important policy issues of the campaign, public opinion was concerned about the economy, inflation and taxation, but Carter did not have a good record on any of them. The major advantage that an incumbent president did have was the potential to use the power of his office for political advantage. Unfortunately, Carter seemed reluctant to do this. Anne Wexler, his lead advisor on outreach, argued that Carter did not focus on his re-election, often seeking GOP support to get his legislation passed. When she mentioned the negative political consequences on his campaign of such action to Carter, she was firmly rebuffed.[75]

To defeat Reagan, two important sources influenced the Carter campaign strategy, the polling data of Caddell and political advice from Jordan. The Iran hostages had taken Jordan away from the campaign since November 1979, but by June 1980 he was back working full time on Carter's re-election. His first task was to provide Carter with a brief on his Republican rival. Jordan talked to Jesse Unruh and Bob Moretti, leading Democratic politicians in California who had dealt with Reagan as governor. Jordan always maintained that he had underestimated Reagan as an opponent,[76] but in a memorandum to Carter in June, he accurately reflected both his opponent's strengths and weaknesses. He described Reagan as 'not dumb but shrewd', that his conservative beliefs could lead him to oversimplify but that he was more moderate than his rhetoric. He described him as an 'uncanny communicator' and that 'people hear him, like him and believe him'. Jordan later warned Carter against launching personal attacks on Reagan as it had wounded Carter when he used this tactic against Ford in 1976. This advice was subsequently ignored by Carter. He may have done this in reaction to another part of the same Jordan memorandum. This suggested that Reagan had a mean temper which, although he had kept under control, would damage him if that became public knowledge. If Carter's later personal attacks had been an attempt to provoke Reagan, it proved misguided.[77]

Jordan's follow-up memorandum later that month outlined the damage that the Kennedy campaign had inflicted on Carter's image and the negative perception of his administration, particularly amongst liberals. Jordan feared that there was a risk that liberal voters would switch to Anderson. Also, at state level, he argued that the primary battles had divided the party in key states like Pennsylvania and New York. He believed that the electorate's pessimism, highlighted in Caddell's polling, meant that the public believed America's problems were unfixable and that there was very little difference between the candidates.[78] Jordan, supported by Rafshoon and Caddell, argued for a low-profile, defensive campaign to continue until the Democratic Convention in August. He wanted to keep Carter out of the media glare and allow the press and Carter's surrogates to focus just on Reagan. Then, after receiving the expected positive poll 'bounce' from the Democratic Convention, he recommended that the White House run a more positive campaign highlighting a clear choice between the candidates, in terms of Carter's vision for the future and the dangers presented by Reagan's policies.[79] This approach was not universally supported in the White House. Many of the domestic policy team, Eizenstat included, feared that the initial low-key approach would not generate the sort of press coverage that the president required. Caddell projected in July 1980 that Reagan could have a 20–25-point lead in the polls after the GOP convention. Dave Rubenstein from Eizenstat's team was concerned that the low profile and the expected post-convention 'bounce' would not be enough to close this gap in the polls given Carter's poor ratings.[80] Carter's aide Hedley Donovan also argued that the 'Rose Garden' strategy had encouraged a bunker mentality with the press ignoring good White House news stories and focusing on the bad.[81]

Carter held healthy leads in the polls over Kennedy and Reagan in January 1980, but these had been reversed by July.[82] Jordan emphasized, 'Our worst fear all along had been that the race would ultimately become a referendum on Carter's presidency instead of a choice between him and Reagan.'[83] Carter was not able to stay out of the headlines before the convention as a series of events forced him to be personally involved in the campaign. A scandal involving his younger brother Billy's dealings with and travels to Libya prompted an independent investigation by the Justice Department. This compelled Carter to endure six weeks of hostile media questioning, including 'how do you think you got into this big mess?'[84] Carter eventually dealt with all the issues arising from the investigation, but 'Billygate' proved to be a major distraction and damaged his image. A further round of OPEC oil price increases triggered another energy crisis that summer. This harmed the president's reputation for competence as many of his legislative proposals on energy that had been recommended a year earlier had still not passed Congress. The divisive Democratic primary campaign enabled the Republicans to utilize Kennedy's campaign rhetoric of 'no more Jimmy Carter' in television adverts targeted at Democratic voters.[85] Jordan had assumed that a low presidential profile would encourage the press to scrutinize Reagan's mistakes on the campaign trail, but he made very few. Errors such as his campaign launch speech defending state's rights in Neshoba, Mississippi, near the location where three civil rights Freedom Summer campaigners were murdered in 1964 and later describing the Vietnam War as a 'noble cause', both called into question Reagan's judgement. However, in general his campaign was disciplined and well run.[86]

For Reagan, his campaign was about promoting his optimistic vision for America. He talked about less government and lower taxation. He focused not so much on specific policies but much more on the failures of Carter. To Reagan's handlers a successful campaign was one that kept Carter's record in the headlines. He was also highly effective in courting the evangelical movement, culminating in his speech in Dallas on 22 August 1980 which led to an endorsement from Jerry Falwell.[87] Such was Reagan's success in exploiting the anger of religious groups with Carter's social policies, one Moral Majority advert described Carter as 'traitor to the South and no longer a Christian'.[88] As a result the Carter campaign were forced to respond with a television advert that reminded the public of the president's deep personal faith.[89]

Carter's ability to affect policy and govern during the long campaign was never more critical than with his handling of the economy. The Carter administration's economic policy was in disarray by 1980. Historian Burton Kaufman described the president's economic team as having 'a bankruptcy of ideas rather than a concerted programme for dealing with a problem that threatened to consume the administration'.[90] Carter's long-term commitment to a balanced budget prevented him from deploying the traditional Democratic Party policies for managing a deficit. His credibility on fiscal restraint was damaged by the proposed $12bn increase in spending to fight recession and unemployment agreed at the Democratic Convention. His attempts to weave this into a coherent programme that would win public support were further hampered by the failure of his administration's policy to curb inflation. The launch of the Carter's fourth anti-inflation policy in March 1980 had been met with cynicism from reporters.[91] The White House was attempting, yet again, to control the wage-price spiral without formal controls. The administration's only effective tool to curb inflation was in the hands of the Federal Reserve and its new Chair, Paul Volcker. His policy of controlling the money supply and interest rates did manage to bring down inflation to nearer 12 per cent, but high interest rates militated against any feel-good factor in the country as economists became increasingly concerned about recession. Volcker was able to ease interest rates during the summer but in early October 1980 Schultz warned Carter of a new interest rate rise later that month due to mortgage and oil price increases.[92] By the time of the election in early November, interest rates had reached nearly 20 per cent, inflation stood at 13 per cent and unemployment at 7.5 per cent. These were the worst election indicators that an incumbent president had faced in an election since Herbert Hoover in 1932.[93] The comparison with Hoover was used by both Kennedy and Reagan in campaign adverts. One by Kennedy used the TV character Archie Bunker who described Carter as 'the most Republican President since Herbert Hoover and may give us a depression that makes Hoover's look like prosperity'.[94]

There were opportunities for Carter to use his office to direct economic policy for political gain. Alonzo McDonald argued that Carter did have the political antennae to sense such prospects, but he always wanted to do the right thing. McDonald quoted an occasion when Carter rejected a concession on energy for the Pennsylvanian steel industry, just before that state's primary election, even though it was supported by the Justice and Treasury departments.[95] This approach was reinforced by Carter's response to the pressure he faced in the summer of 1980 to submit a tax cut to Congress. The economic benefits of a major tax cut had long been the policy of the Republican Party but to Reagan it had become the major component of his campaign. Reagan had co-opted a Republican tax initiative in Congress, the Kemp-Roth bill, and promised to implement this on taking office. There was pressure from within the Democratic Party for Carter to respond with his own tax-cut proposals. This came from conservatives and even from liberals like Ted Kennedy.[96] There was an expectation that as an incumbent president, he would pass tax cuts to help his party win re-election. Carter, however, refused to do so as he did not believe that it was right for the economy whatever the political benefits. He told Secretary Miller, 'I just cannot flip-flop' on taxes.[97] He believed that a tax cut, whilst popular, was irresponsible and would necessitate a 40 per cent cut in non-defence government spending.[98] Carter continued to argue against the GOP proposed tax cut during the election and it became one of the major policy differences between himself and Reagan on the campaign trail. He argued for a more modest tax cut as part of his revitalization programme with half of the benefit going on investment (as opposed to 10 per cent in Reagan's proposals). Carter argued that the Reagan-Kemp-Roth tax plan with its focus on a cut in personal taxation would be inflationary whilst his plan would reduce inflation.[99]

The main parties' economic platforms had some strong similarities, especially on issues such as deregulation and fiscal restraint. Carter's description of Reagan's economic policies as 'Voodoo Economics', a slogan coined by George Bush, his opponent in the primaries but now Reagan's running mate, did result in the Reagan campaign dropping several of its economic proposals. Although the tax cut remained the signature economic policy of Reagan, it was not very popular with the electorate. The polls in July 1980 had Reagan considerably ahead of Carter (83–14) on economic issues, but the public were 53–43 in favour of Carter on the question of the tax cut.[100] The administration's revitalization plan was a response to public dissatisfaction with the economy. Carter's plan would add $5.7bn to the 1981 budget, but journalist Elizabeth Drew said of Carter's failure to communicate his proposal, 'he doesn't seem able to implant it in the national consciousness'. To many, particularly to liberals, the programme did not seem credible given the president's fiscal conservatism, and whilst there was no doubting Reagan's absolute belief in his proposed tax cut, Carter appeared to lack the same degree of conviction for his own economic proposals.[101]

Carter's frustration over his campaign's inability to get his message across led to a serious error of judgement that damaged his standing with the electorate. During 1980, even in polls where Carter was not viewed favourably, 83 per cent still believed that he was a man of moral principles.[102] The White House campaign, in seeking to highlight Reagan's perceived weaknesses, had relied upon political surrogates, particularly the vice president, to attack those weaknesses. They focused on Reagan's inability to grasp complex issues, claiming that he proposed simplistic solutions to difficult problems and too often 'shoots from the hip'.[103] However, Carter's advisors complained that such speeches were not receiving fair coverage in the media. This was not necessarily due to bias but the media's difficulty in covering simultaneously three presidential candidates.[104] Despite earlier warnings from Jordan over the failure of similar tactics in 1976,[105] Carter, supported by Caddell, personally attacked Reagan in three important speeches. In Atlanta on 16 September he came close to accusing him of being a racial bigot.[106] At a labour conference in California six days later he argued that the election was a decision between war and peace, thus suggesting that Reagan would take America into war.[107] Finally, at a Democratic fundraiser in Chicago on 6 October, despite acknowledging the criticism of his approach, he argued that Reagan would be divisive and that if Carter lost the election, 'Americans might be separated black from white, Jew from Christian, North from South, rural from urban'.[108] The media heavily criticized these speeches.[109] Carter later argued that the press took these attacks out of context,[110] but they damaged his public image as a moral man. The Reagan campaign responded with a television advertisement featuring Nancy Reagan defending her husband, and accusations of 'meanness' forced Carter in a television interview with Barbara Walters to promise to tone down his remarks.[111]

Another issue that Carter had to deal with during the campaign was press cynicism over his attempts to resolve the Iranian hostage crisis. He faced accusations as early as April 1980 from Kennedy that he was using announcements on the hostages for political purposes.[112] The press, already wary of being manipulated by Rafshoon's communications tactics in 1978, hinted that a hostage release would be stage-managed by the White House. McDonald argued that every television network believed that Carter's Rose Garden strategy was not a method to help deal with the hostages but a political tactic. The public shared this view. A poll on 30 September showed an increase from 19 to 44 per cent of people who believed that Carter would manipulate the hostage crisis for political gain.[113] The press continued to build expectations of a hostage release as Election Day approached. The problem was further complicated for Carter by signs in September of a serious attempt by some in the Iranian regime to negotiate a settlement. Unfortunately for the White House this gave rise to a series of failed negotiations that continued right up until Election Day. Carter therefore was faced with the worst of both worlds. The media portrayed him as either a cynic manipulating the release of the hostages for political gain or as a weak president unable to secure their freedom.

All of this demonstrated how far Carter's carefully crafted image of competence and trust had been damaged by November 1980. The electorate's scepticism of his handling of the hostages and accusations of meanness all contributed to a decline in poll numbers. In addition, his claims of competence were not just contradicted by his legislative failures but by a growing narrative, popularized by talk show hosts and satirists, which focused on Carter's perceived weirdness. This image was reinforced by a story in August 1979 about Carter, whilst in a boat fishing, being attacked by a wild rabbit. This story which ran for a number of weeks was badly mishandled by the White House and it opened up Carter to media ridicule. All of these factors resulted in the public perception of the president in 1980 being much less credible than the candidate who won in 1976.[114]

Despite these difficulties, the polls showed that Carter was gaining ground on Reagan. The White House message to the public that whatever Carter's difficulties he remained the safe choice in comparison with Reagan was gaining some traction. So, despite having low job approval, the polls indicated that by 9 October the gap had closed to just four points, 43–39.[115] It was Carter's belief that in a televised debate with Reagan his superior ability and experience would enable him to overtake his opponent. Unable to agree on three debates as he had wanted, Carter had to settle for the one. This took place on 28 October in Cleveland, Ohio. It was watched by 80.6 million Americans, a record which lasted until the Hillary Clinton-Donald Trump debates of 2016. As incumbent, Carter had not only to win the debate but be seen to win it. He sought to identify his opponent with a dangerous future but without appearing shrill or exaggerating the risks of a Reagan presidency.[116] He argued that Reagan was outside the mainstream of the Republican Party and his attitude to nuclear arms control was dangerous. During the debate he extended this theme to domestic policy arguing that Reagan's negative attitude to Social Security, Medicare and Health insurance typified the differences between the two parties. He also emphasized the complexity of the office and, by implication, his own experience in comparison to Reagan's. He said early in the debate that 'I've had to make thousands of decisions, and each one of those decisions has been a learning process'. He was mainly on the defensive on his economic record, particularly high inflation, but did attack Reagan's proposals for tax cuts claiming they would be inflationary. He did promote his economic programme and argued that he had created 9 million jobs whilst in office. He was more positive in promoting his energy policy, highlighting the administration's success in conservation.[117] Reagan was very well prepared, having debated Anderson the previous month and by acquiring a leaked copy of Carter's briefing books for the debate. He handled detailed questions well, stood up to pressure and always remained calm and affable. In their closing statements Carter argued for his experience whilst Reagan focused on the president's record by asking Americans whether, since Carter's election, they felt better off and more secure.[118] This was a telling intervention as it directed the public to examine Carter's record in office. In his diaries Carter reluctantly admitted that Reagan had done better in the debate than he had anticipated even though Carter felt that he had won all the key arguments.[119]

After the debate, the White House focused more on promoting Carter's programme for the future. The campaign sought to contradict Republican advertisements which suggested that Carter was a do-nothing president and to emphasize those Reagan policies that he was already implementing such as increased military spending and deregulation.[120] Whilst Carter continued to argue that Reagan was a man unsuited to the office, he also tried to promote his economic revitalization programme with an emphasis on investment, job creation and reduced inflation. He argued that his programme would reap the rewards of the tough decisions that had been made during his presidency.[121] In his later speeches he sought to shore up his support in the Democratic Party by focusing on traditional Democratic audiences such as labour and the minorities. To Black leaders in Atlanta, Carter emphasized his administration's help for the poor through energy policy and job creation (1.3 million additional black jobs).[122] On Labor Day his remarks focused on the work of the Economic Revitalisation Board, Labor law reform, urban renewal and job creation programmes.[123] Carter's main problem remained that he could not promote his domestic policies as a major success and continually had to fall back on a critique of Reagan's own policies. White House criticisms of Reagan's plans on tax or energy for example were framed in terms of why they would not work, rather than being contrasted with Carter's own plans. The most telling indicator of where the Carter campaign team believed his strength lay was in their choice of television adverts. Most of the one-minute adverts emphasized foreign policy and Carter's experience, his role as peacemaker and the absence of war on his watch. In one advertisement

Carter's military service was even highlighted, something that was not discussed in 1976.[124] Carter's message to the American people on domestic policy was a negative one; it was that there were no easy answers to their problems and Reagan would make matters worse.

The final days before the election saw the hostage crisis again took centre stage with the suggestion of new terms from Tehran raising hopes of a breakthrough. This proved to be another false alarm. Carter had to go on television two days before the election to deny that there was any deal.[125] On the Monday before Election Day, the front page of newspapers showed Iranian students trashing the American seal at the embassy in Tehran. This visual reminder of his administration's impotence was extremely damaging to the president.[126] Carter himself noted the symbolic importance of Election Day being the anniversary of the taking of the first hostage.[127]

Both candidates elicited high negative feelings from the public with the result that many voters made their decision very late. It was in the period between 1 and 4 November that Reagan dramatically increased his lead over Carter as most undecided voters opted for the Republican candidate.[128] On 4 November 1980 Carter suffered the worst defeat for an incumbent president since Herbert Hoover in 1932. Reagan won forty-four states, prevailing in the electoral college 489–49. He won the popular vote 51–41 per cent, with Anderson gaining 6.6 per cent. Reagan, unlike Carter in 1976, had 'coattails' with his party gaining thirty-three seats in the House and twelve in the Senate which resulted in a GOP majority in the upper chamber for the first time since 1954. Republicans also gained four governorships and five state legislatures.[129] Post-election polling confirmed that there was a late swing against Carter on all the main policy issues, and he lost support in all voter groups except non-whites.[130] In addition a Harris poll found that those who believed that the best government was one that governed least, a core Reagan message, had increased from one-third in 1974 to three-fifths in 1980.[131] But the polls also showed that the result was less of a victory for Reagan and the GOP than a rejection of Carter and the Democrats. A *Time* magazine poll found that 63 per cent of voters said they voted to reject Carter and only 25 per cent saw it as a mandate for more conservative policies. Barely one in four voters supported Reagan in the ideological sense.[132] A measure of the lasting strength of the negative reaction to Carter was Reagan's successful use of anti-Carter rhetoric in his campaign for re-election against Mondale in 1984.[133] Over 40 years later the GOP are still using Carter tropes against President Joe Biden.[134]

Carter, in public at least, was initially non-committal as to the reasons why he believed he had lost. He acknowledged, however, that his drop in the polls just before Election Day may have been due to the last-minute dashed hopes of the hostage release. When pressed, he accepted that the Kennedy challenge had 'crippled him' with core constituencies.[135] When talking to Jordan two months after his defeat, Carter was more forthcoming. He described 1980 as 'pure hell, the Kennedy challenge, Afghanistan, having to put the SALT treaty on the shelf, the recession, Ronald Reagan, and the hostages … always the hostages! It was one crisis after another'.[136] The idea that the 1980 result was somehow pre-determined has been promoted by authors like Skowronek.[137] He argued that Carter's defeat was inevitable as he was ideologically out of step with the conservative mood of the country, and therefore in trying to find moderate solutions he found himself attacked by both conservatives and liberals. However, the assumption that 1980 was a conservative landslide was not borne out by the figures. The electoral returns saw a 2 per cent drop in turnout and the Democrats lost more votes than the Republicans gained.[138] Jordan did not accept that the election was a conservative watershed, arguing that 'it was not an ideological tidal wave; it was instead an expression of frustration with the Democratic Party and doubt that it could provide solutions to America's problems'.[139] The electorate was not conservative and even strongly liberal on some social issues. It followed therefore, in ideological terms, that promoting the middle ground could have been a winning strategy. Carter could have tried to use the Democratic Party as a vehicle for such a centrist strategy but, as he acknowledged, the party was 'never his', and the Kennedy challenge sapped 5–6 per cent of that vote away from him.[140]

If Carter's defeat was not 'inevitable' what were the factors that contributed to his failure? The hostages appear to have been in the minds of White House staff. Aide Tim Kraft complained that the money spent on a largely ineffective media campaign would have been better used on 'two more helicopters in Iran' for the abortive rescue mission.[141] In separate interviews in 1986 and 1997, Carter endorsed the view that if the hostages had been released, he would have won. He also spoke of general press cynicism and the television news broadcasts of Walter Cronkite and Ted Koppel. They highlighted in every broadcast the length of time the hostages had been held whilst questioning the administration's motives in seeking their release.[142] Rafshoon found that the hostage crisis received more television coverage (444 days) than the US ten-year involvement in the Vietnam War.[143] Carter did receive public support for his handling of this crisis, and it certainly benefitted him early in his campaign against Kennedy. However, the stalled negotiations in early November 1980 were a further reminder to the American public of Carter's failure to secure their release, and this almost certainly widened the margin of Reagan's victory. But it should be noted that Reagan himself believed that the hostages were not the main factor in his success and that their release would not have changed the result. The Reagan campaign was very conscious of the 'risk' of an 'October Surprise' with the hostages being released and worked hard to mitigate any impact on their candidate.

Another important factor in Carter's defeat was the ineffectiveness of his campaign. Unlike in 1976, the 1980 campaign did not have the benefit of Jordan's detailed planning. Although Jordan's absence was attributed to the hostage crisis, advisors like Lance argued that the White House and Jordan should have been actively planning for 1980 as soon as Carter took office.[144] Jordan admitted that he was distracted by Iran but argued that his increased involvement would not have affected the result.[145] However, there were mistakes made by the White House that contributed to the president's defeat. Carter's fundamental problem was that he did not have a positive record on domestic policy to sell to the electorate and so he was always going to be on the defensive unless he could focus the election on Reagan himself. A major error was Carter's decision to make personal attacks on Reagan to demonize him. This failed and only damaged Carter's image as a moral leader. Whereas in 1976 he stood on his good character, in 1980 he was being painted as mean, remote and indifferent. Hugh Sidey of *Time* magazine summed up the press mood: 'The past few days have revealed a man capable of far more petty vituperation than most Americans thought possible even in this political season.'[146] To win Carter had to convince the electorate that not only was Reagan a threat domestically and abroad but that his vision for a better future was less compelling than Carter's own. In his convention speech, Carter summarized his problem with trying to create a positive vision. He argued that presidents must look to the long term and hence 'sometimes ask for sacrifice when the listeners would rather hear the promise of comfort'.[147] Rafshoon argued that the president needed to portray 'hope'.[148] Carter attempted in the run-up to the election to create a programme for long-term change. The Commission for National Agenda for the Eighties attempted to establish such a programme modelled on a similar initiative under President Eisenhower. Although its final report was not produced until December 1980, it was evident by August of that year that any hopes Carter had of reaching a consensus on a wide range of national issues that could be used in his campaign were to be dashed by ideological, sectional and interest group dissent.[149]

Reagan's success in building an early lead in the polls forced Carter to rely on the more liberal elements of the party and resulted in a liberal platform being foisted on him. This included an economic plan which was seen as too liberal for Carter and the electorate. His attempts to explain this programme lacked the conviction, clarity and the simple optimism of Reagan's message. Even Eizenstat was not convinced by Carter's programme, commenting, 'We presented no attractive new alternative, only thin gruel and more of the same.'[150] Hence the public was often confused and even bored with Carter's vision for future prosperity, and liberals were unconvinced whether Carter, if elected, would really implement such a programme.

The Jimmy Carter of 1980 portrayed himself as the same man who had run in 1976 but had now, as president, gained critical experience. But the public remained confused about his ideology and in 1980 he had a record to defend which was vulnerable to attack from his opponents. He therefore needed even more of the support of a liberal Democratic Party than he did in 1976. His basic approach to politics had not changed. His political competitiveness, which resulted in personal attacks on Reagan, was not a new phenomenon; he had been equally harsh on Ford in 1976 and Carl Sanders in 1970. His approach to the nation's problems also remained unchanged. He continued to articulate the complexity of issues and the need for sacrifice. This may have struck a chord with the public in 1976 but by 1980 they longed for a simpler, more optimistic vision for the future. This was something that Carter, with his engineering background, his 'preachy' style and his inherent pessimism, was unable to provide.

The critical factor in the campaign for his opponents was Carter's leadership as president, particularly on the economy. Reagan's comment at the end of the televised debate about whether the public felt better off under Carter drew attention to the administration's poor economic performance since taking office.[151] Unemployment was higher (7.6 v 7.0 per cent), interest rates were higher (15.3 v 6.4 per cent) and above all inflation was higher (12.5 v 5.8 per cent).[152] Polling data from Gallup suggested that the reasons for voting were mainly economic, especially concern about inflation.[153] This coupled with the president's failure to bring home the hostages put the White House on the back foot for most of the campaign. The Carter of 1976 promised to make government work, but the electorate saw little evidence of this. His failure to achieve his legislative goals even with a Democratic Congress contradicted his claim of competence. His campaign tried to focus on Reagan's perceived weaknesses and his own good character and experience. But it soon became reliant upon the electorate's pessimism that no one in office could fix the country's problems and perhaps Carter was the safer option. This was a high-risk strategy as voter apathy could easily change to discontent with unhappy voters opting for change.[154]

The economic gloom increased the negative atmosphere that pervaded Carter's presidency following his 'malaise' speech in July 1979. The continuing hostage crisis added to this general pessimism. The destruction of the US embassy's seal in the final days of the election highlighted Carter's perceived lack of leadership and became a symbol of his failure. Reagan ran an effective campaign with few mistakes and gave an impressive performance in the TV debate. The focus on Carter's record, especially on domestic policy, resulted in the electorate deciding that Reagan's more positive message was a risk worth taking. The perception of Carter as a good man doing his best was no longer enough. As a result, their rejection of the Carter presidency was decisive.

Carter revisited

Jimmy Carter's comprehensive election defeat in November 1980 was a bitter blow for any politician to take, particularly as it was against an opponent who appeared to be diametrically opposed to everything Carter stood for. His relationship with Reagan after the election was not helped by a tense transition meeting in the White House at which Carter felt (perhaps incorrectly) that Reagan was not paying attention to the detailed briefing he was receiving. As Reagan built his team for what promised to be a conservative 'revolution', Carter's final State of the Union message to Congress was a forty-page self-justification of his policies.[1] This was despite his wife, ever the realist, pointing out that many of the policies he was highlighting such as Arms Control, Human Rights and Conservation, were the reasons he lost.[2] During the 1980s and early 1990s, Carter's post-presidency was marked politically by major Democratic politicians trying to avoid being associated with what was widely regarded as a failed presidency. Walter Mondale, standing in 1984 against Reagan, was linked by the GOP campaign with Carter's economic failures. Bill Clinton, despite being elected in 1992, was reluctant to hire 'Carter re-treads' even when their experience would have been helpful.[3] As president, Clinton often found himself being compared to Carter when his policies were seen to have failed. This trend was to continue with later Democratic Presidents Barack Obama and Joe Biden.[4]

It was during the 1990s, however, that media focus moved away from Carter's 'failed' presidency to publicize his actions as a private citizen. Initially it was activities such as working as a volunteer carpenter building houses for the poor as part of Habitats for Humanity, a non-profit Christian organization. The press contrasted this with ex-President Reagan who was earning $2 million on speaking tours in Japan.[5] A more positive profile was also helped by the Clinton administration's use of Carter's mediation skills in Haiti and North Korea in 1994. These missions made use of Carter's diplomatic strengths. A journalist described him as being able to 'deal regularly with inhabitants of godforsaken villages and renegade leaders whom American officials ordinarily refuse to touch'.[6] Underpinning this new positive image of Carter was the work of the Carter Center. Founded by Carter and his wife in partnership with Emory University in Atlanta, this organization's remit was 'to prevent and resolve conflicts, enhance freedom and democracy, and improve health'.[7] Over the years the Center has established programmes to eradicate diseases such as guinea worm and river blindness, as well as immunization campaigns. In addition, Carter has been involved in mediating disputes and supervising elections in countries all over the world. He has also spoken out increasingly on women's rights, leaving his own church, the Southern Baptist Convention, in October 2000 over the issue and establishing a Women's Forum in February 2015.[8] Carter received recognition for his campaigning on conflict resolution, human rights and social welfare in October 2002 when he was awarded the Nobel Peace Prize.

Forty years after he left the White House, Jimmy Carter began to receive the public recognition for not only his post-presidency but for his personal qualities, character and on many of the issues he campaigned for in 1976. New biographies by Jonathan Alter and Kai Bird have reflected a more positive view of the Carter Presidency. This enhanced image has been helped by the marked contrast of Carter's character with that of President Donald Trump. During the 2020 election campaign, Carter was perceived as representing the 'anti-Trump', received visits from Democratic candidates Senators Cory Booker and Amy Klobuchar.[9] The eventual election of fellow Democrat Joe Biden in 2020, who like Carter campaigned on the issue of competence, reinforced this image. Carter's restoration was symbolized by President Biden and his wife visiting Carter and his wife in Plains in April 2021. But despite this the conservative press has continued to use the image of Carter to draw a negative comparison with his Democratic successors.[10] His image has been used more recently to attack President Biden as the spectre of stagflation and foreign policy failures have drawn parallels with the Carter administration.[11] So, despite an increase in public recognition and respect for the man, the image of a failed president fuelled by conservative media has remained strong in the public psyche.

This negative view of the Carter presidency is partly rooted in his electoral defeat in 1980 and the subsequent success of Reagan but it is also based on the perceived failures of his policies. Carter created an expectation that his administration would not only be competent but would make substantial reforms. In his inaugural address he did try to dampen this expectation by saying that 'we cannot afford to do everything',[12] but his inability to prioritize greatly hampered his legislative programme. Tip O'Neill, House Speaker during both the Carter and Reagan presidencies, highlighted the contrast in tactics used by Reagan to pass his tax cut legislation by saying, 'They only put one legislative bill in play at a time' and 'they kept their eye on it all the way through'[13] – a strategy that Carter was unable to follow.

On the critical issue of the economy his administration failed to deliver any substantial improvements. His 1977 stimulus package did help the poor initially but the population in poverty grew from 11.4 to 15 per cent during 1978–80. Yet it was his failure to control inflation that cost him dearly. Carter tried to persuade the American public of the value of his numerous anti-inflation initiatives but to no avail. It was only his appointment of Volcker to head the Federal Reserve that did eventually result in bringing inflation under control. However, this was at the cost of a recession that damaged Carter in the 1980 election. His public commitment to balancing the budget was also a failure as the impact of a recalcitrant Congress, oil price rises and the Soviet invasion of Afghanistan made this objective impossible. The one economic programme that Carter was publicly committed to was tax reform but again the eventual legislation passed proved to be a victory for congressional conservatives. It did not remove many of the tax loopholes and delivered a tax cut that mainly benefitted the well off.

Carter's energy policy was an example of his administration attempting to pass comprehensive legislation that addressed a complex problem facing the country. This demonstrated the scope of Carter's ambition but also his naivety in expecting such a complicated bill to pass without amendment. The final legislation was a significant step forward for energy conservation and in establishing a new Department of Energy, but it did not measure up to the expectations set by the president. It also highlighted Carter's inability to persuade the American public of the seriousness of the problem and the need for sacrifice. This contrasted with Reagan's simpler message that government should not be interfering with the energy market.

Carter was equally unsuccessful in his goal of reforming healthcare and welfare as both bills never got out of committee stage. The complexity of these issues was matched only by the strength of the opposition from both wings of his own party. The failure of Carter's Health bill would prove to be damaging to his chances of re-election as it provoked a major split with liberals in his party. There was legislation that Carter did successfully steer through Congress, such as government reform, deregulation and Social Security reform, but none of these, whilst important, had a high public profile. The one exception to this was on the environment. His administration passed a raft of legislation that reinforced environmental safeguards such as the Clean Air and Water

Acts, strengthened the Environmental Protection Agency and established a national environmental compensation scheme. Carter's signature legislation was the Alaskan Lands Act passed just before he left office. Many of Carter's environmental policies were overturned by his successor but Carter's Alaskan legislation, which protected over 157 million acres of land, would stand as a symbol of his administration's environmental credentials. In some ways Carter's legislative record can be regarded as credible, particularly given the parlous state of the economy and divisions in Congress, but not when measured against the goals he publicly set himself.

There has been serious debate over Carter's inability to manage the conflicting ideologies on key policies. However, the argument that a more effective leader could have resolved such conflicts is not supported by any compelling evidence and does not consider the political climate at the time or Carter's ideology and character. Carter's mishandling of his relationship with Senator Long, for example, did damage his legislative strategy but it was doubtful whether given Long's views on taxation for example, it would have changed the fate of his administration's Tax Reform bill. The assumption that Carter was attempting to steer an ideological path between liberal and conservative factions assumed that he saw politics in ideological terms, but he always denied this and there is little evidence in his behaviour as president to support such an argument. There is evidence to support the arguments of Erwin Hargrove that Carter was non-ideological, dealing with each policy on its merits.[14] This was reinforced by Carter's belief that as president he better represented the public good than both interest groups and even members of congress. His early communication strategy of town hall meetings and radio phone-ins also supported a 'Trustee' approach as espoused by Charles Jones;[15] however, it should be noted that the administration's strategy of reaching out directly to the public, known as the 'People Programme', was largely abandoned by the end of 1978.

Carter believed that no matter how complex the problem there was a solution that could transcend 'normal' politics and gain public support. He was as president dedicated to delivering a solution on policy that was comprehensive, simple and easy to sell to the public. It often resulted in Carter attempting to integrate opposite views on policy rather than transcend them, but this approach, with its focus on solutions, was consistent with his engineering background. In the 1976 election Carter argued that he was neither conservative nor liberal, and that he took policy positions that 'to me are fair and rational'.[16] As president he saw policy issues in technical terms and perceived his role as ensuring that 'a good process open and comprehensive would provide wide ranging policy options, the best of which would prevail on the strengths of their merits'.[17] To Carter the process of study and rational argument with experts, not interest groups, to enable him to provide the best solution was much more important than ideology. This idea of a technocratic presidency proved impossible to operate in practice.

To many politicians facing a national audience, the straddling of the ideological divide by taking a neutral stance was often used as a tactic to increase support, but with Carter this was a central belief. This lack of a core ideology or guiding belief other than his faith caused Carter major difficulties. Historians and former White House staff remain divided on Carter's ideology with a range of labels being associated with his presidency from conservative to liberal, populist, neo-liberal Democrat and even conservative liberal. The need to define Carter ideologically has resulted in him also being linked with the New Democrats of the 1990s, most recently by Eizenstat.[18] This Third Way approach was an attempt by members of the Democratic Party to frame policy that responded to the decline of the New Deal coalition and a more conservative electorate. Some of Carter's policies certainly reflected this, his fiscal conservativism in conjunction with being socially liberal. However, Carter saw policy only in terms of technical effectiveness and it being in line with his personal moral viewpoint. The idea that Carter would think in terms of an ideological framework is not born out by the evidence. To Carter policy represented a problem that required the best solution which had to be developed by experts without the 'encumbrance' of ideology. To a president trained as an engineer there was no such thing as a third way or middle way only a right way. The difficulty for Carter was that although he was clear about his non-ideological stance, this did not prevent others from trying to 'label' him during the 1976 campaign and subsequently when he was in office. This resulted in many misconceptions about his administration which hampered his effectiveness.

To the press and the public Carter was an enigma, and so during the 1976 campaign he was often criticized for being all things to all men. His attempt to deal with this perception of 'fuzziness' on issues partly prompted his misguided interview in *Playboy*. Attempts to frame him ideologically against his policy stances often resulted in confusion. A good example of this was on Civil Rights. Carter's inaugural address as governor of Georgia announced the 'end of segregation', and appeared to northern politicians to introduce a new liberal politician from the South to the national stage. Carter may have seemed to signify radical change – he certainly was not a George Wallace – but his speech merely confirmed the new realities and was as much a message for the North as for the South. His presidency did not bring any major changes in legislation or reform other than positively enforcing the law. Despite this approach, as his presidency developed, disputes over policy increasingly took on an ideological tone. Issues like healthcare and taxation were bellwether policies for liberals and conservatives respectively, with the Carter administration caught in the middle trying to reach consensus over the heads of both parties and interest groups.

Carter's non-ideological stance did not preclude him supporting some policies that could be labelled as such or from taking into account trends in public opinion. The strategic direction of his economic policy may have shifted in his early presidency, but he could still be described as a fiscal conservative. Equally he maintained a consistently liberal stance on issues such as women's rights, protecting the environment and, internationally, on human rights. He also recognized the conservative trend in the electorate on issues such as the need for a strong military and dissatisfaction with government inefficiency. This would often make him more comfortable with conservative members of congress than liberals, even though it was the latter who voted for him more frequently.[19] The major difficulty for Carter was that the Democratic Party had become more liberal and the party platforms in 1976 and particularly in 1980 did not fully reflect his own views on policy.

The consequence of Carter's non-ideological stance was that he became increasingly isolated from the ideological 'tides' that were polarizing America in the 1970s. Many of the social movements that supported him in 1976 had by 1980 become radicalized. Carter's chief weakness, as Hargrove put it, 'seems to have been an inability to appreciate the seriousness of the contradictions that confronted him, a belief that all good things must be compatible.'[20] To Carter, the rhetoric used by Phyllis Schlafly and Bella Abzug was equally incomprehensible. Nowhere was this demonstrated more than in his dealings with the Religious Right. He could not accept that this group were by 1978 a political force with strong conservative views. Their expectations of Carter as president were based on his 'born again' credentials but he refused to base his policies on their common faith. Carter's consistent refusal to stake out an ideological position led many to misunderstand his views and resulted in disappointment and often anger. The desertion of liberal voters to Anderson and evangelicals to Reagan in the 1980 election were good examples of this phenomenon. Carter's failure to recognize the political dangers of ideological conflict and what was to become his untenable position in a fast-shrinking political centre contributed to his defeat in 1980. A possible solution to this problem could have been found if Carter had mapped out a coherent vision for the future that linked all his policies. However, as one of his successors, George H. W. Bush, said of himself, he did not 'do the vision thing'. Jordan described Carter as 'having a curiosity about process not people … he doesn't understand the personal element of politics'.[21] Carter was wedded to a methodology where the right process delivered the best outcomes. Even if he were inclined to do so, Carter would have faced a major difficulty in articulating a coherent vision without exposing the ideological contradictions of his positions. So, if Carter's presidency cannot be described effectively in ideological terms, what was the impact of his character?

The historian Thomas Reeves in his study of President Kennedy asserted that a president needs a strong moral compass to be effective.[22] Other historians have used this argument to focus on flaws in the character and/or private lives of presidents such as Nixon and Clinton. But what would be the impact of a president with a strong moral character; would this enhance his presidency? To win the 1976 election, Carter promoted his suitability for the presidency by highlighting his good character. His emphasis on his faith, his promise 'to never lie' to the American public and to make the government work for the people perfectly suited the needs of an electorate at that time that mistrusted Washington politicians after Watergate and were concerned about 'big government'. Carter claimed that he would be a president who would always do the right thing for the American people and would provide rational solutions to that nation's problems that would not be influenced by 'selfish' interest groups. Carter often described the nation's problems in moral terms, one example being the energy challenge which he described as the 'moral equivalent of war'. Whilst he kept his religious beliefs separate from presidential decisions, his Baptist upbringing influenced his behaviour as president, particularly a sense of always doing the 'right thing'. Yet to pass legislation as president he had to overcome his reluctance to bargain with Congress. His wariness of interest groups, which he regarded with suspicion, extended to members of congress whom he believed were servants of the local as opposed to the national interest. His mistrust of the motives of such groups continued throughout his presidency and was even reflected in his Farewell Address.[23] In line with his engineering background, he believed that if the correct process were followed, the policy recommended would not only be the best solution but one which everyone would accept. Early in his administration he told cabinet members who were developing specific policies to ignore the political consequences of their proposals; he would deal with such issues. This was a naïve attitude that bemused and annoyed important congressional leaders.

Throughout his presidency Carter remained determined to do the right thing whatever the political consequences. His policy agenda, which included major complex legislation on energy, health and tax, could not be delivered even with a workable majority in Congress, which he rarely had. Eizenstat stated, 'He seemed sometimes to like going against the political grain to do what was right.'[24] This trait was seen in the way Carter took personal responsibility for policy failures rather than allowing his subordinates to take the blame. As his friend Bert Lance commented, because of this moral position, 'he never made a popular decision'.[25] It was also true that he never made a decision that was not carefully calculated and thought out. Carter presented an image of someone with strong moral beliefs who could be trusted but who could also deal with Washington politics, although that moral stance did appear to waiver at times. Carter's character, his strong moral position on issues, the perception of him being a good man remained his strongest political asset even in the dark days of 1980. However, there were other less positive character traits that damaged his effectiveness as president.

A pastor once asked Carter, when he first ran for the Georgia Senate, why he was getting into the 'sordid' world of politics. He answered, 'How would you like to be the pastor of a church with 80k members?'[26] His ambition and competitiveness overcame his distaste for operating 'in the hothouse of Washington … where politics is a contact sport'.[27] He had a keen sense of his self-image but not so much how others saw him. He was not above striking deals with members of congress or interest groups, particularly near election time. But his stubbornness did damage his effectiveness as president. For example, he continued to refuse any form of 'coaching' on improving his speaking style even though it could have made him a more effective speaker on television. He also became frustrated about his failure to persuade the public on his policies, especially on energy. This resulted in him developing a hectoring tone which appeared to blame his audience for policy failures. This trait extended to his dealings with politicians. Senators Jackson and Kennedy were known to 'grind their teeth' as they walked out of White House meetings, livid that Carter had talked down to them.[28]

Another one of Carter's traits was his pride in his abilities which at times bordered on arrogance. He argued that his rational approach to solving the country's most serious problems would result in the best solutions. This technocratic persona was established during the 1976 campaign when Carter chose not to exploit his military service as a naval officer on a nuclear submarine but to highlight from this experience his engineering and scientific background. This was a significant decision because he was giving up a major advantage as the only twentieth-century president who had longer military service than

Carter was Dwight D. Eisenhower. He became the candidate who would bring competence back to government, make it more efficient and eliminate waste. Like Reagan, Carter recognized the problems of 'big government' but retained his faith in it as a force for good. He believed that with reform the government would deliver better solutions for the country. The difficulty with the solutions that Carter sought to deliver was that they were complex and not easily the subject to change. His energy policy, for instance, could not sustain changes to any part of the legislation that were suggested by Congress because it would compromise the whole package. Carter was confident that he could gain public support by explaining these complex issues but often his powers of persuasion were found wanting. Also, his policies were attacked if not as a whole then piecemeal by interest groups who often used emotional and simplistic arguments that Carter found difficult to counteract. Ultimately the difficulty with emphasizing his competence as president was that to sustain this image, Carter had to demonstrate a legislative record of success and this he could not do.

Carter's effectiveness in Washington was hampered by his personal isolation in the White House. UK Prime Minister James Callaghan's political office described Carter in a briefing as 'admired and respected rather than loved … a rather distant calculating man'.[29] Elected as an outsider, Carter made little attempt to engage personally with the Washington elite. This would be in marked contrast with his successor. He did not like mixing with 'unsavoury politicians' and his wife talked of the disdain he had for the social engagements expected of him as president.[30] His solitary nature was part of his character. It was reflected in his failure to attend Navy reunions[31] and even his current detachment from other former presidents.[32] His decision-making process invariably had him reading documents on his own. He was a loner in a highly social profession. All of this limited his ability to influence key opinion makers in Washington.

In the 1976 election Carter highlighted elements of his background and character to gain public support. His emphasis on his morality, his faith and his competence were exactly what the American public wanted from their presidential candidates after the trauma of Vietnam and Watergate. Carter may have emphasized some elements of his character and background over others, for example, scientist over military, but he was clear about who he was, and this did not change during his presidency. Character traits that were strengths on the campaign trail were not necessarily as effective when he was in government. His belief that campaigning was a positive political activity, whilst deal-making in government with politicians and interest groups after the election was somehow tawdry, limited his ability to legislate. For a modern president moral character is not enough to be successful; a high level of political skill is also necessary. Carter, as a moral exemplar, fitted the public need in 1976 but the American public required something different in 1980. The electorate wanted clear simple answers to the nation's problems and a positive vision of the future. They had grown tired of the explanations of the complexity of problems and the calls for self-sacrifice. They wanted to see their lives improved after four years. For Carter to 'sell' that message would require not only changes in policy but also a level of pragmatism that would have been out of character from someone who remained unchanged in his core beliefs throughout his presidency. Carter saw the presidency as an opportunity for him to provide rational solutions that would solve the underlying problems faced by the United States. He did not feel constrained by ideology or the need to satisfy interest groups because he believed that he had the character, skills and detailed knowledge to convince the public that he would find the right solutions. To Carter being right was everything but 'often being president is about more than being right'.[33] He chose to address such substantive issues as energy and healthcare which required a presidential leadership that was transformational. He needed to be able to change public opinion and have the practical skills to persuade an ideologically divided Congress to pass key legislation. Reagan proved he had those skills; Carter didn't.

Changes in the political, economic and social environment of the 1970s had an impact on Carter's presidency. For Carter very few of these factors were favourable to him. The power of his office since Watergate had been constrained by the legislature. He inherited a Congress that was jealous of its powers and governed by a new complex committee structure that made the legislative process unwieldy. To achieve success, he had to be able to sell his policies to the public and negotiate with senior members of congress. This was to prove a major problem for Carter. His ability to reach out to the public was limited by his uninspiring rhetoric on television and the cynicism of both public and press. He was further affected by the fragmentation of the old New Deal coalition in the Democratic Party and the rise of conservative sentiment across the country. This created a vacuum that was filled by well-funded interest groups which by their nature took a narrow position on political issues. Carter's refusal to create an overall vision for his policies made it very difficult for him to build a base of support in Congress and in the country.

Another major factor which Carter inherited was the weakness of the economy. He was the first modern Democratic president to operate under the restriction of very low growth and had to face oil price rises that drove up inflation. 'Stagflation' was a new problem for America and one to which his neo-Keynesian economic advisors had no effective solution. As well as all these factors over which Carter had little or no control, any new president would need at least some luck. Carter had none. As Robert Strauss, the chair of Carter's 1980 campaign committee, colourfully said: 'Poor bastard, he used up all his luck getting here. We've had our victories and defeats, but we've not had a single piece of luck.'[34] His term of office saw the oil price rises, the Soviet invasion of Afghanistan and above all else the hostage crisis in Tehran. Whilst Carter was hindered by the environment in which he operated he was by no means helpless and did have resources that could have given him the potential to deliver a credible programme. Yet one of the consequences of Carter's ideological neutrality was that he created expectations on both sides of the ideological divide, conservative evangelicals being a case in point. He was further restricted by his failure to articulate a prioritized agenda supported by a vision of what he was attempting to achieve for the country. His legislative proposals were trying to address either serious underlying problems such as energy and healthcare which were difficult to pass or technical issues like deregulation and government reform which, although more straightforward, excited very little public interest.

The perception of a president's record, particularly in terms of domestic policy, is judged by their ability to pass legislation, but as Hargrove asked: 'When less skilful leaders lack political support, is the failure due to limited skills or to political circumstances?'[35] Carter did make mistakes in his legislative strategy, especially on prioritization and his management of relationships, but his scope for achieving reforms was limited by the ideological and regional divide in Congress. The public perception of Carter in 1979, as demonstrated by Caddell's polling data, was that he had no major achievements domestically but there was a general view that no one could have done any better, particularly on the economy. This was not a compelling recommendation for a politician who stood in 1976 on his competence, his ability to deliver solutions. In the 1980 election Carter did not substantively defend his domestic record and even his memoirs focus mainly on foreign policy. Carter could not point to a domestic policy equivalent of a Middle East Peace deal. But in discussing such failures as healthcare and welfare reform, consideration should be given to the policy failures of later Democratic presidents who benefitted from much greater congressional support.

The limits on presidential power in the 1970s meant that to be successful any new president had to be able to reach out and persuade the American public and deal effectively with key congressional politicians and interest groups. The support of a Democratic Party would have been helpful to the president but as early as June 1977 Rafshoon was describing the Democratic National Committee as a 'foreign power'.[36] To enable Carter to be successful he needed not only the right personal skill set but to have the support of a well-run White House organization. There were many criticisms of the early Carter administration. These included a congressional liaison which had been under resourced, confused policy coordination and the inexperience of the Georgians he brought with him to Washington. This criticism was largely unfair and often tinged with anti-southern snobbery from the Washington elite. As with many new administrations, Carter's took time to adjust but certainly by 1978 the White House was operating well as subsequent comments from former staff bear out. As the quality and the experience of staff improved, units like congressional liaison, the press office and especially outreach became highly effective, and as a result some of their roles and processes were to be replicated by subsequent administrations. This was despite the continuing perception in Washington that Carter and his staff were outsiders. This view was fuelled by the reluctance of the Carter team to engage personally with Washington society. One Carter decision that did have a significant legacy was the role played by the vice president. The trust and the formal responsibilities given by Carter to Walter Mondale became the benchmark for subsequent politically active vice presidents like Al Gore, Dick Cheney and Joe Biden. Also, though to a lesser extent, the role of Rosalynn Carter became the model for the politically active First Lady, Hillary Clinton. Whilst Carter's White House organization became more effective in supporting his policy initiatives, it was still dependent upon the president's decision-making and ability to persuade the American public and key politicians of the wisdom of his policies.

Carter was a highly intelligent, self-disciplined president who worked extremely hard. He was often criticized for being indecisive and too involved in the detail, but this was based upon a misunderstanding of his leadership style and how he absorbed information. It was the case that he wanted to understand the detail of policy, believing this analysis or homework would enable him to balance conflicting views. He was comfortable with complexity but needed to understand the detail so he could come to a rational decision and explain it to the public. Carter's preferred method of assimilating information was reading. He was intelligent enough to understand technical detail and his skill at speed reading meant that he digested large documents quickly. The assumption that these substantial policy papers were examples of Carter's inability to delegate and delayed his decision making was erroneous. It was ironic that his successor, Ronald Reagan, was to be criticized for making major policy decisions on single page memoranda. It is true that early in his administration there were examples of Carter commenting upon minor even obscure issues, but this dramatically declined after his first year. There were few, if any, of his major policies that Carter did not fully delegate to his cabinet whom he expected to use their expertise to deliver the best solution. Where meetings on policy took place that did involve him, they were more often than not called by cabinet members or his staff because they wanted more guidance. Indeed, Mondale believed that he delegated too much.[37] Despite the marked contrast between Reagan and Carter in the policy papers they received neither man spent much time in the development of their policies. Despite press criticism Carter was not indecisive. Jordan rather colourfully commented that 'anyone who watched him operate knows that he is a mean son of a bitch. The one thing he is not is indecisive'.[38]

Carter, however, made errors in his approach to legislation which demonstrated both a lack of understanding of how Washington operated and a general naivety. He did not have a structured agenda which was essential to pass legislation. This was despite the efforts of his staff to provide one and the efforts of Mondale to help him. The result of this was his legislative programme was stuck in Congress and under the control of congressional leaders whom he was unable to influence. He might have been more successful if he were more effective in persuading the American public and building coalitions to support his programmes, but this would prove to be his greatest political weakness.

Historians have analysed the skills needed for presidents to be successful leaders. Many have focused upon the importance of a president's ability to persuade the public and senior politicians to support them. Carter was an excellent campaigner and highly effective in interactive environments like press conferences, town hall meetings and radio phone-ins. Yet his speeches in set piece environments such as television were not persuasive. His speaking style often came across as 'holier than thou' and his messages of sacrifice failed to inspire the public. By April 1979 even Carter had recognized that his television addresses were not working. Rafshoon and the speechwriting team attempted to compensate for this weakness by trying to manage his message and the communications channels he used but this was criticized as media manipulation by the press. Carter stubbornly resisted attempts to persuade him to articulate a vision for his administration that linked his programmes together and could be communicated to the public. His message of rational but complex policies could not be sold to a public that craved simple solutions and a positive vision for the future. This rhetorical deficit became a major issue when Carter faced

Ronald Reagan in 1980 because Reagan's message provided a clear, simple and optimistic vision for America.

Carter had many of the skills required to be a successful president. He had intelligence, a strong work ethic and, after some early problems, a strong organization to support him. He often made bold decisions but his inability to persuade his audience, be it the public or members of congress, was a major weakness as a leader. A change in speaking style and creating a vision he simply did not have was never an option for a stubborn man proud of his southern heritage and convinced that he was proposing the best policies for the country. Facing someone with the rhetorical ability of Reagan, Carter was always going to be at a disadvantage, but it was difficult if not impossible to run an effective campaign when his domestic record as president delivered few positive achievements and the economy was in such a poor state.

Jimmy Carter is currently viewed by historians as a 'below average' president. In the C-Span survey of 2021, Carter was ranked twenty-sixth out of forty-three and below every post-war president except Richard Nixon and George W. Bush.[39] His successor influenced his immediate legacy. His heavy defeat to Ronald Reagan was followed by what was widely regarded as two successful terms of office, and the dismantling of many of Carter's policies. Reagan is ranked ninth in the same survey. Confusion over the ideological significance of his administration has also affected Carter's rating. Conservatives and liberals criticized him severely for failing to deliver on their agendas, even though Carter did not ever endorse these programmes in their entirety. He therefore suffered and has continued to suffer for his insistence on what he regarded as a rational, non-ideological approach to policy. His record in terms of domestic policy, whilst containing both major and minor achievements, was largely unsuccessful in comparison with the ambitious programme he set out in 1976. It would be difficult to argue, however, that this was entirely due to Carter's personal failings. The political environment inside Congress and in the nation was not amenable to Carter's remedies for the nation's ills. His failure to prioritize and his inability to persuade his audience did not help but it could equally be argued that he was unlucky with crises that he faced that were beyond his control. His election in 1976 was a major personal victory but it would be difficult to envisage Carter winning at any other time. What was required for victory in 1976 had changed in 1980, and Carter was far too moral a man and, truth be told, too stubborn to change his policies and his image to challenge Reagan effectively.

Carter's declining years and the change in the political climate in the run-up to the 2020 election signalled a more positive view of Carter and his presidency. Whilst his position in the 2021 C-Span Presidential Survey remains low overall there has been a marked improvement in historians' view of his position under the category 'Moral Authority' from fourteenth to seventh.[40] The post-revisionist historians such as Alter have focused on his personal skills, calling him 'frighteningly competent',[41] his morality and his prescience over policies such as Health and the Environment. However, whilst his reputation may, indeed should, improve in relation to other presidents, analysis of his record domestically should not change his position dramatically. His undoubted personal capability and his successful post-presidency should not hide his weaknesses, in particular his failure to persuade both Congress and the American people to support him.

A post-revisionist interpretation of Carter is overdue, and this book supports the claim that many of Carter's achievements have been underrated; also, that some of the criticism of his failures has been unfair given the environment in which he operated. However, there is a risk of historians being seduced by the 'afterglow' of Carter's post-presidency and favourable comparison with the Trump administration. This can result in insufficient weight being given to the opportunities that he missed to achieve a more substantive legacy. President Biden's engagement with Carter has already resulted in the GOP making unfavorable comparisons with Biden's policy failures, particularly on inflation.[42] It highlights how the negative view of Carter's presidency has persisted in the public mind. Despite his achievements in office there were errors of judgement which often were the result of Carter's character flaws and political failings. These included his failure to engage effectively with key politicians in Congress, his reluctance to prioritize legislation for an already overloaded legislature and his unwillingness to articulate a clear vision for the country. Carter's belief that policy developed by independent experts would be accepted by Congress and the public bore no relationship to the realities of US politics in the 1970s, let alone politics today.

This book concludes that some of Carter's difficulties with the political elite, interest groups and the media arose from their misunderstanding of who he was and how he thought. His refusal to accept a 'label' often resulted in an inaccurate picture of the ideological orientation of his policies. This misleading portrayal resulted in expectations that Carter could or would not fulfil and consequently an adverse reaction from a wide range of groups which felt his action or often inaction represented a betrayal of their values. This misreading of Carter extended to myths about his leadership style. Descriptions of a president who was mired in policy detail and indecisive are not supported by the evidence. In his domestic policies he delegated widely on all key issues except energy and made difficult decisions throughout his term in office. From this point of view, a new understanding of Carter is required. Nevertheless, whatever his qualities, history should come to regard Jimmy Carter as a good, possibly even a great man but never better than an average president. Whatever his personal qualities and the difficult challenges he faced, Carter's overall record in domestic policy was more disappointing than successful.

Notes

Preface

1   Burton Kaufman and Scott Kaufman, *The Presidency of James Earl Carter* (Lawrence: University of Press of Kansas, 2006).

2   Kaufman and Kaufman, *The Presidency of James Earl Carter* and Haynes Johnson, *In the Absence of Power. Governing America* (New York: Viking, 1980).

3   Fred Greenstein, *The Presidential Difference: Leadership Style from FDR to George W Bush* (Princeton: Princeton University Press, 2004); John P Burke, *Presidential Transitions: From Politics to Practice* (Boulder: Lynne Rienner, 2000); James Pfiffner, *The Modern Presidency* (Boston: Wadsworth Engage Learning, 2008) and Richard Neustadt, *Presidential Power, and the Modern Presidents. The Politics of Leadership from Roosevelt to Reagan* (New York: Free Press, 1990).

4   Stuart Eizenstat, 'President Carter, the Democratic Party, and the Making of Domestic Policy', in Herbert Rosenbaum and Alex Ugrinsky, eds, *The Presidency and Domestic Policy of Jimmy Carter* (Westport: Greenwood, 1994), 15.

5   John Dumbrell, *The Carter Presidency: A Re-evaluation* (Manchester: Manchester University Press, 1993).

6   M Glen Abernathy, Dilys M Hill and Phil Williams, *The Carter Years: The President and Policy Making* (London: Frances Pinter, 1984).

7   Erwin Hargrove, *Jimmy Carter as President: Leadership and Politics of the Public Good* (London: Louisiana State University Press, 1988).

8   Jonathan Alter, *His Very Best. Jimmy Carter. A Life* (New York: Simon and Schuster, 2020); Kai Bird, *The Outlier. The Unfinished Presidency of Jimmy Carter* (New York: Crown, 2021) and Nancy Mitchell, *Jimmy Carter in Africa. Race and the Cold War* (Washington DC: Stanford University Press, 2016).

9   Frye Gaillard, *Prophet from Plains* (Athens: University of Georgia Press, 2007), 15.

10 Thomas Reeves, *A Question of Character: A Life of John F Kennedy* (New York: Collier Macmillan, 1991).

Chapter 1

1   https://www.youtube.com/watch?v=bwykRTPJwoI

2   Alter, *His Very Best*, 199.

3   Jimmy Carter, *Why Not the Best? Presidential Edition* (Eastbourne: Kingsway, 1977).

4   Peter Bourne and Jimmy Carter, *A Comprehensive Biography from Plains to the Presidency* (New York: Scribner, 1997), 77.

5   Patrick Anderson, *Electing Jimmy Carter. The Campaign of 1976* (Baton Rouge: Louisiana State University Press, 1994), 93–4.

6   James A Speer, 'Jimmy Carter Was a Baptist President', in Rosenbaum and Ugrinsky, *Presidency and Domestic Policy of Jimmy Carter*, 88–92.

7   Stuart Eizenstat Interview, *Miller Center*, 4–5.

8   *Governor Carter's Inaugural Address*, 12 January 1971, https://www. jimmycarterlibrary.gov/assets/documents/inaugural_address_gov.pdf

9   Gary Fink, *Prelude to the Presidency. The Political Character and Legislative Style of Jimmy Carter* (Westport: Greenwood, 1980), 177.

10 Bert Lance Interview, *Miller Center*, 14.

11 Fink, *Prelude to the Presidency*, 35–42.

12 Ibid., 75 and 117.

13 Betty Glad, *Jimmy Carter. In Search of the Great White House* (New York, London: WW Norton and Company, 1980), 205.

14 Lance Interview, *Miller Center*, 25.

15 Jimmy Carter Interview, *Miller Center*, 47 and Jimmy Carter, *Government as Good as Its People* (New York: Simon and Schuster, 1977), 49.

16 Carter, *Why Not the Best?*

17 Address Announcing Candidacy for the Democratic Presidential Nomination at the National Press Club, 12 December 1974, *APP*.

18 Jerry Jasinowski, 'The First Two Years of the Carter Administration: An Appraisal', *PSQ*, Vol. 9: 11–15.

19 Carter, *Government as Good as Its People*, 45.

20 Peter N Carroll, *It Seemed like Nothing Happened. The Tragedy and the Promise of the 1970s* (New York: Holt Pritchard and Rinehart, 1982), 206–11.

21 Ibid., 235.

22 Mark Rozell, *The Press and Carter Presidency* (Boulder, London: Westview, 1989), 4.

23 Eric Davis, 'Legislative Reform and the Decline of Presidential Influence on Capitol Hill', *British Journal of Political Science*, Vol. 8: 465–77.

24 Comments by James C Free, in Rosenbaum and Ugrinsky, *Presidency and Domestic Policy of Jimmy Carter*, 318.

25 Nelson Polsby, *Consequences of Party Reform* (Oxford: Oxford University Press, 1983), 34–5.

26 Ibid., 54–9 and 61.

27 Leslie Wheeler, *Jimmy Who? An Examination of Presidential Candidate Jimmy Carter: The Man, His Career, His Stands on the Issues* (New York: Barron's Woodbury, 1976), 96.

28   Bruce J Schulman, *The Seventies. The Great Shift in American Culture, Society and Politics* (Cambridge: Da Capo Press, 2001), 212.

29   Daniel Horowitz, *Jimmy Carter, and the Energy Crisis of the 1970s. The Crisis of Confidence Speech of 15 July 1979* (Boston: Bedford/St Martins, 2005), 5.

30   Schulman, *The Seventies*, 151.

31   Carroll, *It Seemed like Nothing Happened*, 187–8.

32   Robert Shogan, *Promises to Keep. Carter's First One Hundred Days* (New York, London: Crowell and Company, 1977), 30.

33   E Stanley Godbold, *Jimmy, and Rosalyn Carter. The Georgia Years 1924–1974* (Oxford: Oxford University Press, 2010), 227–8.

34   William Leuchtenburg, *Shadow of FDR. From Harry Truman to Barak Obama* (Ithaca, London: Cornell University Press, 2009), 177–8.

35   Reo Christenson, 'Carter and Truman. A Reappraisal of Both', *PSQ*, Vol. 13: 313–23.

36   Clark Clifford, *Counsel to the President* (New York: Random House, 1991), 620.

37   Dom Bonafede, 'The Carter White House: The Shape Is There but No Specifics', *National Journal*, 25 December 1976.

38   Shogan, *Promises to Keep*, 43.

39   Iwan Morgan, 'Jimmy Carter, Bill Clinton, and New Democratic Economics', *Historical Journal*, Vol. 47: 1015–39.

40   Press Cartoons, Jody Powell Subject Files, Box 56, *JCPL*.

41   Eizenstat, 'Democratic Party and Domestic Policy', 6.

42   Jimmy Carter, *Keeping Faith: Memoirs of a President* (New York: Bantam, 1982), 102.

43   Clifford, *Counsel to the President*, 618.

44   Leo P Ribuffo, 'Jimmy Carter and the Selling of the President 1976–1980', in Rosenbaum and Ugrinsky, *Presidency and Domestic Policy of Jimmy Carter*, 144.

45   Address Announcing Candidacy for the Democratic Presidential Nomination at the National Press Club, 12 December 1974, *APP*.

46   Anderson, *Electing Jimmy Carter*, 2.

47   'Man of the Year: Hello I Am Jimmy Carter and …', *Time* Magazine, 3 January 1977.

48   Peter Meyer, *James Earl Carter. Man, and the Myth* (Kansas City: Sheed, Andrews and McNeil, 1978), 146–8.

49   Zbigniew Brzezinski, *Power and Principle: Memoirs of a National Security Advisor* (New York: Farrar, Strauss and Giroux, 1983), 21–2.

50   Hargrove, *Carter as President*, 1–12.

51   Ribuffo, 'Selling of a President', 144–5.

52   Colin Campbell, *Managing the Presidency: Carter, Reagan, and the Search for Executive Harmony* (London: University of Pittsburgh Press, 1986), 60.

53   Andrew Melman, Jimmy Hoover, *NYT*, 7 February 1979.

54   Jack Knott and Aaron Wildavsky, 'Jimmy Carter's Theory of Governing',
     The Wilson Quarterly (1976–), Vol. 1: 46–67.

55   For influence of Carter the engineer, see above.

56   Sean P Cunningham, *American Politics in the Post War Sunbelt: Conservative
     Growth in a Battleground Region* (New York: Cambridge University Press,
     2014), 174.

57   David L Holmes, *The Faiths of Post War Presidents: From Truman to Obama*
     (Athens: University of Georgia Press, 2012), 162–6.

58   Randall Balmer, *Redeemer. The Life of Jimmy Carter* (New York: Basic Books,
     2014), 41.

59   Carter Interview *Playboy Magazine,* November *1976.*

60   Bert Lance with Bill Gilbert, *The Truth of the Matter. My Life in and out of Politics*
     (New York: Summit Books, 1992), 40.

61   Rafshoon to Carter, 25 July 1978, Presidential Files, Staff Secretary (SS)
     Box 86, JCPL.

62   Eizenstat, 'Democratic Party and Domestic Policy', 5–6.

63   Lloyd Cutler Interview, *Miller Center,* 18.

64   Jules Witcover, *Marathon – Pursuit of the Presidency 1972–76* (New York: Viking,
     1977), 114–15.

65   Carl Biven, *Jimmy Carter's Economic Policy in the Age of Limits* (Chapel Hill,
     London: University of North Carolina Press, 2002), 17.

66   Bourne, *Plains to the Presidency,* 201.

67   Ibid., 255.

68   Gregory Domin, *Jimmy Carter – Public Opinion and the Search for Values
     1977–1981* (Macon: Mercer University Press, 2003), 16.

69   Witcover, *Marathon,* 118.

70   Garland Haas, *Jimmy Carter, and the Politics of Frustration* (London: McFarland,
     1992), 46.

71   Dixie Whistles a Different Tune, *Time,* 31 May 1971.

72   Kaufman and Kaufman, *Presidency of James Earl Carter,* 11–12.

73   Polsby, *Consequences of Party Reform,* 204.

74   Witcover, *Marathon,* 110–14.

75   Ibid., 212.

76   Drew, *American Journal,* 271.

77   Charles O Jones, *Trustee President. Jimmy Carter and the United States Congress*
     (Baton Rouge, London: Louisiana State University Press, 1988), 19.

78   Anderson, *Electing Jimmy Carter,* 65.

79   http://www.livingroomcandidate.org/commercials/1976

80   Carter, *Government as Good as Its People.*

81   Ibid.

82 Andrew Downer Crain, *The Ford Presidency. A History* (Jefferson: McFarland, 2009), 272.

83 Ibid., 272–5.

84 Address Accepting the Presidential Nomination at the Democratic National Convention in New York City, July 1976, *APP*.

85 Presidential Debate, 23 September 1976, *APP*.

86 Michael G Krukones, 'Campaigner and President: Jimmy Carter's Campaign Promises and Presidential Performance', in Rosenbaum and Ugrinsky, *Presidency and Domestic Policy of Jimmy Carter*, 141.

87 Paul Light, *The President's Agenda: Domestic Policy Kennedy – Clinton* (Baltimore, London: Johns Hopkins University Press, 1999), 98.

88 Kandy Stroud, *How Jimmy Won. The Victory Campaign from Plains to the White House* (New York: William Morrow, 1977), 432.

89 Drew, *American Journal*, 476–7.

90 Anderson, *Electing Jimmy Carter*, 99.

91 Schulman, *The Seventies*, 124.

92 Jonathan Moore and Janet Fraser, eds, *Campaign for President: Managers Look at '76. Proceedings of a Conference on the 1976 Presidential Campaign Decision Making* (Cambridge: Ballinger Publishing, 1977), 5.

93 Carter, *A Government as Good as Its People*, 165.

94 Eizenstat Speech, 17 November 1977, SS Box 54, *JCPL*.

95 Stephen Hess, *Organizing the Presidency* (Washington DC: Brookings Institution Press, 2002), 123.

Chapter 2

1 Inaugural Address of President Jimmy Carter, 20 January 1977, *APP*.

2 Alter, *His Very Best*, 298.

3 William Safire, Pedestrian Inaugural, *New York Times,* 24 January 1977.

4 Address Announcing Candidacy for the Democratic Presidential Nomination at the National Press Club, 12 December 1974, *APP*.

5 Ibid.

6 Ribuffo, 'Selling the President', 141 (Carter had 51 positions in campaign and 186 separate pledges).

7 Reinhold Neibuhr, Theologian (1892–1971).

8 Carter, *Keeping Faith*, 65.

9 Lance, *Truth of the Matter,* 127–8.

10 Hedrick Smith, *The Power Game: How Washington Works* (New York: Ballentine Books, 1988), 339.

11 Mondale to Carter, 27 March 1978, SS Box 69 and 3 January 1979, SS Box 102, *JCPL*.

12 Esther Peterson and Winifred Conkling, *Restless: The Memoirs of Labor and Consumer Activists* (Washington DC: Caring Publishing, 1995), 256.

13 Agenda update, 9 January 1978, SS Box 58, *JCPL*.

14 James Giglio, *The Presidency of John F Kennedy* (Lawrence: University Press of Kansas, 2006), 99.

15 Rafshoon to Carter, 10 November 1978, SS Box 97 and Mondale to Carter, 21 November 1978, SS Box 97, *JCPL*.

16 Jordan to Carter, 21 November 1978, SS Box 52, *JCPL*.

17 Jimmy Carter, *White House Diaries* (New York: Picador, 2010), 24.

18 Carter to Rex Scouten, 5 March 1977, SS Box 10, Carter to Staff, 29 September 1977, SS Box 44 and Carter to Greg Schneiders 11 February 1977, SS Box 7, *JCPL*.

19 James Fallows, 'The Passionless President', *Atlantic Monthly* (May 1979), 75–81.

20 Carter, *Diaries*, 39 and 60.

21 Hamilton Jordan, *Crisis: The Last Years of the Carter Presidency* (New York: Michael Joseph, 1982), 42.

22 Harrison Welford, 'Staffing the Presidency; an Insider's Comments', *Political Science Quarterly*, Vol. 93: 10–12.

23 Kenneth J Thompson, *The Carter Presidency. Fourteen Intimate Perspectives of Jimmy Carter* (Lanham, MD: University Press of America, 1990), 214.

24 Bert Carp Interview, *Miller Center*, 26 and 68–9.

25 Eizenstat, 'Democratic Party and Domestic Policy', 5–6.

26 Powell to Carter, 21 July 1977 SS Box 35, *JCPL*.

27 Carter to Sarah McClendon, 20 September 1977, SS Box 42, *JCPL*.

28 Bruce Mazlish and Edwin Diamond, *Jimmy Carter. A Character Portrait* (New York: Simon and Schuster, 1979), 236.

29 Carl Brauer, *Presidential Transitions: Eisenhower to Reagan* (New York: Oxford University Press, 1986), 180–1.

30 James W Riddlesperger Jr and James D King, 'Political Constraints, Leadership Style, and Temporal Limits: The Administration of Jimmy Carter', in Rosenbaum and Ugrinsky, *Presidency and Domestic Policy of Jimmy Carter*, 357.

31 Bourne, *Plains to the Presidency*, 358.

32 Burke, *Presidential Transitions*, 37.

33 Kaufman and Kaufman, *Presidency of James Earl Carter*, 29.

34 Eizenstat to Carter, December 1976, SS Box 3, *JCPL*.

35 Stuart Eizenstat, *President Carter: The White House Years* (New York: St Martin's Press, 2018), 103.

36 Knott and Wildavsky, *Theory of Governing*, 53.

37   Lance Interview, *Miller Center,* 41–2.

38   Alonzo McDonald Interview, *Miller Center, 106.*

39   Bourne, *Plains to the Presidency,* 272.

40   Carter Interview, *Miller Center,* 8–9. Note: Sherman Adams worked for Eisenhower, Bob Haldeman for Nixon both as chief of staff.

41   Dumbrell, *Carter Presidency,* 31–2.

42   Michael Nelson, ed, *The Presidency and the Political System* (Washington DC: Congressional Quarterly Inc, 1988), 163.

43   Robert Lipshutz to Carter, 31 March 1977, SS Box 13, *JCPL.*

44   James McIntyre Interview, *Miller Center,* 6.

45   Gene Eidenberg, *Jimmy Carter Library Exit Interview Project,* 13, *JCPL.*

46   Eizenstat Interview, *Miller Center,* 27.

47   Carter, *Keeping Faith,* 35.

48   Thompson, *Fourteen Intimate Perspectives,* 122.

49   Carter, *Keeping Faith,* 49.

50   Phil Walden to Carter, 18 December 1976, SS Box 1, *JCPL.*

51   Carter to Califano, 27 January 1978, SS Box 60, *JCPL.*

52   Carter, *Diaries,* 344.

53   Jordan Interview, *Miller Center,* 33.

54   Mondale to Carter, 11 February 1977, SS Box 7, *JCPL.*

55   Carter to Cabinet, 27 April 1977, Powell, Box 39, *JCPL.*

56   Copy of Post Article, 6 April 1977, Chief of Staff, Box 33, *JCPL.*

57   Jordan to Carter, April 1978, Chief of Staff, Box 33, *JCPL.*

58   Eizenstat to Carter, 2 September 1977, SS Box 40, *JCPL.*

59   Carter to Staff, 24 January 1978, Chief of Staff, Box 37, *JCPL.*

60   Landon Butler Interview, *Miller Center,* 6.

61   Anne Wexler Interview, *Miller Center,* 5–6.

62   Joseph Califano, *Governing America: An Insider's Report from the White House and the Cabinet* (New York: Simon and Schuster, 1981), 410.

63   *President's News* Conference, 30 November 1977, *APP.*

64   Jon R Bond and Richard Fleisher, 'Carter and Congress: Presidential Style, Party Politics, and Legislative Success', in Rosenbaum and Ugrinsky, *Presidency and Domestic Policy of Jimmy Carter,* 287–91.

65   Thompson, *Fourteen Intimate Perspectives,* 121.

66   Anne Wexler, Exit Interview, *JCPL,* 6.

67   Ibid., 75 and Clifford, *Counsel to the President,* 628.

68   Carter Interview, *Miller Center,* 19.

69   Eizenstat Interview, *Miller Center,* 21.

70   Anderson, *Electing Jimmy Carter,* 68.

71   Bird, *The Outlier,* 287.

72   Barbara Kellerman, 'Introversion in the Oval Office', *PSQ*, Vol. 13: 383–9.

73   All Quiet on the Potomac, *NYT*, 12 May 1977.

74   Eizenstat, *White House Years*, 112.

75   Jordan to Carter, April 1977, Chief of Staff, Box 34, *JCPL*.

76   Lance, *Truth of the Matter*, 112–13.

77   Lance Interview, *Miller Center*, 27 and Lance, *Truth of the Matter*, 98.

78   Lance to Carter, 21 September 1977, SS Box 43, *JCPL*.

79   Bird, *The Outlier*, 236.

80   Lance, *Truth of the Matter*, 103.

81   Eizenstat to Carter, 22 March 1978, SS Box 68, *JCPL*.

82   Carter, *Diaries*, 109.

83   Faye Lind Jensen, 'An Awesome Responsibility: Rosalyn Carter as First Lady', *PSQ*, Vol. 20, No. 4: 769–75.

84   Anne Wexler Interview, *Miller Center*, 63.

85   McIntyre Interview, *Miller Center*, 98–9.

86   McIntyre Interview, *Miller Center*, 11.

87   Califano, *Governing America*, 65–6.

88   Shirley Anne Warshaw, 'The Carter Experience with Cabinet Government' in Rosenbaum and Ugrinsky, *Presidency and Domestic Policy of Jimmy Carter*, 381–2.

89   Comments by James Free in Rosenbaum and Ugrinsky, *Presidency and Domestic Policy of Jimmy Carter*, 318.

90   Bob Bergland Interview, *Miller Center*, 39–40.

91   Brzezinski, *Power and Principle*, 521.

92   Kraft – Time Study, 2 June 1977, SS Box 24, *JCPL*.

93   Eizenstat Interview, *Miller Center*, 96–7.

94   President's News Conference, 29 May 1979, *APP*.

95   Charles O Jones, 'Carter and Congress: From the Outside in', *British Journal of Political Science*, Vol 15: 269–98.

96   Alter, *The Very Best*, 174.

97   Robert Mann, *Legacy to Power. Senator Russell Long of Louisiana* (New York: Paragon House, 1992), 360.

98   Douglas Brinkley, *Unfinished Presidency. Jimmy Carter's Journey beyond the White House* (New York, London: Penguin Books, 1998), 5–6.

99   Eizenstat, *White House Years*, 678–9.

100 Laura Kalman, *Right Star Rising: A New Politics, 1974–1980* (New York: WW Norton and Company, 2010), 210.

101 Alter, *The Very Best*, 328.

102 Bourne, *Plains to the Presidency*, 213.

103 Les Francis, *Exit Interview*, 10–11, *JCPL*.

104 Johnson, *Absence of Power*, 253–4.

105 Speer, 'Carter Was a Baptist President', 102–5.

106 Carter, *Diaries*, 75.

107 Democratic Majorities: House 292–143 and Senate 62–38.

108 Carter Interview, *Miller Center*, 7–8.

109 Frank Moore to Carter, December 1976, Plains File, Box 41, *JCPL*.

110 Carter, *Diaries*, 183.

111 Carter to O'Neill, 1 October 1979, Susan Clough File, Box 42, *JCPL*.

112 John Farrell, *Tip O'Neill, and the Democratic Century* (Boston, New York: Little Brown, 2001), 460–1 and 329.

113 Frank Moore Interview, *Miller Center*, 76.

114 Moore to Carter, 23 August 1977, Frank Moore, Office of Congressional Liaison, Box 19, *JCPL*.

115 Dan Tate to Carter, 18 April 1977, SS Box 15, *JCPL*.

116 Moore to Carter, 28 October 1980, Frank Moore, Box 37, *JCPL*.

117 Tate to Carter, 9 October 1978, SS Box 95, *JCPL*.

118 Glad, *In Search of the Great White House*, 421.

119 Moore to Carter, December 1976, Plains Files, Box 41, *JCPL* and Moore Interview, *Miller Center*, 29–30.

120 Jones, 'Carter and Congress', 269–98.

121 Moore Interview, *Miller Center*, 7.

122 Jones, 'Carter and Congress.'

123 *Washington Star* Article, 21 February 1977, SS Box 5, *JCPL* and *Congressional Weekly Report xxxv* no. 9, 26 February 1977: 361–3.

124 Moore, *Exit Interview*, 6–7, *JCPL*.

125 Moore Interview, 2-3k calls a day, *Miller Center*, 5–6.

126 Moore to Carter, 26 March 1977, SS Box 13, Tate to Moore, 29 July 1977, SS Box 34, Tate to Jordan, 29 September 1977, SS Box 45 and Carter note, 20 June 1977, SS Box 26, *JCPL*.

127 Califano, *Governing America*, 148.

128 Farrell, *Tip O'Neill*, 514–16 and Carter, *Diaries*, 209.

129 William F Mullen, 'Perceptions of Carter's Legislative Successes and Failures. Views from the Hill and Liaison Staff', *PSQ*, Vol. 12: 522–33.

130 Cabinet Minutes, 7 February 1977, SS Box 5, *JCPL*.

131 David Barber, *Race for the Presidency: The Media and the Nomination Process* (Englewood, New Jersey: Prentice Hall, 1978), 437.

132 Jones, 'Carter and Congress.'

133 *Congressional Weekly Report,* Vol 3, 3 February 1979: 195–200.

134 Moore Legislative Report, 18 March 1978, SS Box 68, *JCPL*.

135 Moore to Carter, 1 June 1977, SS Box 23, *JCPL*.

136   Moore to Carter, 30 March 1977, SS Box 13, *JCPL* and Moore Interview, *Miller Center*, 72.

137   Carp Interview, *Miller Center,* 70.

138   Moore to Carter, February 1978, Chief of Staff, Box 34, *JCPL.*

139   Carter, *Diaries,* 252.

140   Senators to Carter, 14 February 1977, Eizenstat, Box 315, *JCPL.*

141   Paul E Scheele, 'President Carter and the Water Projects: A Case Study in Presidential and Congressional Decision Making', *PSQ,* Vol. 8: 348–54.

142   Mann, *Legacy to Power,* 341.

143   Jeffrey K Stine, 'Environmental Policy during the Carter Presidency', in Gary Fink and Hugh Davis Graham, eds, *The Carter Presidency Policy Choices in the Post New Deal Era* (Lawrence: University of Kansas Press, 1998), 185–7.

144   Scheele, 'President Carter and the Water Projects', 348–54.

145   Scott A Frisch and Sean O'Kelly, *Jimmy Carter, and the Water Wars. Presidential Influence and the Politics of Pork* (Amherst: Cambria Press, 1981), 73.

146   Dumbrell, *Carter Presidency,* 40–1.

147   Carter to Powell, 25 February 1977, Powell, Box 39, *JCPL.*

148   Eizenstat to Carter, 20 June 1977, Eizenstat, Box 315, *JCPL* and Eizenstat Interview, *Miller Center,* 61.

149   Lance, *Truth of the Matter,* 114.

150   *WP* article, 9 January 1978, SS Box 91, *JCPL.*

151   Carter Interview, *ABC News,* 10 August 1977.

152   Carter, *Keeping Faith,* 105.

153   Mondale to Carter, 23 November 1977, Chief of Staff, Box 37, *JCPL.*

154   Mullen, 'Perception of Carter's Legislative Successes and Failures', 522–33.

155   Francis to Carter, 18 July 1977, SS Box 32, *JCPL.*

156   Speer, 'Carter was a Baptist President', 107.

157   Don Richardson, ed, *Conversations with Carter* (Boulder: Lynne Rienner, 1998), 28 December 1977, 148.

158   Bird, *The Outlier,* 110.

159   Barry Jagoda Papers, Donated Historical Materials, Box 5, October 1976 *JCPL.*

160   Richardson, *Conversations with Carter,* 17 October 1997.

161   Harold Barger, *The Impossible Presidency. Illusions and Realities of Executive Power* (Glenview: Scott, Foreman, 1984), 127.

162   Moore, *Carter Library Exit Interview Project,* 8, *JCPL.*

163   Lance, *Truth of the Matter,* 88–9 and Powell Interview, *Miller Center,* 84–5.

164   'Good Old Boy Network' article, 31 August 1977, SS Box 39, *JCPL.*

165   Mazlish and Diamond, *Character Portrait,* 181.

166   Thompson, *Fourteen Intimate Perspectives,* 68.

167   Carter Interview, *Playboy,* November 1976.

168 Carter, *Keeping Faith,* 131–3.

169 Carter, *Diaries,* 130.

170 Carter, *Keeping Faith,* 125.

171 Powell to Carter, 17 January 1978, SS Box 59 and Rafshoon to Carter, 25 August 1978, Box 90, *JCPL.*

172 Carter, *Diaries,* 192–3.

173 Hedley Donovan to Carter, 24 October 1979, SS Box 137, *JCPL.*

174 Carter, *Diaries*, 211.

175 'White House Staff Swells despite Carter's Pledge to Make Deep Cutbacks', *WP*, 31 March 1977, SS Box 13, *JCPL.*

176 Powell to Carter, 25 February 1977, SS Box 9, *JCPL.*

177 Robert Locander, 'Carter and the Press. The First Two Years', *PSQ*, Vol. 10: 106–20.

178 Powell to Carter, 14 December 1977, SS Box 55, *JCPL.*

179 Alter, *His Very Best*, 302.

180 Schneiders to Carter, 8 March 1977, SS Box 10, *JCPL.*

181 Cabinet Minutes, 21 March 1977, SS Box 12, *JCPL.*

182 Fallows, 'The Passionless President.'

183 Wexler, *Carter Library Exit Interview Project,* 4, *JCPL.*

184 Dan F Hahn, 'The Rhetoric of Jimmy Carter', *PSQ*, Vol. 14 (Part 2): 265–88.

185 Harold Holzer, *The President vs The Press* (New York: Dutton, 2020), 296.

186 Lance Interview, *Miller Center,* 7.

187 John Anthony Maltese, '"Rafshoonery": The Effort to Control the Communications Agenda of the Carter Administration' in Rosenbaum and Ugrinsky, *Presidency and Domestic Policy of Jimmy Carter,* 437–8.

188 Esther Peterson, *Exit Interview,* 8–9, *JCPL.*

189 Dumbrell, *Carter Presidency*, 213.

190 Ibid., 14. (One such joke was Carson as Carnac the Magnificent who held up the envelope to his head, divined the answer inside as 'Yes and no, pro and con, for and against' then opened the envelope and said, 'Describe Jimmy Carter's position on three major issues.')

191 Walt Wurfel, *Exit Interview,* 1–2, *JCPL.*

192 Ray Jenkins to Watson, 19 December 1980, Plains Box 116, *JCPL.*

193 Rafshoon to Carter, 19 July 1978, SS Box 85, *JCPL* and Rafshoon Interview, *Miller Center*, 27.

194 Jenkins Interview, *Miller Center,* 22.

195 Rafshoon, *Exit Interview,* 3, *JCPL.*

196 Powell Interview, *Miller Center,* 78.

197 Brinkley, *Unfinished Presidency*, x.

198 Wexler Interview, *Miller Center*, 60.

199 Rafshoon Interview, *Miller Center,* 13.

200 Ibid., 20.

201   Fallows, *Exit Interview,* 8–9, *JCPL.*

202   Ibid.

203   Carter to Rafshoon, 5 March 1979 SS Box 115N, *JCPL* and Robert Schlesinger, *White House Ghosts* (New York: Simon and Schuster, 2008), 86–7.

204   Rafshoon, *Carter Library Exit Interview Project,* 7, *JCPL.*

205   Alter, *His Very Best,* 306–7.

206   Carter Interview, *Playboy,* November 1976.

207   Gordon Stewart, *Exit Interview,* 10, *JCPL.*

208   Address to the Nation on Energy, 18 April 1977 and Anti-Inflation Program Address to the Nation, 24 October 1978, *APP.*

209   Fallows, 'The Passionless President.'

210   Carter, *Government as Good,* 8.

211   Article, 20 January 1979, Speechwriters Subject Files, Box 29, *JCPL* and President's News Conference, 26 January 1979, *APP.*

212   Barber, *Race for the Presidency,* 435.

213   Eizenstat, *White House Years,* 57.

214   Humphrey Memorial Speech, 15 July 1978, SS Box 58, *JCPL.*

215   Eizenstat to Carter, 29 April 1978, SS Box 74, *JCPL*, https://www.presidency.ucsb. edu/documents/los-angeles-california-remarks-the-100th-anniversary-luncheon-the-los-angeles-county-bar and https://www.presidency.ucsb.edu/documents/law-day-address-the-university-georgia-athens-georgia

216   Hahn, 'Rhetoric of Jimmy Carter', 265–8.

217   William Leuchtenberg, 'Jimmy Carter and the Post-New Deal Presidency', in Fink and Graham, *Carter Presidency,* 10.

218   Eizenstat, *White House Years,* 108.

219   Fallows, *Exit Interview, JCPL,* 13.

220   Rafshoon, *Exit Interview,* 9, *JCPL.*

Chapter 3

1   Address Accepting the Presidential Nomination at the Democratic National Convention, July 1976, *APP.*

2   Duane Windsor, 'Budget Strategy in the Carter Administration', in Rosenbaum and Ugrinsky, *Presidency and Domestic Policy of Jimmy Carter,* 393, Table 18.1.

3   Biven, *Carter's Economy,* 200–1.

4   Rick Perlstein, *Reaganland and America's Right Turn. 1976–1980* (New York: Simon and Schuster, 2020), 206.

5   Stuart Eizenstat, 'Economists and the White House Decisions', *Journal of Economic Perspectives* (Summer 1992): 65–71.

6　Biven, 'Economic Advice in the Carter Administration', in Rosenbaum and Ugrinsky, *Presidency and Domestic Policy of Jimmy Carter,* 616.

7　Hargrove, *Carter as President*, 97.

8　Perlstein, *Reaganland,* 280.

9　Biven, *Carter's Economy,* 126.

10　Charles Schultze Interview, *Miller Center,* 70.

11　Carter, *Keeping Faith,* 118.

12　Hugh Carter to Carter, Periodicals, 8 February 1977, SS Box 7, Travel Costs, Note to Department Heads, no date, SS Box 90 and Sale of Yacht, Hugh Carter to Carter, 23 March 1977, SS Box 13, *JCPL.*

13　Lance, *Truth of the Matter,* 112–13.

14　Jim McIntyre Interview, *Miller Center,* 42.

15　Eizenstat to Carter, 3 June 1977, SS Box 24 and Blumenthal to Carter, 15 June 1977, SS Box 27, *JCPL.*

16　Lance, *Truth of the Matter,* 59.

17　Schultze Interview, *Miller Center,* 14.

18　Schultze to Carter, 27 December 1977, SS Box 57, *JCPL.*

19　Personal Note, Schultze to Carter, no date SS Box 53, *JCPL.*

20　Carter, *Diaries,* 344.

21　Lance, *Truth of the Matter,* 108.

22　Briefing to Carter, no date, Eizenstat Box 257, *JCPL.*

23　Blumenthal to Carter, 14 March 1979, C of S Box 34, *JCPL.*

24　Carter Interview, *Miller Center,* 13–14.

25　Carter, *Diaries,* 345.

26　McIntyre Interview, *Miller Center,* 56.

27　Schultze Interview, *Miller Center,* 33.

28　McIntyre Interview, *Miller Center,* 44 and 24.

29　Draft memo to Carter, 20 September 1978, Eizenstat Box 155, *JCPL.*

30　Biven, *Carter's Economy,* 40–5.

31　EPG membership, SS Box 6, *JCPL.*

32　Schultze to Carter, 5 March 1977, Rafshoon Box 18, *JCPL.*

33　Jordan to Carter, 13 July 1977, C of S Box 37, *JCPL.*

34　McIntyre Interview, *Miller Center,* 35.

35　Carter Interview, *Miller Center,* 19–20.

36　McIntyre Interview, *Miller Center,* 98–9.

37　Eizenstat to Carter, 1 March 1980, SS Box 152, *JCPL.*

38　McIntyre Interview, *Miller Center,* 53–4.

39　Okun Speech to Brookings Institution, 6 October 1977, SS Box 49, *JCPL.*

40　Carter to Schultze, Lance and Blumenthal, 25 June 1977, SS Box 27, *JCPL.*

41　Briefing for Carter, 20 November 1976, SS Box 2 and Burns to Carter, 31 March 1977, SS Box 15, *JCPL.*

42   Eizenstat to JC, 13 August 1977, SS Box 36, *JCPL*.

43   Biven, *Jimmy Carter's Economy*, 237–42.

44   Schultze Interview, *Miller Center*, 40.

45   Appointing Lyle Gramley to Fed board, 13 February 1980, SS Box 151, *JCPL*.

46   Schultze to Carter, 11 April 1980, SS Box 158, *JCPL*.

47   Schultze to Carter, 25 September 1980, CEA Schultze Box 54, *JCPL*.

48   Mark A Peterson, *Legislating Together: The White House and Capitol Hill from Eisenhower to Reagan* (Cambridge, MA; London: Harvard University Press, 1990), 220–1.

49   *Congressional Weekly Report XXXV no. 37,* 10 September 1977: 1905–15.

50   Mann, *Legacy to Power*, 339.

51   Tate to Moore, 8 December 1977, SS Box 54, *JCPL*.

52   Mann, *Legacy to Power*, 368.

53   Ibid., 339–40.

54   Ibid., 358–9.

55   Califano, *Governing America*, 130.

56   Carp Interview, *Miller Center,* 37.

57   Abernathy, *Carter Years*, 36.

58   Schultze to Carter, November 1976, SS Box 1, *JCPL*.

59   Biven, *Carter's Economy*, 70.

60   Economic Recovery Program: Message to Congress, 31 January 1977 and Report to the American People; Remarks from the White House Library, 2 February 1977, *APP*.

61   Kaufman and Kaufman, *Presidency of James Earl Carter*, 37.

62   Jones, *Trustee President*, 130–4.

63   Eizenstat to Carter, 31 January 1977, SS Box 5, *JCPL*.

64   Blumenthal to Carter, 3 February 1977, SS Box 6, *JCPL*.

65   FM legislative report, 15 February 1977, SS Box 8, *JCPL*.

66   Eizenstat and Moore to all White House and Cabinet Staff, 24 February 1977, SS Box 9, *JCPL*.

67   Tate to Moore, 23 February 1977, *FM Box 50, JCPL*.

68   Moore report on ERP, 5 February 1977, SS Box 5, *JCPL*.

69   Schultze to Carter, 2 March 1977, SS Box 9 and Schultze to Carter, 18 March 1977, SS Box 14, *JCPL*.

70   Schultze briefing for Carter, 29 March 1977, SS Box 13, *JCPL*.

71   Tate to Carter, 5 April 1977, FM Box 80, *JCPL*.

72   Carter note to Senators, 6 April 1977, SS Box 10, *JCPL*.

73   Mondale to Carter, 13 April 1977, SS Box 15, *JCPL*.

74   Schultze Interview, *Miller Center*, 24–7.

75   Tate to Carter, 18 April 1977, SS Box 15, *JCPL*.

76   Perlstein, *Reaganland*, 298.

77 Blumenthal to Carter, 11 May 1977, SS Box 20, *JCPL*.
78 Eizenstat to Carter, 6 October 1977, SS Box 45, *JCPL*.
79 EPG note, no date, SS Box 25, *JCPL*.
80 Eizenstat to Carter, 24 May 1977, SS Box 22, *JCPL*.
81 Patrick Andelic, *Donkey Work. Congressional Democrats in Conservative America 1974–1992* (Lawrence: University Press of Kansas, 2019), 84.
82 Schultze to Carter, 22 June 1977, SS Box 27, *JCPL*.
83 Eizenstat and Schultze to Carter, 6 October 1977, SS Box 45, *JCPL*.
84 Andelic, *Donkey Work*, 89.
85 McIntyre to Carter, 24 October 1977, SS Box 47, *JCPL*.
86 Address Accepting the Presidential Nomination at the Democratic National Convention, July 1976, *APP*.
87 Report to the American People – Remarks from the White House Library, 2 February 1977, *APP*.
88 Campaign briefs, no date, Speechwriters Staff Offices, Jim Fallows Files Box 8, *JCPL*.
89 Eizenstat to Carter, 3 June 1977, SS Box 24, *JCPL*.
90 Blumenthal to Carter, 8 February 1977, SS Box 7, *JCPL*.
91 Carter, *Diaries*, 53–4.
92 Eizenstat to Carter, 16 May 1977, SS Box 21, *JCPL*.
93 Fallows to Carter, 6 February 1977, Eizenstat Box 287, *JCPL*.
94 Califano to Blumenthal, 11 July 1977, Eizenstat Box 287 and Eizenstat to Carter, 14 July 1977, SS Box 42, *JCPL*.
95 Eizenstat to Carter, 22 June 1977, SS Box 27, *JCPL*.
96 Carter to Blumenthal and Laurence Woodworth, 29 June 1977, SS Box 28, *JCPL*.
97 Moore to Carter, 29 August 1977, SS Box 39, *JCPL*.
98 Blumenthal to Carter, 3 August 1977, Eizenstat Box 286, *JCPL*.
99 Mondale to Carter, 16 September 1977, SS Box 42 Califano to Carter, 15 September 1977, Eizenstat Box 288, *JCPL*.
100 Blumenthal to Carter, 16 September 1977, SS Box 42, *JCPL*.
101 Mondale to Carter, 26 October 1977, SS Box 48, *JCPL*.
102 Bob Ginsburg to Eizenstat, 17 May 1978, DPS Subject Files Rubenstein Box 84, *JCPL*.
103 Wexler to Carter, 10 July 1978, Eizenstat Box 289 and Moore and Eizenstat to Carter, 19 July 1978, SS Box 85, *JCPL*.
104 Article in Washington Outlook, 7 August 1978, SS Box 87, *JCPL*.
105 Blumenthal to Carter, 20 September 1978, SS Box 91, *JCPL*.
106 Eizenstat to Carter, 10 October 1978, Eizenstat Box 289, *JCPL*.
107 Schultze to Carter, 27 September 1978, SS Box 92, *JCPL*.
108 Perlstein, *Reaganland*, 218.

109 Eizenstat to Carter, 6 November 1978, Eizenstat Box 289, *JCPL*.

110 Carter, *Keeping Faith*, 84.

111 Iwan W Morgan, *Deficit Government. Taxing and Spending in Modern America* (Chicago: Ivan Dee, 1995), 146.

112 Leuchtenburg, 'Jimmy Carter and the Post-New Deal Presidency'.

113 Biven, *Carter's Economy*, 67.

114 Pat Caddell to Carter, 21 December 1976, SS Box 1, *JCPL*.

115 Schultze to Mondale, 19 January 1977, Eizenstat Box 144, *JCPL*.

116 Biven, *Jimmy Carter's Economy*, 128–32.

117 Eizenstat to Carter, 2 December 1976, SS Box 1, *JCPL* and Schultze Interview, *Miller Center*, 28–9.

118 Rosenbaum and Ugrinsky, *Presidency and Domestic Policy of Jimmy Carter*, 383.

119 Fred Kahn Interview, *Miller Center*, 106.

120 Schultze to Carter, 29 March 1977, SS Box 13, *JCPL*.

121 Arthur Burns to Carter, 31 March 1977, SS Box 14, *JCPL*.

122 Draft to Eizenstat, 1 April 1977, Eizenstat Box 44, *JCPL*.

123 Schultze to Carter, 6 April 1977, SS Box 14, *JCPL*.

124 Anti-Inflation Program Statement Outlining Administration Actions, 15 April 1977, *APP*.

125 Biven, *Carter's Economy*, 134–5.

126 Carter to Senator Tower, 20 September 1977, SS Box 42, *JCPL*.

127 Schultze to Carter, 7 December 1977, SS Box 54, *JCPL*.

128 Schultze to Carter, 7 January 1978, SS Box 57, *JCPL*.

129 President's News Conference, 11 April 1978, *APP*.

130 Schultze to Carter, 6 May 1978, SS Box 74, *JCPL*.

131 Carter to Meany, 11 May 1978, Eizenstat Box 143, *JCPL*.

132 Schultze to Carter, 3 June 1978, SS Box 79 and Eizenstat and Ginsburg to Carter, 18 September 1978, SS Box 92, *JCPL*.

133 Blumenthal to Carter, 13 September 1977, SS Box 92, *JCPL*.

134 Anti-inflation Address to the Nation, 24 October 1978, *APP*.

135 Editorial, *Wall Street Journal*, 31 October 1978 and Schultze Interview, *Miller Center*, 65.

136 Kahn Interview, *Miller Center*, 8–14.

137 Ibid., 123 and 129.

138 Butler to Jordan, 4 October 1978, SS Box 95, *JCPL*.

139 Wexler to Carter, 6 December 1978, SS Box 98, *JCPL*.

140 Kaufman and Kaufman, *Presidency of James Earl Carter*, 167–8.

141 Schultze to Carter, 13 March 1979, CEA Schultze Box 9, *JCPL*.

142 Kennedy to Carter, 1 June 1979, Rubenstein Box 64, *JCPL*.

143 Eizenstat to Carter, 15 September 1979, SS Box 131, *JCPL*.

144 Kaufman and Kaufman, *Presidency of James Earl Carter*, 175.

145 Iwan Morgan, 'Monetary Metamorphosis: The Volcker Fed and Inflation', *Journal of Political History*, Vol. 24, No. 4, 2012: 545–71.

146 Al From to Kahn and Eizenstat, 14 August 1979, Rubenstein Box 64, *JCPL*.

147 Erwin Hargrove and Samuel Morley, *President's Council of Economic Advisors* (Boulder: Westview, 1984), 499–500.

148 Kahn to Carter, 13 October 1979, SS Box 135, Schultze to Carter, 24 October 1979, SS Box 137 and Miller and Schultze to Carter, 14 November 1979, SS Box 140, *JCPL*.

149 Anti-Inflation Program Remarks Announcing the Administration's Program, 14 March 1980, *APP*.

150 From to Kahn, 7 March 1980, SS Box 154, *JCPL*.

151 Kahn to Carter, 2 April 1980, SS Box 157, *JCPL*.

152 Wexler, McDonald and Eizenstat to Carter, 9 April 1980 and From to Khan, 17 April 1980, Wexler Box 26, *JCPL*.

153 Kahn to Carter, 22 April 1980, SS Box 159, *JCPL*.

154 Hargrove, *Council of Economic Advisors,* 484.

155 Kahn to Carter, 5 November 1979, SS Box 138, *JCPL*.

156 Schultze to Carter, 21 January 1980, SS Box 148, *JCPL*.

157 Schulman, *The Seventies*, 133.

158 Perlstein, *Reaganland*, 408.

159 Windsor, 'Budget Strategy in the Carter Administration', 404–5.

160 Ibid., 403.

161 Douglas Bennet to Moore, 29 April 1977, SS Box 18, *JCPL*.

162 Eizenstat, *White House Years*, 7.

163 McIntyre Interview, *Miller Center*, 55.

164 Windsor, 'Budget Strategy in the Carter Administration', 387–407.

165 Joe Onek to Carp and Eizenstat, 9 May 1977, Eizenstat Box 154, *JCPL*.

166 McIntyre to Carter, 24 May 1977, SS Box 77, *JCPL*.

167 Hargrove, *Carter as President*, 98–9.

168 Perlstein*, Reaganland*, 379.

169 Wexler to Jordan, 30 May 1978, Wexler Box 67, *JCPL*.

170 Bo Cutter to Jordan 30 May 1978, Wexler Box 67, *JCPL*.

171 Hargrove, *Carter as President,* 100.

172 Moore to EPG, 5 March 1980, Eizenstat Box 154, *JCPL*.

173 Schultze to Carter, 27 December 1979, Schultze Files Box 52, *JCPL*.

174 Eizenstat to Carter, 1 March 1980, SS Box 152, *JCPL*.

175 Eizenstat to Carter, 26 March 1980, SS Box 156, *JCPL*.

176 Eizenstat to Carter, 26 May 1980, SS Box 163 and Tate to Moore, 28 May 1980, SS Box 164, *JCPL*.

177   Comments by McIntyre in Rosenbaum and Ugrinsky, *Presidency and Domestic Policy of Jimmy Carter,* 418–19.

178   Steven Roberts, 'Carter and Congress: Doubt and Distrust Prevail', *New York Times*, 5 August 1979.

179   Hargrove, *Carter as President*, 69–70; Iwan W Morgan, *Age of Deficits. Presidents and Unbalanced Budgets from Jimmy Carter to George W Bush* (Lawrence: University of Kansas, 2009), 75 and Biven, *Carter's Economy*, 253–6.

180   Ann Mari May, 'Monetary Policy and the Carter Presidency', *PSQ*, Vol. 23: 669–711.

181   Morgan, 'Jimmy Carter, Bill Clinton and the New Democratic Economics', 1015–39.

182   Anthony Campagna, *Economic Policy in the Carter Administration* (Westport: St Martin's Press, 1992), 205.

183   Morgan, *Age of Deficits*, 74.

184   Sidney Melman, 'Jimmy Hoover?' *NYT*, 7 February 1979 and Sidney Weinstein, 'Carter's Hoover Syndrome', *New Leader*, 24 March 1980, 5.

185   Ibid.

186   Eizenstat, *White House Years*, 876.

187   *NYT Magazine*, 13 July 1980.

Chapter 4

1   Marilu Hunt McCarthy, 'Economic Aspects of Carter Energy Program', in Rosenbaum and Ugrinsky, *Presidency and Domestic Policy of Jimmy Carter,* 555 and Crain, *Ford Presidency*, 74.

2   Crain, *Ford Presidency*, 74.

3   Hunt McCarthy, 'Economic Aspects of Carter Energy Programme', 555.

4   Ibid., 559–60.

5   Crain, *Ford Presidency*, 106–8.

6   Ibid., 13.

7   Horowitz, *Jimmy Carter, and the Energy Crisis of the 1970s,* 10.

8   James Schlesinger Interview, *Miller Center,* 13.

9   Presidential Campaign Debate, 23 September 1976, *APP.*

10   Grenville Garside to Senator Jackson, 19 November 1976, SS Box 1, *JCPL.*

11   Arlon Tussing to Jackson, 19 November 1976, SS Box 1, *JCPL.*

12   Dan Dreyfus to Carter, 13 December 1976, SS Box 1, *JCPL.*

13   Schlesinger Interview, *Miller Center,* 12.

14   Crain, *Ford Presidency*, 69–70 and 194–5.

15   Omi Warden to Carter, 18 December 1976 and Dave Freeman (ERDA) to Carter, 17 December 1976, SS Box 1, *JCPL*.

16   Schlesinger Interview, *Miller Center,* 89.

17   Ibid., 19.

18   Dumbrell, *Carter Presidency*, 22.

19   John C Barrow, 'An Age of Limits: Jimmy Carter and the Quest for a National Energy Policy', in Fink and Graham, *Carter Presidency*, 160–1.

20   Inaugural Address, 21 January 1977, *APP.*

21   Report to the American People, 2 February 1977, *APP.*

22   Hunt McCarthy, 'Economic Aspects of Carter Energy Policy', 563–5.

23   Hargrove, *Carter as President*, 48–9.

24   Tate to Moore, 3 February 1977, SS Box 5, *JCPL*.

25   Schlesinger to Carter, 16 February 1977, SS Box 8 and Briefing to Carter, 28 February 1977, SS Box 9, *JCPL*.

26   Carter to Schlesinger, 29 March 1977, SS Box 13, *JCPL*.

27   Schultze to Carter, Impact described as 0.2–0.4 per cent, 15 April 1977, SS Box 15, *JCPL*.

28   Eizenstat to Carter, 10 February 1977, SS Box 7 and Califano to Carter, 18 April 1977 SS Box 18, *JCPL*.

29   Schlesinger to Carter, 31 March 1977, SS Box 13, *JCPL*.

30   Barrow, 'Quest for National Energy Policy', 162.

31   Carter, *Energy Addresses and News Conferences*, 18, 20 and 22 April 1977, *APP.*

32   Domin, *Public Opinion and Values*, 40.

33   Russell D Motter, 'Seeking Limits: The Passage of the National Energy Act as a Microcosm of the Carter Presidency', in Rosenbaum and Ugrinsky, *Presidency and Domestic Policy of Jimmy Carter*, 576.

34   Carter, *Keeping the Faith*, 91.

35   Address to the Nation on Energy, 18 April 1977, *APP.*

36   Carter's Address to Joint Session of Congress, 22 April 1977, *APP.*

37   Radio-Television News Directors Association – Interview with Members of the Board of Directors of the Association, 29 April 1977, *APP.*

38   Portsmouth, New Hampshire Town Hall Meeting, 25 April 1979, *APP.*

39   Hunt McCarthy, 'Economic Aspects of Carter Energy Programme', 560–3.

40   Carter, *Keeping the Faith,* 97.

41   Motter, 'Seeking Limits: Passage of the National Energy Act', 578.

42   Ibid.

43   Caddell to Carter, 2 May 1977, Jody Powell Papers Box 30, *JCPL*.

44   Meg Jacobs, *Panic at the Pump. The Energy Crisis and the Transformation of American Politics in the 1970s* (New York: Hill and Wang, 2017), 73–83.

45   *Congressional Quarterly Weekly Report*, Vol. XXXV, No 40, 1977.

46   Barbara Kellerman, *Political Presidency. Practice of Leadership* (New York, Oxford: Oxford University Press, 1999), 199–202.

47   Carter, *Carter Diaries*, 118.

48   Schlesinger Interview, *Miller Center*, 28–9.

49   Motter, 'Seeking Limits: Passage of the National Energy Act', 576.

50   Farrell, *Tip O'Neill*, 471.

51   Motter, 'Passage of the National Energy Act', 579.

52   Moore to Carter, Weekly Legislative Report, 30 May 1977, SS Box 23, *JCPL*.

53   Schlesinger, *Interview Miller Center*, 6 and 30.

54   Ibid., 5.

55   Mann, *Legacy to Power*, 347.

56   Moore to Carter, 18 May 1977, SS Box 21, *JCPL*.

57   Schlesinger, Eizenstat and McIntyre to Carter, 1 November 1977, SS Box 48, *JCPL*.

58   Eizenstat and Schlesinger to Carter, 12 October 1977, Eizenstat Box 199, *JCPL*.

59   Schultze, Eizenstat, Schlesinger, Jordan, Moore, McIntyre and Larry Woodworth to Carter, Strategy on Energy Conference, 1 November 1977, SS Box 48, *JCPL*.

60   Moore and Eizenstat to Carter, 18 October 1977, SS Box 46 and Eizenstat, Butler and Kitty Schirmer to Carter, 19 October 1977, SS Box 47, *JCPL*.

61   Moore and Tate to Carter, 17 October 1977, SS Box 46, *JCPL*.

62   Eizenstat and Schirmer to Carter, 8 December 1977, Eizenstat Box 198, *JCPL*.

63   Eizenstat, *White House Years*, 161.

64   Jones, *Trustee President*, 141.

65   Call to Jackson, 9 January 1978, SS Box 57, Meeting with Long, 18 January 1978, SS Box 65 and Eizenstat and Schlesinger to Carter, 27 March 1978, SS Box 69, *JCPL*.

66   Motter, 'Seeking Limits: Passage of the National Energy Act', *NYT* and CBS poll, 18 January 1978, 582.

67   Congressional Quarterly Weekly Report. Vol. XXXV. 24 December 1977: 2231–6.

68   Eizenstat, *White House Years*, 191.

69   Motter, 'Seeking Limits: Passage of the National Energy Act', 586.

70   Rafshoon to Carter, 7 June 1978, Eizenstat Box 198, *JCPL*.

71   Hunt McCarthy, 'Economic Aspects of Carter Energy Programme', 562.

72   Eizenstat and Moore to Carter, 16 October 1978, Frank Moore Box 36, *JCPL*.

73   Poll of Senators, no date, Eizenstat Box 250, *JCPL*.

74   Rafshoon to Carter, 23 February 1979, SS Box 108, *JCPL*.

75   Moore to Carter, 23 March 1979, SS Box 110, *JCPL*.

76   Schultze, Blumenthal, Juanita Kreps, Schlesinger and Henry Owen to Carter, 23 March 1979, Eizenstat Box 250, *JCPL*.

77   Energy Address to the Nation, 5 April 1979, *APP*.

78   ABC Harris Poll, 6 April 1979, DPS Rubenstein Energy Files Box 97, *JCPL*.

79   Eizenstat to Carter, Energy Program Report 1, 21 April 1979, SS Box 114, *JCPL*.

80   Jacobs, *Panic at the Pumps*, 210.

81   Ibid., 210.

82   Eizenstat to Carter, 25 April 1979, SS Box 114, *JCPL*.

83   Eizenstat to Carter, 4 and 7 May 1979, Eizenstat Box 322, *JCPL*.

84   Jacobs, *Panic at the Pump*, 219–21.

85   Horowitz, *Jimmy Carter, and the Energy Crisis*, 19.

86   Jacobs, *Panic at the Pump*, 222.

87   Achsah Nesmith, Walter Shapiro and Gordon Stewart to Rafshoon and Hertzberg, 29 June 1979, Speechwriters Subject Files Box 8, *JCPL*.

88   Eizenstat, McIntyre, Califano and Graciela Olivare to Carter, 11 July 1979, SS Box 123 *JCPL*.

89   Eizenstat to Carter, 7 July 1979, SS Box 123, *JCPL*.

90   Address to the Nation on Energy and National Goals: 'The Malaise Speech', 15 July 1979, *APP*.

91   Horowitz, *Jimmy Carter and the Energy Crisis of 1970's*, 120–41.

92   Schlesinger to Carter and reply, 20 July 1979, SS Box 124, *JCPL*.

93   Carter to Schlesinger, 5 December 1977, SS Box 53 and Carter to Schlesinger, 6 March 1979, SS Box 109, *JCPL*.

94   Rubenstein to Eizenstat, 10 July 1979, DPS Rubenstein Energy Files Box 98, *JCP*.

95   Schlesinger Interview, *Miller Center*, 10–11, 23 and 84.

96   Schlesinger to Carter, 13 July 1979, SS Box 123, *JCPL*.

97   Address to the Nation on Energy and National Goals: 'The Malaise Speech', 15 July 1979, *APP*.

98   Rafshoon to Staff, 20 July 1979, DPS Rubenstein Energy Files Box 98, *JCPL*.

99   Wexler to Carter, 31 July 1979, SS Box 125, *JCPL*.

100 Wexler, Jordan, Powell and Eizenstat to Carter, SS Box 130, *JCPL*.

101 Energy Legislation, 23 and 25 July 1979, SS Box 125 and Moore to Carter, Energy calls, 8 August 1979, SS Box 127, *JCPL*.

102 Moore to Carter, Energy Legislation, 23 July 1979, SS Box 125, *JCPL*.

103 Jack Watson to Carter, 14 August 1979 and Caddell to Carter, 7 August 1979, SS Box 126, *JCPL*.

104 Moore telegraph to Carter, 17 August 1979, SS Box 127, *JCPL*.

105 Article in *WSJ*, 31 August 1979, SS Box 129, *JCPL*.

106 Eizenstat to Carter, 8 September 1979, SS Box 129, *JCPL*.

107 Abernathy, *Carter Years*, 19.

108 Tate to Carter, 26 November 1979, SS Box 140, *JCPL*.

109 Eizenstat to Carter, 27 April 1980, DPS Rubenstein Energy Files Box 103, *JCPL*.

110 Eizentstat and Schirmer to Carter, 1 April 1980, Eizenstat Box 322, *JCPL*.

111 Gus Speth to Carter, 31 March 1980, SS Box 156, *JCPL*.

112 Eli Strobbha (Council of Environmental Quality) to Eizenstat, 14 April 1980, DPS Rubenstein Energy Files Box 102, *JCPL*.

113 Undated, Speechwriters Subject Files Box 2 and 22 September 1980, Plains Files President's Daily Diary Box 16, *JCPL*.

114 Jacobs, *Panic at the Pump*, 268.

115 George C Edwards, 'Exclusive Interview: President Jimmy Carter', *PSQ*, Vol. 38: 1–13.

116 Eizenstat and Schirmer to Carter, 19 January 1980, SS Box 147, *JCPL*.

117 Jones, *Trustee President*; Hargrove, *Carter as President* and Morris, *American Moralist*.

118 Motter, 'Seeking Limits: Passage of the National Energy Act', 576–7.

119 Kaufman and Kaufman, *Presidency of James Earl Carter*.

120 Address to the Nation on Energy and National Goals: 'The Malaise Speech', 15 July 1979, *APP*.

121 Richardson, *Conversations with Carter*, 1 June 1979, 172–5.

122 Moore to Carter, 8 August 1979, SS Box 127, *JCPL*.

123 Horowitz, *Jimmy Carter, and the Energy Crisis*, 120–41.

124 Barrow, 'Quest for National Energy Policy', 174.

125 Carter to Eizenstat, 4 March 1980, DPS Rubenstein Energy Files Box 101 and Eizenstat to Carter, 26 March 1979, DPS Rubenstein Energy Files Box 97, *JCPL*.

126 Barrow, 'Quest for National Energy Policy', 170–2.

127 Address to the Nation on Energy, 18 April 1977, *APP*.

Chapter 5

1   Jordan to Carter, undated/late April 1977, Chief of Staff Box 37, *JCPL*.

2   'Our Nation's Past and Future': Address Accepting the Presidential Nomination at the Democratic National Convention, 15 July 1976, *APP*.

3   Carter's National Health Speech to Student National Medical Association (SNMA) DC, 16 April 1976, DPS James Mongan and Joe Onek Box 48, *JCPL*.

4   Rafshoon to Carter, 10 November 1978, SS Box 97, *JCPL*.

5   Agenda update, 9 January 1978, SS Box 58 and Mondale to Carter, 15 January 1979, SS Box 102, *JCPL*.

6   McIntyre, Eizenstat and Moore to Carter, 2 June 1978, SS Box 79, *JCPL*.

7   Moore Interview, *Miller Center*, 16.

8   Robert Finbow, 'Presidential Leadership or Structural Constraints? Failure of President Carter's Health Insurance Proposals', *PSQ*, Vol. 28: 169–86.

9   Warshaw, 'Carter Experience with Cabinet Government', 381 and President's News Conference, 17 January 1979, *APP*.

10   Taylor Dark, 'Organized Labor and the Carter Administration: Origins of Conflict', in Rosenbaum and Ugrinsky, *Presidency and Domestic Policy of Jimmy Carter*, 767.

11   Rafshoon Interview, *Miller Center*, 34.

12   Jordan Interview, *Miller Center*, 42.

13   Arnie Miller to Carter, 6 December 1978, SS Box 100 and Jordan to Carter, 18 July 1979, C of S Box 33, *JCPL*.

14   Kathy Cade to Rosalyn Carter, 24 May 1979, SS Box 118, *JCPL*.

15   Califano, *Governing America*, 29–30.

16   Califano to Carter, 9 August 1977, SS Box 40, *JCPL*.

17   Warshaw, 'Carter Experience with Cabinet Government', 378–9.

18   Carter to Califano, 3 March 1977, SS Box10, 30 June 1977, SS Box 28 and 27 January 1978, SS Box 60, *JCPL*.

19   Califano to Carter, 10 June 1977, SS Box 24, *JCPL*.

20   Califano, *Governing America*, 65–6 and Carter, *White House Diaries*, 185–8.

21   Ibid., 308 and Carter to Califano, 3 January 1979, SS Box 102, *JCPL*.

22   Rafshoon Interview, *Miller Center*, 36.

23   Carter Interview, *Miller Center*, 13–14.

24   Blumenthal to Carter, 28 April 1977, SS Box 19, *JCPL*.

25   Organisational review of EPG, undated, SS Box 23, *JCPL*.

26   Moore and Eizenstat to Carter, 18 October 1977, SS Box 47, *JCPL*.

27   Schultze to Carter, 2 May 1977, SS Box 19, *JCPL*.

28   Eizenstat to Carte, 12 August 1977, SS Box 36, *JCPL*.

29   Social Security Financing Legislation Letter to Congressional Leaders, 10 April 1978, *APP*.

30   Califano to Powell, 5 January 1979, Eizenstat Box 277, *JCPL*.

31   Patricia Harris to Miller, Marshall, McIntyre, Eizenstat, Schultze and Kahn, 18 January 1980, DPS Rubenstein Subject Files, *JCPL*.

32   Lou Cannon, *Governor Reagan. His Rise to Power* (New York: BBS Public Affairs, 2003), 349–33.

33   Rafshoon to Carter, 22 September 1978, SS Box 93, *JCPL*.

34   James T Paterson, 'Jimmy Carter and Welfare Reform', in Fink and Graham, *Carter Presidency*, 117.

35   Report to the American People, 2 February 1977, *APP.*

36   Laurence E Lynn and David de F Whitman, *The President as Policy Maker: Jimmy Carter and Welfare Reform* (Philadelphia: Temple University Press, 1981), 202–3.

37   Carter to Califano, 21 March 1977, SS Box 11 and Carter to Califano, 15 October 1977, Eizenstat Box 318, *JCPL*.

38   Lynn and Whitman, *Carter, and Welfare Reform*, 140.

39   Ibid., 53.

40   Califano to Carter, 9 February 1977, SS Box7, *JCPL*.

41 Schultze Interview, *Miller Center*, 62.

42 Jordan to Carter, Undated/late April 1977, Chief of Staff Box 37, *JCPL*.

43 Paterson, 'Carter, and Welfare Reform', 125.

44 Califano to Carter, 5 January 1977, SS Box 1, *JCPL*.

45 Hargrove, *Carter as President*, 55–60.

46 Lynn and Whitman, *Carter, and Welfare Reform*, 157 and 99–102.

47 David Rosenbaum, Much Dollars Figure in Welfare Costs, *NYT*, 26 June 1977.

48 Califano to Carter, 12 April 1977, SS Box 17, *JCPL*.

49 Eizenstat, Schultze and Lance to Carter, 20 May 1977, SS Box 22, *JCPL*.

50 Welfare Reform Remarks at a News Briefing on Goals and Guidelines, 2 May 1977, *APP*.

51 Eizenstat, Carp, Bill Spring and Raines to Carter, 26 April 1977, SS Box 18, *JCPL*.

52 Califano to Carter, 29 April 1977, SS Box 19, *JCPL*.

53 Eizenstat, Carp, Spring and Raines to Carter, 26 April 1977, SS Box 18, *JCPL*.

54 Lynn and Whitman, *Carter, and Welfare Reform*, 207–8.

55 Watson and Jim Parnham to Carter, 23 May 1977, SS Box 22 and Eizenstat to Carter, 25 May 1977, SS Box 22, *JCPL*.

56 Welfare Reform Remarks at a News Briefing on Goals and Guidelines, 2 May 1977, *APP*.

57 Califano to Carter, 13 June 1977, SS Box 24, *JCPL*.

58 Lynn and Whitman, *Carter, and Welfare Reform*, 136–7.

59 Paterson, 'Carter, and Welfare Reform', 128–30.

60 Lynn and Whitman, *Carter, and Welfare Reform*, 40.

61 Califano to Carter, 25 July 1977, SS Box 33, *JCPL*.

62 Lance to Carter, 25 July 1977, SS Box 34, *JCPL*.

63 Eizenstat, Carp, Raines and Spring to Carter, 27 July 1977, SS Box 34, *JCPL*.

64 Welfare Reform Message to Congress, 6 August 1977, *APP*.

65 Lynn and Whitman, *Carter, and Welfare Reform*, 232–5.

66 Califano to Carter, 30 November 1977, SS Box 53, *JCPL*.

67 Lynn and Whitman, *Carter, and Welfare Reform*, 238.

68 Califano to Carter, 9 March 1978, SS Box 66 JCPL.

69 Eizenstat to Carter, 23 May 1978, SS Box 77, *JCPL*.

70 McIntyre to Carter, 9 June 1978, SS Box 82, *JCPL*.

71 Eizenstat, McIntyre, Schultze, Bob Bergland, Califano and Marshall to Carter, 23 December 1978, SS Box 101, *JCPL*.

72 Jim Mongan and Florence Prioleau to Eizenstat, 17 March 1980, Human Resources Prioleau Box 21, *JCPL*.

73 Lynn and Whitman, *Carter, and Welfare Reform*, 255–79.

74 Ibid., 268–71.

75 David Rosenbaum, President Stresses Welfare Limit despite Warning, 27 May 1977, *NYT*.

76   24 January 1977, SS Box 4, *JCPL.*

77   General briefing on Hospital Cost Containment, Date unknown, Eizenstat
      Box 217, *JCPL.*

78   Peterson, *Legislating Together*, 20.

79   Wexler Interview, *Miller Center,* 48.

80   Eizenstat to Carter, 11 February 1977, SS Box 9, *JCPL.*

81   Califano to Carter, 20 April 1977, SS Box 17, *JCPL.*

82   Healthcare Legislation Message to the Congress, 25 April 1977, *APP.*

83   State of the Union Address Delivered before a Joint Session of the Congress,
      23 January 1979, *APP.*

84   Jordan and Moore to Carter, 23 January 1979, SS Box 104, *JCPL.*

85   Hospital Cost Containment Remarks Announcing Proposed Legislation, 6 March
      1979, *APP.*

86   Preparation for meeting with Carter, 22 October 1979, Alonzo McDonald
      Box 12, *JCPL.*

87   Harris, McIntyre, Eizenstat, Kahn and Frank Press to Carter, 21 December 1979,
      SS Box 150, *JCPL.*

88   Eizenstat to Carter, 13 February 1980, SS Box 150, *JCPL.*

89   Carter Interview, *Miller Center*, 228–9.

90   Califano, *Governing America*, 98.

91   Speech to SNMA, 16 April 1976, DPS Mongan and Onek Box 48, *JCPL.*

92   Califano, *Governing America*, 88.

93   Timothy Stanley, *Kennedy vs Carter. The Battle for the Democratic Party's Soul*
      (Lawrence: University of Kansas Press, 2010), 52.

94   Califano, *Governing America*, 99–103.

95   Bourne to Jordan, 20 June 1977 and Bourne to Jordan and Eizenstat, 1 August
      1977 Eizenstat Box 240, *JCPL.*

96   Jordan to Bourne, 8 July 1977, Eizenstat Box 240, *JCPL.*

97   Onek and Bob Havely to Eizenstat, 8 September 1977, Eizenstat Box 240, *JCPL.*

98   Califano to Carter, 3 November 1977, Eizenstat Box 240, *JCPL.*

99   Bourne to Carter, 12 December 1977, SS Box 53, *JCPL.*

100 Eizenstat, Onek and Havely to Carter, 20 December 1977, SS Box 56, *JCPL.*

101 Butler to Jordan and Eizenstat, 12 January 1978, Eizenstat Box 241, *JCPL.*

102 Califano, *Governing America*, 100.

103 Eizenstat to Carter, 8 February 1978, SS Box 62, JCPL.

104 Onek to Eizenstat and Butler, 13 March 1978, Eizenstat Box 241, *JCPL.*

105 Eizenstat briefing for meeting with Kennedy and Labour, 6 April 1978, SS
      Box 69, *JCPL.*

106 Califano to Carter, 15 May 1978, Eizenstat Box 241, *JCPL.*

107 Califano to Carter, 30 May 1978, SS Box 78, *JCPL.*

108 Eizenstat to Carter, 31 May 1978, SS Box 78, *JCPL*.

109 Schultze and McIntyre to Carter, 14 June 1978, SS Box 81, *JCPL*.

110 Briefing Eizenstat and Onek to Carter, 21 June 1978, DPS Mongan and Onek Box 49, *JCPL*.

111 Eizenstat and Onek to Carter, undated, Eizenstat Box 242, *JCPL*.

112 Richard Moe, Health Care for All – A Cautionary Tale from the 1970s, *History New Network*, 14 April 2019.

113 Perlstein, *Reaganland*, 561.

114 Press release, 28 July 1978, DPS Mongan and Onek Box 50, *JCPL*.

115 No date, Eizenstat Box 242, *JCPL*.

116 Richard Moe to Mondale, 14 August 1978 and Eizenstat to Mondale, 22 August 1978, Eizenstat Box 242, *JCPL*.

117 Onek to Eizenstat, 27 November 1978, Eizenstat Box 241, *JCPL*.

118 Eizenstat, McIntyre and Schultze to Carter, 17 January 1979, SS Box 103, *JCPL*.

119 Eizenstat to Carter, 22 February 1979, SS Box 108, *JCPL*.

120 McIntyre to Carter, 15 May 1979, Eizenstat Box 241 and Schultze to Carter, 16 May 1979, SS Box 117, *JCPL*.

121 Eizenstat and Onek to Carter, 16 May 1979, SS Box 117, *JCPL*.

122 Differences between Kennedy and Carter Healthcare Plans, Undated, DPS Rubenstein Subject Files Box 59, *JCPL*.

123 Califano to Carter, 6 June 1979, Eizenstat Box 241, *JCPL*.

124 National Health Plan Remarks Announcing Proposed Legislation, 12 June 1979, *APP*.

125 Kennedy press release, 12 June 1979, Eizenstat Box 243, *JCPL*.

126 Eizenstat to Carter, Undated, Eizenstat Box 243, *JCPL*.

127 Alex Wadden, 'Found and Lost: A Third Way on Health Care', in Mark White, ed, *The Presidency of Bill Clinton: The Legacy of a New Domestic and Foreign Policy* (London: I.B. Tauris, 2012), 92–119.

128 Califano, *Governing America*, 108–9.

129 Carter, *Keeping the Faith*, 463.

130 Carter Speech to SNMA, 16 April 1976, DPS Mongan and Onek Box 48, *JCPL*.

131 Lance, *Truth of the Matter*, 178.

132 Andelic, *Donkey Work*, 115.

Chapter 6

1 Butler to Carter, 22 December 1980, Plains Box 16, *JCL*.

2 Dubofsky and Dulles, *Labor in America*, 357–8.

3 Dark, 'Organized Labor and the Carter Administration', 776.

4   Mervyn Dubofsky and Foster Rhea Dulles, *Labor in America, a History* (Wheeling: Harlan Davidson, 1999), 381.

5   Ibid., 355–7.

6   Ibid., 377–80.

7   Butler to Carter, 22 December 1980, Plains Box 16, *JCL*.

8   Isabel D Harrison, State and Labour in the US: The Carter Administration and the AFL-CIO, 1976–1980: Political Strategy and the National Accord, Unpublished PhD Dissertation, (Oxford University, 1989).

9   Butler to Carter, 16 July 1978, SS Box 124, *JCPL*.

10   Leuchtenberg, 'Jimmy Carter and the Post-New Deal Presidency', 14–16.

11   Dark, 'Organized Labor and the Carter Administration', 764.

12   Ray Marshall Interview, *Miller Center*, 4–6.

13   Carp Interview, *Miller Center*, 46–7.

14   Dubofsky and Dulles, *Labor in America*, 349–50.

15   Jordan to Carter, no date, SS Box 4, *JCPL*.

16   David Rubenstein to Eizenstat and Butler, 15 February 1977, Chief of Staff Butler Box 85, *JCPL*.

17   Eizenstat and Butler to Carter, 23 February 1977, SS Box 8, *JCPL*.

18   Formal AFL-CIO statement, 22 February 1977, Chief of Staff Butler Box 85, *JCPL*.

19   Tracy Roof, *American Labor, Congress, and the Welfare State* (Baltimore: Johns Hopkins University Press, 2011), 152.

20   Dark, 'Organized Labor and the Carter Administration', 767.

21   Eizenstat and Ben Johnston to Carter, undated, SS Box 8, *JCPL*.

22   Roof, *American Labor*, 155–6.

23   Gary M Fink, 'Fragile Alliance: Jimmy Carter and the American Labor Movement', in Rosenbaum and Ugrinsky, *Presidency and Domestic Policies of Jimmy Carter*, 788–9.

24   Eizenstat and Johnston to Carter, 27 June 1977, DPS Rubenstein Box 66, *JCPL*.

25   Eizenstat to Carter and Jordan to Carter, 30 June 1977, SS Box 29, *JCPL*.

26   Sar Levitan and Martha Cooper, *Business Lobbies and the Public Good* (Baltimore: Johns Hopkins University Press, 1984), 134.

27   Marshall to Carter, 19 May 1978, SS Box 76, Moore and Bob Thomson to Carter, 13 June 1978, SS Box 80 and Eizenstat and Johnston to Carter, 19 June 1978, SS Box 81, *JCPL*.

28   Moore, Thomson and Nik Edes to Carter, 10 July 1978, SS Box 84, *JCPL*.

29   Mondale to Carter on 1979 Agenda, 21 November 1978, SS Box 98, *JCPL*.

30   Butler to Carter, 10 July 1978, SS Box 84, JCPL.

31   Dubofsky and Dulles, *Labor in America*, 382.

32   Comments by Harold P Coxsen, in Rosenbaum and Ugrinsky, *Presidency and Domestic Policy of Jimmy Carter*, 808.

33 Melvyn Dubofsky, Jimmy Carter and the End of the Politics of Productivity, in Fink and Graham, *Carter Presidency*, 105–6.

34 Leuchtenberg, 'Jimmy Carter and the Post-New Deal Presidency', 22–3.

35 Carter announcement, 22 February 1978, DPS Eizenstat Box 230, *JCPL*.

36 Fink, 'Fragile Alliance: Jimmy Carter and the American Labor Movement', 790–3.

37 Doug Fraser to Carter, 8 November 1977, SS Box 52 and George Meany to Carter, 20 October 1978, SS Box 95, *JCPL*.

38 Meany to Carter, 9 November 1978, SS Box 98, *JCPL*.

39 Remarks and a Question-and-Answer Session at the Annual Convention of the Communications Workers of America, 16 July 1979, *APP*.

40 Dubofsky, End of the Politics of Productivity, 108–9.

41 Marshall and Bob Strauss to Carter and Schultze and Barry Bosworth to Carter, Meetings with Labour, 9 May 1978, SS Box 75, *JCPL*.

42 Butler to Carter, 10 May 1978, SS Box 75, *JCPL*.

43 Marshall to Carter, 18 September 1978, SS Box 92, *JCPL*.

44 Butler to Carter, 22 December 1980, Plains Box 16, *JCPL*.

45 Butler to Carter, 7 December 1978, SS Box 100, *JCPL*.

46 Abernathy, *Carter Years*, 47–8.

47 Miller to Carter, 14 September 1979, SS Box 130 and Butler to Jordan, 28 February 1980, SS Box 152, *JCPL*.

48 Lane Kirkland to Carter, 21 December 1979, SS Box 144, *JCPL*.

49 Carter, *Diaries*, 308.

50 Richard Pettigrew to Carter, 28 November 1977, Chief of Staff Box 34, *JCPL*.

51 Fraser to Carter, 8 November 1977, SS Box 52, *JCPL*.

52 Eizenstat and Schirmer to Carter, 3 February 1977, SS Box 5, *JCPL*.

53 Dubofsky, End of the Politics of Productivity, 111.

54 Dubofsky and Dulles, *Labor in America*, 382.

55 Roof, *American Labor*, 151–2.

56 Perlstein, *Reaganland*, 316.

57 Ibid., 318.

58 Dark, 'Organized Labor and the Carter Administration', 764.

59 Fink, 'Fragile Alliance: Jimmy Carter and the American Labor Movement', 799 and List of Union reps at Camp David, undated, Eizenstat Box 162, *JCPL*.

60 Carter to Meany on Crown of St Stephen, undated, Chief of Staff Butler Box 85, *JCPL*.

61 Fink, 'Fragile Alliance: Jimmy Carter and the American Labor Movement', 784.

62 Carter to Meany, Handwritten Note Wishing Happy Birthday, 15 August 1977, Chief of Staff Butler Box 85, *JCPL*.

63 Untitled draft, 13 January 1978, SS Box 58, *JCPL*.

64 Charles Warren, Speth and Marion Edey to Carter, Environmental Lobby, 25 August 1977, SS Box 39, *JCPL*.

65 Butler to Carter, 25 January 1977, SS Box 3, *JCPL*.

66 Eizenstat and Butler to Carter, 3 March 1977, SS Box 10 and Eizenstat and Butler to Carter, 13 January 1978, Eizenstat Box 136, *JCPL*.

67 Jordan to Carter, 22 August 1977, SS Box 37 and Meany to Carter, undated, Chief of Staff Butler Box 86, *JCPL*.

68 Summary of actions taken by President Carter, undated, SS Box 33, *JCPL*.

69 Copy of article, 25 February 1978, SS Box 65 and Carter to Butler, 25 February 1978, Chief of Staff Butler Box 86, *JCPL*.

70 Butler to Carter, 28 February 1978, Chief of Staff Butler Box 86, *JCPL*.

71 Jordan to Carter, 25 April 1978, SS Box 73, *JCPL*.

72 Butler to Jordan, 11 January 1978, Chief of Staff Butler Box 86, *JCPL*.

73 Remarks at the United Steelworkers of America Convention, 20 September 1978, *APP*.

74 Laurie Lucey to Butler, 25 September 1978, Chief of Staff Butler Box 86, *JCPL*.

75 Dubofsky and Dulles, *Labor in America*, 382.

76 Untitled, 22 December 1980, Plains Box 16, *JCPL*.

77 Butler and Moe to Mondale, 19 January 1979, Chief of Staff Butler Box 114, *JCPL*.

78 Dark, 'Organized Labor and the Carter Administration', 771.

79 Ibid., 771–2.

80 Ibid.

81 28 September 1979, Chief of Staff Butler Box 87, *JCPL*.

82 Fink, 'Fragile Alliance: Jimmy Carter and the American Labor Movement', 797.

83 Process of consulting AFL-CIO confirmed, no date, Chief of Staff Butler Box 86, *JCPL*.

84 Butler to Jordan, 4 June 1980, SS Box 165, *JCPL*.

85 Butler to Carter, 10 April 1980, SS Box 157, *JCPL*.

86 Eizenstat to Carter, 14 September 1979, SS Box 130, *JCPL*.

87 Dark, 'Organized Labor and the Carter Administration', 773–4.

88 Butler to Jordan, 4 January 1980, Chief of Staff Butler Box 142, *JCPL*.

89 Butler to Jordan, 6 February 1980, SS Box 150, *JCPL*.

90 Bernie Aronson to Butler, 30 May 1980, Chief of Staff Butler Box 145, *JCPL*.

91 Butler to Jordan, 1 May 1979, Chief of Staff Butler Box 114, Wexler and Moe to Jordan, undated, Chief of Staff Jordan Box 79 and Butler to Moe, 30 May 1980, Chief of Staff Butler Box 145, *JCPL*.

92 Butler to Jordan, 18 April 1979, Chief of Staff Jordan Box 79, *JCPL*.

93 Eizenstat to Carter, 21 July 1980, Chief of Staff Jordan Box 79, *JCPL*.

94 Harrison, State and Labour in the US.

95 Butler to Carter, 24 August 1980, SS Box 173, *JCPL*.

96   Harrison, State and Labour in the US.
97   Marshall to Carter, 7 March 1978, Chief of Staff Butler Box 93, *JCPL*.
98   Eizenstat and Bill Johnston to Carter, 30 March 1977, SS Box 13, *JCPL*.
99   Dubofsky and Dulles, *Labor in America*, 369.
100 Butler to Carter, 24 August 1980, SS Box 173, *JCPL*.
101 Eizenstat, *White House Years*, 647.

Chapter 7

1   Bruce Schulman in David Horowitz, *Jimmy Carter, and the Energy Crisis of the 1970s. The Crisis of Confidence Speech of 15 July 1979* (Boston, New York: Bedford Books, 2005), 2.
2   James Hunter, *Culture Wars: The Struggle to Define America* (New York: Basic Books, 1991).
3   Writer Joe Queenan in Thomas Borstelmann, *The 1970s: A New Global History from Civil Rights to Economic Inequality* (Princeton: Princeton University Press, 2012), 2.
4   Adee, American Civil Religion, in Rosenbaum and Ugrinsky, *Presidency and Domestic Policy of Jimmy Carter*, 77–8.
5   Ibid., 79.
6   Carter Law Day Speech, University of Georgia, 4 May 1974, *APP*.
7   Robert Freedman, 'The Religious Right and the Carter Administration', *The Historical Journal*, Vol. 48: 231–60.
8   Ibid.
9   Ibid.
10   Borstelmann, *The 1970s*, 84 and 250.
11   Freedman, 'Religious Right', 231–60.
12   Balmer, *Redeemer*, 100–1.
13   Carter Interview, *Playboy*, November 1976.
14   John Kennedy's speech to Greater Houston Ministerial Association, 12 September 1960, *APP*.
15   President's News Conference, 9 November 1978, *APP*.
16   Freedman, 'Religious Right', 231–60.
17   Balmer, *Redeemer*, 103.
18   Borstelmann, *The 1970s*, 250.
19   Schulman, *Seventies*, 202.
20   Thomas Edsall with Mary Edsall, *Chain Reaction: The Impact of Race, Rights and Taxes on American Politics* (New York: WW Norton and Company, 1991), 132–3.
21   Freedman, 'Religious Right', 231–60.
22   Edsall with Edsall, *Chain Reaction*, 132–3.

23 Carter, *Diaries*, 454.
24 Memo Strickland to Carter, 3 December 1976, Box 91, Chief of Staff, *JCPL*.
25 Robert Maddox Exit Interview, 8 December 1980, *JCPL*.
26 Ibid., 12–13.
27 Carter, *Diaries*, 394.
28 William Martin, *With God on Our Side: The Rise of the Religious Right in America* (New York: Broadway Books, 1996), 189.
29 Maddox Exit Interview, 8 December 1980, *JCPL*.
30 Balmer, *Redeemer*, 134.
31 Sacramento, California Remarks at a 'Get Out the Vote' Rally, 3 November 1978, *APP*.
32 Freedman, 'Religious Right', 231–60.
33 Ibid.
34 Edsall and Edsall, *Chain Reaction*, 132–3.
35 Maddox Exit Interview, 8 December 1989, *JCPL*.
36 Susan Faludi, *Backlash: The Undeclared War against Women* (London: Chatto and Windrush, 1992), 264.
37 Freedman 'Religious Right', 231–60.
38 Speer, 'Carter was a Baptist President', 92.
39 Bergland Interview, *Miller Center*, 9.
40 John Kennedy Televised Address to the Nation, 11 June 1963, *APP*.
41 Governor Carter's Inaugural Address, 12 January 1971, https://www.americanrhetoric.com/speeches/jimmycarterlawday1974.htm
42 Randy Sanders, 'The Sad Duty of Politics: Jimmy Carter and the Issue of Race in His 1970. Gubernatorial Campaign', *Georgia Historical Quarterly*, Vol. LXXVI: 612–38.
43 Balmer, *Redeemer*, 8.
44 Carter, *Why Not the Best?* 45.
45 Borstelmann, *The 1970s*, 244.
46 Dumbrell, *Carter Presidency*, 88.
47 Carter, *Diaries*, 4.
48 Borstelmann, *The 1970s*, 245.
49 Hugh Davis Graham, 'Civil Rights in the Carter Presidency', in Fink and Graham, *Carter Presidency*, 202–3.
50 Kaufman and Kaufman, *Presidency of James Earl Carter*, 36.
51 Eizenstat to Carter, 28 January 1977, SS Box 4, *JCPL*.
52 Schulman, *Seventies*, 69–70.
53 Walter Mondale, *The Good Fight: A Life in Liberal Politics* (New York: Scribner, 2010), 179.
54 Bell, *Taking Care of the Law*, 30.

55   Annie Gutierrez to Eizenstat, 18 February 1977, DPS Eizenstat Box 149, *JCPL*.

56   Mondale, *Good Fight*, 177–81.

57   Drew Days to Eizenstat, 12 August 1977, Department of Justice, Attorney General, Box 114, *NARA*.

58   Califano to Carter, 7 September 1977, DPS Eizenstat Box 149, *JCPL*.

59   Eizenstat to Carter and Eleanor Holmes Norton to Carter, 9 September 1977, SS Box 40, *JCPL*.

60   Holmes Norton to Wade McCree, 12 September 1977, DPS Eizenstat Box 149, *JCPL*.

61   Eizenstat and Bob Lipshutz to Carter, 6 June 1977, DPS SS Box 39, *JCPL*.

62   Eizenstat to Carter and Mondale, 16 September 1977, SS Box 41, *JCPL*.

63   Jordan to Carter, undated, DPS Eizenstat Box 149, *JCPL*.

64   Bunny Mitchell to Kraft, 12 September 1977, SS Box 40, *JCPL*.

65   Schulman, *Seventies*, 69–70.

66   Memorandum from the President on Equality for Women, 20 July 1978, *APP*.

67   Graham, 'Civil Rights in the Carter Presidency', 204–6.

68   10 December 1977, Department of Justice, Attorney General Box 114, *NARA*.

69   Interview with the National Black Network Question-and-Answer Session with Representatives of the Network, 18 July 1977, *APP*.

70   Carter note to Cabinet and Heads of Agencies, 25 March 1977, SS Box 12, *JCPL*.

71   Valerie Pinson to Carter, 7 September 1977, SS Box 40 and Louis Martin Exit Interview, 3–4, *JCPL*.

72   Anderson, *Electing Jimmy Carter*, 39–40.

73   Carter to Eizenstat and Harris, 16 February 1978, Harris Papers Box 113, *LC*.

74   Carroll, *It Seemed Like Nothing Happened*, 192.

75   Days to Civiletti, 21 April 1980, Justice Department, Attorney General Box 133, *NARA*.

76   Stephanie A Slocum-Schaffer, *America in the 70s* (Syracuse: Syracuse University Press, 2003), 150.

77   Watson to Carter, 16 August 1979, SS Box 127, *JCPL*.

78   Carter to Parren Mitchell, 8 February 1977, Harris Papers Box 112, *LC*.

79   Louis Martin to Carter, 12 March 1979, Louis Martin Papers, Box 2, *LC*.

80   Harris to Carter, no date, Harris Papers Box 114, *LC*.

81   Undated, Martin Box 2, *LC*.

82   https://ropercenter.cornell.edu/?s=jimmy+carter

83   Carter Speech to Black Leaders, 5 January 1981, SS Box 185, *JCPL*.

84   Dumbrell, *Carter Presidency*, 89.

85   Thomas Sullivan to Bell, 9 May 1979, Attorney General Box 114, *NARA*.

86   Martin to Carter, 13 September 1978, Martin Box 2, *LC*.

87   Borstelmann, *The 1970s*, 81.

88 Freedman, 'The Religious Right', 231–60.

89 Schulman, *Seventies*, 186.

90 Eizenstat, *White House Years*, 103–15.

91 Ibid., 114.

92 Carter, *Diaries*, 127.

93 Briefing, undated, ERA Box 128, *LC*.

94 Schulman, *Seventies*, 168–70.

95 Borstelmann, *The 1970s*, 84.

96 Ibid., 256.

97 Freedman, 'Religious Right', 231–60.

98 Mark Siegel to Carter and Rosalyn Carter, 5 March 1977 and Rick Hutcheson to Carter, 3 March 1977, SS Box 10, *JCPL*.

99 Equal Rights Amendment Remarks at a White House Reception for Supporters of the Amendment, 23 October 1979, *APP*.

100 Liz Carpenter and Mildred Jeffery to Carter, 19 April 1978, ERA Box 120, *LC*.

101 Illinois ERAmerica and Weddington to Carter and Rosalyn Carter, 21 April 1980, SS Box 163, *JCPL*.

102 Sarah Weddington to Carter and Rosalyn Carter, 28 May 1979, SS Box 119, *JCPL*.

103 Carter, *Diaries*, 253–4.

104 Response to letter in *Ridgway Report*, 14 September 1980, ERA Box 2, *LC*.

105 Watson to Carter, 12 April 1980, SS Box 158, *JCPL*.

106 Carter, *Diaries*, 276–7.

107 7–8 March 1980, ERA Box 120, *LC* and Hutcheson to Carter, 21 March 1978, SS Box 69, *JCPL*.

108 Susan M Hartman, 'Feminism, Public Policy and the Carter Administration', in Fink and Graham, *Carter Presidency*, 232–6.

109 Carter, *Diaries*, 71.

110 Califano, *Governing America*, 65–6.

111 https://www.brainyquote.com/quotes/bella_abzug_688092

112 Martin Schram, *Washington Post*, 'The Story behind Bella's Departure', 13 January 1979 and Hartman, 'Feminism, Public Policy and the Carter Administration', 228.

113 Ibid., 228 and Weddington to Carter, 22 November 1978, SS Box 93, *JCPL*.

114 Schulman, *Seventies*, 187–9.

115 https://www.theage.com.au/politics/federal/losing-my-religion-for-equality-20090714-dk0v.html

116 Borstelmann, *The 1970s*, 84.

117 Eizenstat, *White House Years*, 839.

118 Carroll, *It Seemed Like Nothing Happened*, 272.

119 Carter, *Diaries*, 378 and Dumbrell, *Carter Presidency*, 80.

120 Faludi, *Backlash*, 306.

121 Slocum-Schaffer, *America in the 70s*, 130–1.

122 Governor Carter's Inaugural Address, 12 January 1971. https://www.americanrhetoric.com/speeches/jimmycarterlawday1974.htm

123 Carter, *Why Not the Best?* 137.

124 Jeffrey Stine, 'Environmental Policy during the Carter Presidency', in Fink and Graham, *Carter Presidency*, 180 and Kenneth J Morris, *Jimmy Carter. American Moralist* (Athens, London: University of Georgia Press, 1996), 198.

125 Carter, *Diaries*, 527 and 41.

126 Eizenstat, *White House Years*, 260.

127 Scheele, 'Carter and the Water Projects.'

128 Environment Message to Congress, 23 May 1977, *APP.*

129 Eizenstat to Carter, 8 February 1977, SS Box 7, *JCPL.*

130 Stine, 'Environmental Policy in the Carter Presidency', 180.

131 Eizenstat and Schirmer to Carter, 14 April 1977, SS Box 15, *JCPL.*

132 Eizenstat to Carter, 20 April 1977, SS Box 17, *JCPL.*

133 Speth to Carter, 16 August 1979, SS Box 127, *JCPL.*

134 Kaufman and Kaufman, *Presidency of James Earl Carter*, 209.

135 Eizenstat to Carter, 13 September 1977, SS Box 41, *JCPL.*

136 Eizenstat, Cecil Andrus and Bob Bergland to Carter, 29 November 1978, SS Box 98, *JCPL.*

137 Dateline: Alaska Cantwell, *Associated Press*, 15 January 1979 and https://www.youtube.com/watch?v=fGeI-9cLoDg

138 Press Briefing, 12 July 1980, Congressional Liaison Evelyn Small, Box 320, *JCPL.*

139 Eizenstat to Carter, 8 August 1980, SS Box 175, *JCPL.*

140 Moore, Bob Schule and Gary Fontana to Carter, 23 July 1980, SS Box 169, *JCPL.*

141 Eizenstat, 'Democratic Party and the Making of Domestic Policy', 10.

142 Carp Interview, *Miller Center*, 47–8.

143 Eizenstat, *White House Years*, 272–3 and Stine, 'Environmental Policy', 180.

144 *Governor Carter's Inaugural Address*, 12 January 1971.

145 Eizenstat, *White House Years*, 260.

Chapter 8

1   Address to the Nation on Energy and National Goals: 'The Malaise Speech', 15 July 1979, *APP.*

2   Maddox to Carter, 3 October 1978, SS Box 93, *JCPL.*

3   Caddell to Carter, 12 July 1979, Chief of Staff Butler, Box 142, *JCPL.*

4   Caddell report, 23 April 1979, Powell Papers, Press Offices, Box 40, *JCPL.*

5   Horowitz, *Jimmy Carter and the Energy Crisis*, 17.

6   Nesmith, Schapiro and Stewart to Rafshoon and Hertzberg on energy speech, 26 September 1979, Speechwriters Subject Files, Box 8, *JCPL*.

7   Rafshoon and Hertzberg to Carter, 1 April 1979, SS Box 112, *JCPL*.

8   Lance, *Truth of the Matter*, 178.

9   Horowitz, *Jimmy Carter and the Energy Crisis*, 94–6.

10   Eizenstat, *White House Years*, 670–2 and 680.

11   Ribuffo, 'Selling the President', 155.

12   Hugh Carter to President Carter, 17 July 1979, SS Box 124, *JCPL*.

13   *New Republic*, 4 August 1979.

14   Remarks at the Annual Convention of the National Association of Counties, 16 July 1979, *APP*.

15   Nelson, *Presidency, and the Political System*, 16.

16   Joseph Kraft, 'Self-inflicted Wounds', *WP*, 29 July 1979.

17   Jordan to Carter, 17 July 1979, Chief of Staff Box 37, *JCPL* and Carter, *Diaries*, 345–6.

18   Polsby, *Consequences of Party Reform*, 126–7.

19   Alonzo McDonald Interview, *Miller Center*, 16–43.

20   Carp Interview, *Miller Center*, 60.

21   Kaufman and Kaufman, *Presidency of James Earl Carter*, 184.

22   Jack Germond and Jules Witcover, *Blue Smoke and Mirrors. How Reagan Won and Why Carter Lost the Election of 1980* (New York: Viking, 1981), 45.

23   Morris, *American Moralist*, 5.

24   Kennedy speech at Faneuil Hall Boston, 7 November 1979, General, Adam Clymer Personal Papers, *JFK*.

25   Brinkley, *Unfinished Presidency*, 5.

26   Greenstein, *Presidential Difference*, 128.

27   Dumbrell, *Carter Presidency*, 51–2.

28   McDonald Interview, *Miller Center*, 72–3.

29   Motter, 'Seeking Limits: Passage of National Energy Act', 571.

30   Carter, *Diaries,* 527.

31   Glad, *In Search of the Great White House*, 212–13.

32   Interview with Jordan, 2 March 1995, Ickes to Jordan, Adam Clymer Personal Papers, *JFKPL*.

33   Lisa Bourdeaux to Moore, 28 January 1980, SS Box 147, *JCPL*.

34   Interview with Jordan, 2 March 1995, Ickes-Jordan, Adam Clymer Personal Papers, *JFKPL*.

35   Ted Kennedy, *True Compass* (Boston: Little Brown, 2009), 357.

36   Eizenstat, Edward Kennedy Oral History, 13 July 2000, *Miller Center*, 11.

37   Kennedy, *True Compass*, 364–7.

38   Carey Parker Interview, Edward Kennedy Oral History, 13 October 2008, *Miller Center*, 5.

39   Stuart Eizenstat Interview, Edward Kennedy Oral History, 13 July 2000, *Miller Center, 11.*

40   Jordan, *Crisis.*

41   Eizenstat, *White House Years,* 806.

42   Morgan, *The Age of Deficits,* 66–8.

43   Mondale, Edward Kennedy Oral History, *Miller Center.*

44   Wexler to Carter, 7 December 1979, SS Box 141, *JCPL.*

45   Austin Ranney, ed, *The American Elections of 1980* (Washington, London: American Enterprise Institute for Public Policy Research, 1982), 45.

46   https://www.youtube.com/watch?v=b6qLFAnBIFg

47   Parker Interview, Ted Kennedy Oral History, 13 October 2008, *Miller Center,* 6–7.

48   Bob Shrum to Kennedy, 17 December 1979, 1979 General, Adam Clymer Personal Papers, *JFKPL.*

49   Stanley, *Kennedy vs Carter,* 156 and 96–7.

50   Aronson to Butler, 30 May 1980, Chief of Staff Butler Box 145, *JCPL.*

51   Carter notes of meeting with Kennedy, 5 June 1980, General, Adam Clymer Personal Papers, *JFKPL.*

52   Moore and Tate to Carter, 10 June 1980, SS Box 165, *JCPL.*

53   Ranney, *Elections of 1980,* 116–19.

54   Haas, *Politics of Frustration,* 149.

55   http://www.americanrhetoric.com/speeches/tedkennedy1980dnc.htm

56   Jordan, *Crisis,* 330.

57   Jody Powell, *The Other Side of the Story* (New York: William Morrow, 1984), 250.

58   Carter, *Diaries,* 457.

59   Kennedy Interview, Ted Kennedy Oral History, Date Unknown, *Miller Center.*

60   Ward, *Camelot's End,* 273 and Alter, *The Very Best,* 593.

61   Stanley, *Kennedy vs Carter,* 2 and 196–8.

62   Marshall to Carter, 31 December 1979, SS Box 144, *JCPL* and *NYT,* 12 August 1980, General, Adam Clymer Personal Papers, *JFKPL.*

63   Remarks Announcing Candidacy for the Republican Presidential Nomination, 13 November 1979, *APP.*

64   Michael Deaver, *A Different Drummer: My Thirty Years with Ronald Reagan* (New York: Harper Collins, 2001), 98.

65   Michael Berman Interview, *Miller Center,* 72–3.

66   Morris, *American Moralist,* 415.

67   Iwan W Morgan, *Reagan: American Icon* (London: I.B. Tauris, 2016), 82–112.

68   Ibid., 128–33.

69   Address Accepting the Presidential Nomination at the Republican National Convention in Detroit, 17 July 1980, *APP.*

70   Sandbrook, *Mad as Hell,* 335.

71   Campagna, *Economic Policy in the Carter Administration*, 205.

72   Michael A Genovese, 'Jimmy Carter and the Age of Limits: Presidential Power in a Time of Decline and Diffusion', in Rosenbaum and Urgrinsky, *Presidency and Domestic Policies of Jimmy Carter,* 197–214.

73   Michael Schaller, *Reckoning with Reagan: America and Its President in 1980's* (New York: Oxford University Press, 1992), 5.

74   Interview with Jordan, 2 March 1995, Ickes-Jordan Adam Clymer Personal Papers, *JFKPL*.

75   Wexler Interview, *Miller Center,* 38– 9.

76   Jordan Interview, 2 March 1995, Ickes-Jordan, Adam Clymer Personal Papers, *JFKPL*.

77   Jordan, *Crisis*, 302–4.

78   Ibid., 304–9.

79   Rubenstein to Eizenstat, 1 July 1980, Box 1, DPS Dave Rubenstein Campaign Files, *JCPL*.

80   Ibid.

81   Hedley Donovan, *Roosevelt to Reagan: Reporter's Encounters with Nine Presidents* (New York: Harper, and Row Publishing, 1984), 219–22.

82   *ABC/Harris* Polls, 28 January 1980 and 15 July 1980, DPS Rubenstein 1980 Campaign Files Box 1, *JCPL*.

83   Jordan, *Crisis,* 376–8.

84   President's News Conference, 4 August 1980, *APP.*

85   www.livingroomcandidate.org/commercials/1980

86   Morgan, *Reagan*, 138–9.

87   Ibid., 134–5.

88   Eizenstat, *White House Years*, 868.

89   http://www.livingroomcandidate.org/commercials/1980

90   Kaufman and Kaufman, *Presidency of James Earl Carter*, 204–5.

91   President's Carter News Conference, 14 March 1980, *APP.*

92   Schultze to Carter, 2 October 1980, SS Box 179, *JCPL*.

93   Morgan, *Age of Deficits*, 73.

94   Alter, *His Very Best*, 572.

95   McDonald Interview, *Miller Center,* 58.

96   Carter, *Diaries*, 446–7.

97   McDonald Interview, *Miller Center,* 58–9 and Eizenstat, *White House Years*, 876.

98   McIntyre to Carter, 8 September 1980, SS Box 175, *JCPL*.

99   Interview with the President Question-and-Answer Session with the Editorial Board of Associated Press, 17 October 1980, *APP* and Schultze to Carter, 9 September 1980, SS Box 175, *JCPL*.

100 *ABC/Harris* Poll, 15 July 1980, DPS Rubenstein 1980 Campaign Files Box 1, *JCPL*.

101 Morgan, *Age of Deficits*, 72–3.

102   Morris, *American Moralist*, 287.

103   Reagan Talking Points, August 1980, Election Harris Box 326, *LC*.

104   Germond and Witcover, *Blue Smoke and Mirrors*, 251.

105   Ibid., 243–5.

106   Atlanta, Georgia Remarks at a Meeting with Southern Black Leaders, 16
        September 1980, *APP*.

107   Los Angeles, California Remarks at the California State AFL-CIO Convention,
        22 September 1980, *APP*.

108   Chicago, Illinois Remarks at a Democratic National Committee Fundraising
        Reception, 6 October 1980, *APP*.

109   Timothy Schellhardt, Carter and Meanness, *WP*, 3 November 1980.

110   Carter, *Keeping Faith*, 561.

111   www.livingroomcandidate.org/commercials/1980 and Germond and Witcover,
        Blue Smoke and Mirrors, 261–2.

112   President's News Conference, 17 April 1980, *APP*.

113   Germond and Witcover, *Blue Smoke and Mirrors*, 319.

114   Iwan W Morgan and Mark White, eds, *The Presidential Image. A History from
        Theodore Roosevelt to Donald Trump* (London, New York: I.B. Tauris, 2020), 168–9.

115   *ABC News/Harris* poll, 8 October 1980, DPS Rubenstein 1980 Campaign Files
        Box 1, *JCPL*.

116   Debate brief to Carter, October 1980, SS Box 172, *JCPL*.

117   Presidential Debate in Cleveland, 28 October 1980, *APP*.

118   Morgan, *Reagan*, 141.

119   Carter, *Diaries*, 479.

120   Neustadt to Rubenstein, 6 October 1980, DPS Rubenstein 1980 Campaign
        Files, *JCPL*.

121   Jenkins to Carter, 2 July 1980, SS Box 168, *JCPL*.

122   Remarks at a Meeting of Southern Black Leaders, 18 September 1980, *APP*.

123   Labor Day Remarks at a White House Picnic for Representatives of Organized
        Labor, 1 September 1980, *APP*.

124   www.livingroomcandidate.org/commercials/1980

125   Morgan, *Reagan*, 141–2.

126   McDonald Interview, *Miller Center*, 62.

127   Carter, *Diaries*, 530.

128   Everett Carl Ladd, 'The Brittle Mandate. Electoral De-alignment and the 1980
        Election', *Political Science Quarterly*, Vol. 96: 1–25.

129   Ranney, *American Elections of 1980*, 213.

130   Ibid., 237 and 255.

131   Morgan, *Reagan*, 143.

132   Ibid., 142.

133   http://www.livingroomcandidate.org/commercials/1984

134 Tim Smart, 'The GOP Tries to Cast Joe Biden as Modern-Day Jimmy Carter', *US News and World Report*, 13 May 2021.

135 1980 Presidential Election Remarks with Reporters on the Results of the Election, 5 November 1980, *APP*.

136 Jordan, *Crisis*, 7.

137 Stephen Skowronek, *The Politics That Presidents Make. Leadership from John Adams to Bill Clinton* (Cambridge, London: Belknap Press of Harvard, 1997).

138 Kaufman and Kaufman, *Presidency of James Earl Carter*, 244–5 and Ranney, *Elections of 1980*, 216–17.

139 Jordan, *Crisis*, 378.

140 George C Edwards, 'Exclusive Interview: President Jimmy Carter', 1–13.

141 Rafshoon Interview, *Miller Center*, 52.

142 Carter Interview, 12 May 1986, *USA Today* and Richardson, *Conversations with Carter*, 17 October 1997.

143 Eizenstat, *White House Years*, 784.

144 Lance, *Truth of the Matter*, 97.

145 Jordan, *Exit Interview*, *JCPL*, 5 and 79–81.

146 Perlstein, *Reaganland*, 859.

147 Remarks Accepting the Presidential Nomination at the 1980 Democratic National Convention in New York, 14 August 1980, *APP*.

148 Rafshoon Interview, *Miller Center*, 55.

149 Edward D Berkowitz, 'Jimmy Carter and the Sunbelt Report: Seeking a National Agenda', in Rosenbaum and Ugrinsky, *Presidency and Domestic Policies of Jimmy Carter*, 33–41.

150 Eizenstat, *White House Years*, 876.

151 Presidential Debate in Cleveland, 28 October 1980, *APP*.

152 Windsor, 'Budget Strategy in the Carter Administration', 393.

153 Ranney, *Elections in 1980*, 227.

154 Jordan, *Crisis*, 34–9.

Chapter 9

1 State of the Union Annual Message to Congress, 16 January 1981, *APP*.

2 Brinkley, *Unfinished Presidency*, 32.

3 Russell Riley, *Inside the Clinton White House – An Oral History* (New York: Oxford University, 2016), 93.

4 Tim Stanley, 'Barack Obama Is Facing His Jimmy Carter Moment', *Daily Telegraph*, 25 May 2012.

5 Brinkley, *Unfinished Presidency*, xvi–xvii.

6   Curtis Wilkie, 'Blessed Be the Peacemaker ', *Boston Globe Magazine*, 12 April 1990.
7   https://www.cartercenter.org/index.html
8   https://forum.cartercenter.org/
9   David Siders, 'Democrats Find a Foil For Trump I Jimmy Carter', *Politico*, 13 March 2019.
10   https://legalinsurrection.com/2014/10/branco-cartoon-legacy-building/
11   Michael Barone, 'Joe Biden Is Making Even Jimmy Carter Look Good', *NYT*, 3 September 2021.
12   Inaugural Speech, 20 January 1977, *APP.*
13   Tip O'Neill and William Novak, *Man of the House. The Life and Political Memoir of Speaker O'Neill* (London: Bodley Heath, 1981), 342.
14   Hargrove, *Carter as President*.
15   Jones, *Trustee President*.
16   Carter Interview, *Playboy*, November 1976.
17   Hess, *Organizing the Presidency*, 123.
18   Eizenstat, *White House Years*, 13.
19   Carter, *Keeping Faith,* 102.
20   Hargrove, *Carter as President*, 174.
21   Bourne, *Jimmy Carter*, 206.
22   Reeves, *A Question of Character*.
23   Farewell Address to the Nation, 14 January 1981, *APP.*
24   Eizenstat Interview, *Miller Center*, 54.
25   Lance Interview, *Miller Center*, 43.
26   Rick Perlstein, *The Invisible Bridge* (New York: Simon and Schuster, 2014), 589.
27   Eizenstat, *White House Years*, 197.
28   Brinkley, *Unfinished Presidency*, Introduction.
29   Mitchell, *Carter in Africa*, 657.
30   Eizenstat, *White House Years*, 55 and 112.
31   Donovan, *Roosevelt to Reagan*, 240–1.
32   https://commons.wikimedia.org/wiki/File: Living_US_Presidents_2009.jpg
33   D Bier, *Newsweek*, 5 September 2015.
34   Jordan, *Crisis*, 60.
35   Hargrove, *Carter as President*, xxiii.
36   Rafshoon to Carter, 14 June 1977, SS Box 34, *JCPL*.
37   Mondale, *The Good Fight*, 241.
38   Mitchell, *Carter in Africa*, 656.
39   https://www.c-span.org/presidentsurvey2021/?page=overall
40   https://www.c-span.org/presidentsurvey2021/?category=4
41   Alter, *His Very Best*, xii.
42   Tim Smart, 'GOP Tries to Cast Joe Biden as a Modern-Day Jimmy Carter', *US News*, 13 May 2021.

Selected bibliography

Primary sources

Archives

Jimmy Carter Presidential Library, Atlanta, GA, 3037–1498.
https://www.jimmycarterlibrary.gov/

- – Cabinet Secretary Files
- – Chief of Staff Files
- – Susan Clough Files
- – Council of Economic Advisors Files
- – Domestic Policy Staff Files
- – James Free Papers
- – Barry Jagoda Papers
- – Hamilton Jordan Papers
- – Alonzo McDonald Papers
- – Walter Mondale Papers
- – Office of Congressional Liaison Files
- – Office of Staff Secretary Files
- – Plains Files
- – Jody Powell Papers
- – Press Office Files
- – Speechwriter Files
- – Anne Wexler – Special Assistant to the President Files

Library of Congress, Washington, DC. http://www.loc.gov/rr/

- – Papers of Patricia Roberts Harris
- – Papers of Louis Martin
- – Papers of Abraham Ribicoff
- – Records of ERAmerica

National Archive, Washington DC. https://www.archives.gov/college-park

- – Department of Justice – Attorney General
- – Department of Justice – Civil Rights Division

Online resources

PPUS – Public Papers of the President of the United States. http://presidency.proxied.lsit.ucsb.edu/ws/

APP – *The American Presidency Project* – University of California Santa Barbara, CA 93106, USA. www.presidency.ucsb.edu

Miller Center, University of Virginia – Oral History – https://millercenter.org/the-presidency/presidential-oral-histories/jimmy-carter

Newspapers

New York Times
National Journal
Newsweek
Time
US News and World Report
Washington Post
Wall Street Journal

Memoirs

Anderson, Patrick, *Electing Jimmy Carter. The Campaign of 1976* (Baton Rouge, London: Louisiana State University Press, 1994)

Bell, Griffin and Ronald Ostrow, *Taking Care of the Law* (New York: William Morrow and Company, 1982)

Bourne, Peter, *Jimmy Carter. A Comprehensive Biography from Plains to the Presidency* (New York: Scribner, 1997)

Brzezinski, Zbigniew, *Power and Principle: Memoirs of a National Security Advisor* (New York: Farrar, Strauss and Giroux, 1983)

Califano, Joseph, *Governing America: An Insider Report from the White House and the Cabinet* (New York: Simon and Schuster, 1981)

Carter, Jimmy, *A Government as Good as Its People* (New York: Simon and Schuster, 1977)

Carter, Jimmy, *I'll Never Lie to You* (New York: Ballantine Books, 1976)

Carter, Jimmy, *Keeping Faith: Memoirs of a President* (New York: Bantam Books, 1982)

Carter, Jimmy, *Turning Point, a Candidate, a State and a Nation Coming of Age, 1962 Campaign* (New York, Toronto: Times Press, Random House, 1992)

Carter, Jimmy, *White House Diaries* (New York: Picador, 2010)

Carter, Jimmy, *Why Not the Best? Presidential Edition* (Eastbourne: Kingsway Publishing, 1977)

Carter, Rosalyn, *First Lady from Plains* (Boston: Houghton Mifflin, 1984)

Clifford, Clark, *Counsel to the President* (New York: Random House, 1991)

Deaver, Michael, *A Different Drummer: My Thirty Years with Ronald Reagan* (New York: Harper Collins, 2001)

Donovan, Hedley, *Roosevelt to Reagan: A Reporters Encounters with 9 Presidents* (New York: Harper and Row Publishing, 1984)

Drew, Elizabeth, *American Journal. The Events of 1976* (New York: Random House, 1976)

Drew, Elizabeth, *Portrait of an Election. The 1980 Presidential Campaign* (London, Henley: Routledge and Kegan Paul, 1981)

Eizenstat, Stuart, *President Carter; The White House Years* (New York: St Martin's Press, 2018)

Jordan, Hamilton, *Crisis: The Last Year of the Carter Presidency* (New York: Michael Joseph, 1982)

Kennedy, Edward, *True Compass* (London: Little Brown, 2009)

Lance, Bert with Bill Gilbert, *The Truth of the Matter. My Life in and out of Politics* (New York: Summit Books, 1992)

Mondale, Walter, *The Good Fight: A Life in Liberal Politics* (New York: Scribner, 2010)

O'Neill, Tip and William Novak, *Man of the House. The Life and Political Memoirs of Speaker O'Neill* (London: Bodley Heath, 1987)

Peterson, Esther and Winifred Conkling, *Restless: The Memoirs of Labor and Consumer Activists: Esther Peterson* (Washington DC: Caring Publishing, 1995)

Powell, Jody, *The Other Side of the Story* (New York: William Morrow and Co, 1984)

Vance, Cyrus, *Hard Choices. Critical Years in America's Foreign Policy* (New York: Simon and Schuster, 1983)

Volcker, Paul and Toyoo Gyoten, *Changing Fortunes. The World's Money and the Threat to American Leadership* (New York: Times Books, 1992)

Other primary books

Breitinger, Eckhard, ed, *Presidential Campaign 1976 – Campaign Speeches* (Las Vegas: Lang, 1978)

Horowitz, Daniel, *Jimmy Carter and the Energy Crisis of 1970's. The Crisis of Confidence Speech of 15 July 1979* (Boston, London: Bedford/St Martins, 2005)

Moore, Jonathan, ed, *Campaign for President: Managers Look at 80. Proceedings of a Conference on 1980 Presidential Campaign Decision Making* (Cambridge: Ballinger Publishing Company, 1981)

Moore, Jonathan and Janet Fraser, eds, *Campaign for President: Managers Look at 76. Proceedings of a Conference on the 1976 Presidential Campaign Decision Making* (Cambridge: Ballinger Publishing Company, 1977)

Pechman, Joseph, ed, *Arthur Okun Essays, Economics in Policy Making* (Cambridge MA, London: MIT Press, 1993)

Richardson, Don, ed, *Conversations with Carter* (Boulder, London: Lynne Rienner Publishers, 1998)

Thompson, Kenneth W., ed, *The Carter Presidency: Fourteen Intimate Perspectives of Jimmy Carter* (Lanham MD, New York, London: University Press of America, 1990)

Thompson, Kenneth W., ed, *The Three Press Secretaries* (Lanham, London: University Press of America, 1983)

Articles

Edwards, George C., 'Exclusive Interview: President Jimmy Carter', *Presidential Studies Quarterly*, Vol. 38 (March, 2005): 1–13.

Eizenstat, Stuart, 'Economists and the White House Decisions', *Journal of Economic Perspectives*, Vol. 6 (Summer, 1992): 65–71.

Fallows, James, 'The Passionless President', *Atlantic Monthly* (May 1979): 75–81.

Jasinowski, Jerry, 'The First Two Years of the Carter Administration: An Appraisal', *Presidential Studies Quarterly*, Vol. 9 (Winter, 1979): 11–15.

Schultze, Charles L., 'The President's Plan', *Challenge,* Vol. 22 (July/August, 1979): 28–34.

Wellford, Harrison, 'Staffing the Presidency; An Insider's Comments', *Political Science Quarterly*, Vol. 93 (Spring, 1978): 10–12.

Secondary sources

Books

Abernathy, M. Glen, Dilys M. Hill and Phil Williams, *The Carter Years: The President and Policy Making* (London: Frances Pinter, 1984)

Alter, Jonathan, *His Very Best. Jimmy Carter, A Life* (New York: Simon and Schuster, 2020)

Andelic, Patrick, *Donkey Work. Congressional Democrats in Conservative America 1974–1992* (Lawrence: University Press of Kansas, 2019)

Baker, Peter and Susan Glasser, *The Man Who Ran Washington. The Life and Times of James A Baker III* (New York: Anchor Books, 2020)

Balmer, Randall, *Redeemer. The Life of Jimmy Carter* (New York: Basic Books, 2014)

Barber, David, *Race for the Presidency: The Media and the Nominating Process* (Englewood, New Jersey: Prentice Hall, 1978)

Barber, David, *The Presidential Character: Predicting Performance in the White House* (Englewood Cliffs: Prentice Hall, 1977)

Barger, Harold, *The Impossible Presidency. Illusions and Realities of Executive Power* (Glenview: Scott, Foreman and Company, 1984)

Bird, Kai, *The Outlier. The Unfinished Presidency of Jimmy Carter* (New York: Crown, 2021)

Biven, W. Carl, *Jimmy Carter's Economy: Policy in the Age of Limits* (Chapel Hill, London: University of North Carolina Press, 2002)

Borstelmann, Thomas, *The 1970s: A New Global History from Civil Rights to Economic Inequality* (Princeton, Woodstock: Princeton University Press, 2012)

Brauer, Carl, *Presidential Transitions. Eisenhower to Reagan* (New York, Oxford: Oxford University Press, 1986)

Brinkley, Douglas, *The Unfinished Presidency: Jimmy Carter's Journey beyond the White House* (New York, London: Penguin Books, 1998)

Burke, John P., *Presidential Transitions from Politics to Practice* (Boulder, London: Lynne Rienner Publishers, 2000)

Campagna, Anthony, *Economic Policy in the Carter Administration* (Westport, London: Greenwood Press, 1995)

Campbell, Colin, *Managing the Presidency Carter, Reagan and the Search for Executive Harmony* (London: University of Pittsburgh Press, 1986)

Cannon, Lou, *Governor Reagan. His Rise to Power* (New York: BBS Public Affairs, 2003)

Carroll, Peter N., *It Seemed Like Nothing Happened. The Tragedy and the Promise of the 1970s* (New York: Holt, Pritchard and Rinehart, 1982)

Crain, Andrew Downer, *The Ford Presidency. A History* (Jefferson: McFarland and Company, 2009)

Cronin, Thomas, *State of the Presidency* (Boston: Little Brown, 1980)

Cunningham, Sean P., *American Politics in the Post War Sunbelt* (New York: Cambridge University Press, 2014)

Domin, Gregory, *Jimmy Carter – Public Opinion and the Search for Values 1977–81* (Macon: Mercer University Press, 2003)

Dubofsky, Melvyn and Foster Rhea Dulles, *Labor in America: A History* (Wheeling: Harlan Davidson, 1999)

Dumbrell, John, *The Carter Presidency. A Re-evaluation* (Manchester, New York: Manchester University Press, 1993)

Edsall, Thomas B. and Mary D. Edsall, *Chain Reaction: The Impact of Race, Rights and Taxes on American Politics* (New York: WW Norton and Company, 1991)

Faludi, Susan, *Backlash: The Undeclared War against Women* (London: Chatto and Windrush, 1992)

Farrell, John, *Tip O'Neill and the Democratic Century* (Boston, New York: Little, Brown and Company, 2001)

Fink, Gary, *Prelude to the Presidency: The Political Character and Legislative Style of Jimmy Carter* (Westport, London: Greenwood Press, 1980)

Fink, Gary and Hugh Davis Graham, ed, *The Carter Presidency. Policy Choices in the Post New Deal Era* (Lawrence: University of Kansas Press, 1998)

Frisch, Scott A. and Sean Q. Kelly, *Jimmy Carter and the Water Wars. Presidential Influence and the Politics of Pork* (Amherst, New York: Cambria press, 1981)

Gaillard, Frye, *Prophet from Plains* (Athens: University of Georgia Press, 2007)

Germond, Jack and Jules Witcover, *Blue Smoke and Mirrors. How Reagan Won and Why Carter Lost the Election of 1980* (New York: Viking Press, 1981)

Giglio, James N., *The Presidency of John F Kennedy* (Lawrence: University Press of Kansas, 2006)

Glad, Betty, *Jimmy Carter. In Search of the Great White House* (New York, London: WW Norton and Company, 1980)

Godbold, E. Stanley, *Jimmy, and Rosalyn Carter. The Georgian Years 1924–1974* (Oxford, New York: Oxford University Press, 2010)

Greenstein, Fred I., *Presidential Difference. Leadership Style from FDR to George W Bush* (Princeton, Oxford: Princeton University Press, 2004)

Haas, Garland, *Jimmy Carter and the Politics of Frustration* (Jefferson, London: McFarland and Company, 1992)

Hargrove, Erwin, *Jimmy Carter as President. Leadership and Politics of the Public Good* (London, Baton Rouge: Louisiana State University Press, 1988)

Hargrove, Erwin and Samuel Morley, *President's Council of Economic Advisors* (Boulder, London: Westview Press, 1984)

Hess, Stephen, *Organizing the Presidency 1988* (Washington DC: Brookings Institute Press, 2002)

Holmes, David L., *The Faiths of Post War Presidents. From Truman to Obama* (Athens, London: University of Georgia Press, 2012)

Hunter, James, *Culture Wars: The Struggle to Define America* (New York: Basic Books, 1991)

Jacobs, Meg, *Panic at the Pump. The Energy Crisis and the Transformation of American Politics in the 1970's* (New York: Hill and Wang, 2017)

Johnson, Haynes, *In the Absence of Power. Governing America* (New York: Viking Press, 1980)

Jones, Charles O., *Trustee President. Jimmy Carter and the United States Congress* (Baton Rouge, London: Louisiana State University Press, 1988)

Kaufman, Burton I. and Scott Kaufman, *The Presidency of James Earl Carter* (Lawrence: University Press of Kansas, 2006)

Kellerman, Barbara, *The Political Presidency. Practice of Leadership* (New York, Oxford: Oxford University Press, 1999)

Leuchtenburg, William, *Shadow of FDR. From Harry Truman to Barak Obama* (Ithaca, London: Cornell University Press, 2009)

Levitan, Sar and Martha Cooper, *Business Lobbies and the Public Good* (Baltimore, London: Johns Hopkins University Press, 1984)

Light, Paul, *The President's Agenda. Domestic Policy Kennedy – Clinton* (Baltimore, London: Johns Hopkins University Press, 1999)

Lynn, Laurence E. and David de F. Whitman, *The President as Policy Maker: Jimmy Carter & Welfare Reform* (Philadelphia: Temple University Press, 1981)

Mann, Michael, *Russell Long. A Life in Politics* (Jackson: University Press of Mississippi, 2014)

Mann, Robert, *Legacy to Power. Senator Russell Long of Louisiana* (New York: Paragon House, 1992)

Martin, William, *With God on Our Side. The Rise of the Religious Right in America* (New York: Broadway Books, 1996)

Mattson, Kevin, *What the Heck Are You up to Mr President?* (New York, Berlin, London: Bloomsbury Press, 2009)

Mazlish, Bruce and Edwin Diamond, *Jimmy Carter. A Character Portrait* (New York: Simon and Schuster, 1979)

Meyer, Peter, *James Earl Carter. The Man and the Myth* (Kansas City: Sheed, Andrews and McMeet, 1978)

Mitchell, Nancy, *Jimmy Carter in Africa. Race and the Cold War* (Washington, DC: Stanford University Press, 2016)

Mollenhoff, Clark, *The President Who Failed. Carter out of Control* (London: Macmillan Publishing, 1980)

Morgan, Iwan W., *The Age of Deficits. Presidents and Unbalanced Budgets. From Jimmy Carter to George W Bush* (Lawrence: University of Kansas, 2009)

Morgan, Iwan W., *Deficit Government. Taxing and Spending in Modern America* (Chicago: Ivan Dee, 1995)

Morgan, Iwan W., *Reagan: American Icon* (London, New York: I.B. Tauris, 2016)

Morgan, Iwan W. and Mark White, eds, *The Presidential Image. A History from Theodore Roosevelt to Donald Trump* (London, New York: I.B. Tauris, 2020)

Morris, Kenneth J. and Jimmy Carter, *American Moralist* (Athens, London: University of Georgia Press, 1996)

Nelson, Michael, ed, *The Presidency and the Political System* (Washington DC: Congressional Quarterly, 1988)

Neustadt, Richard E., *Presidential Power and the Modern Presidents. The Politics of Leadership from Roosevelt to Reagan* (New York: The Free Press, 1990)

O'Neill, Timothy J., *Bakke and the Politics of Equality, Friends and Foes in the Public School of Litigation* (Middletown, Scranton: Wesleyan University Press, 1984)

Perlstein, Rick, *The Invisible Bridge* (New York: Simon and Schuster, 2014)

Perlstein, Rick, *Reaganland. America's Right Turn. 1976–1980* (New York: Simon and Schuster, 2020)

Petersen, Mark A., *Legislating Together: The White House and Capitol Hill from Eisenhower to Reagan* (Cambridge, London: Harvard University Press, 1990)

Pfiffner, James F., *The Modern Presidency* (Boston: Wadsworth Engage L Nelson Learning, 2008)

Polsby, Nelson, *Consequences of Party Reform* (Oxford: Oxford University Press, 1983)

Ranney, Austin, ed, *The American Elections of 1980* (Washington, London: American Enterprise Institute for Public Policy Research, 1982)

Reeves, Thomas, *A Question of Character: A Life of John F Kennedy* (New York, Toronto: Collier Macmillan, 1991)

Riley, Russell L., *Inside the Clinton White House – An Oral History* (Oxford: Oxford University Press, 2016)

Roof, Tracy, *American Labor, Congress and the Welfare State* (Baltimore: Johns Hopkins University Press, 2011)

Rosenbaum, Herbert and Alexj Ugrinsky, eds, *The Presidency and Domestic Policies of Jimmy Carter* (Westport, London: Greenwood Press, 1994)

Rozell, Mark J., *The Press and the Carter Presidency* (Boulder, London: Westview, 1989)

Sandbrook, Dominic, *Mad as Hell. Crisis in the 1970s and the Rise of the Populist Right* (New York: Anchor Books, 2011)

Schaller, Michael, *Reckoning with Reagan: America and Its President in 1980's* (New York: Oxford University Press, 1992)

Schlesinger, Robert, *White House Ghosts. Presidents and Their Speechwriters* (New York: Simon and Schuster, 2008)

Schulman, Bruce J., *The Seventies. The Great Shift in American Culture, Society and Politics* (Cambridge: Da Capo Press, 2001)

Shogan, Robert, *Promises to Keep, Carter's First One Hundred Days* (New York, London: Crowell & Company, 1977)

Skowronek, Stephen, *The Politics That Presidents Make. Leadership from John Adams to Bill Clinton* (Cambridge, London: Belknap Press of Harvard University Press, 1997)

Slocum-Schaffer, Stephanie A., *America in the 70's* (Syracuse: Syracuse University Press, 2003)

Smith, Hedrick, *The Power Game. How Washington Works* (New York: Ballentine Books, 1988)

Stanley, Timothy, *Kennedy vs Carter. The 1980 Battle for the Democratic Party's Soul* (Lawrence: University Press of Kansas, 2010)

Stroud, Kandy, *How Jimmy Won. The Victory Campaign from Plains to the White House* (New York: William Morrow and Company, 1977)

Ward, Jon, *Camelot's End. The Democrats' Last Great Civil War* (New York, Boston: Twelves, 2019)

Wheeler, Leslie, *Jimmy Who? An Examination of Presidential Candidate Jimmy Carter. The Man, His Career, His Stands on the Issues* (New York: Barrons Woodbury, 1976)

White, Mark, *The Presidency of Bill Clinton: The Legacy of a New Domestic and Foreign Policy* (London: I.B. Tauris, 2012)

Wilson, Robert, ed, *Character above All: The Presidents from FDR to George Bush* (New York: Simon and Schuster, 1995)

Witcover, Jules, *Marathon – Pursuit of the Presidency 1972–1976* (New York: Viking Press, 1977)

Wooten, James, *Dasher: The Roots and Rising of Jimmy Carter* (New York: Summit Books, 1978)

Zelizer, Julian, *Jimmy Carter* (New York: Times Books, 2010)

Articles

Capinger, Christopher, 'The Politics of Trustee Governance: Jimmy Carter's Fight for a Standby Gasoline Rationing Plan', *Presidential Studies Quarterly*, Vol. 26 (Summer, 1996): 187–206.

Christensen, Reo M., 'Carter and Truman. A Reappraisal of Both', *Presidential Studies Quarterly*, Vol. 13 (Spring, 1983): 313–23.

Davis, Eric, 'Legislative Liaison in the Carter Administration', *Political Science Quarterly*, Vol. 94 (Summer, 1979): 287–301.

Davis, Eric, 'Legislative Reform and the Decline of Presidential Influence on Capitol Hill', *British Journal of Political Science*, Vol. 8 (October, 1979): 465–79.

Feigenbaum, Edward D., 'Organization and Decision Making in the Ford and Carter White Houses', *Presidential Studies Quarterly*, Vol. 10 (Summer, 1980): 364–77.

Finbow, Robert, 'Presidential Leadership or Structural Constraints? Failure of President Carter's Health Insurance Proposals', *Presidential Studies Quarterly*, Vol. 28 (Winter, 1998): 169–86.

Fink, Gary, 'Ray Marshall. Jimmy Carter's Ambassador to Organized Labor', *Labor History*, Vol. 37 (Fall, 1996): 463–79.

Flanagan, Robert, 'National Accord as a Social Contract', *Industrial and Labor Relations Review*, Vol. 34 (October, 1980): 35–50.

Fleischer, Richard and Jon R. Bond, 'Assessing Presidential Support in the House. Lessons from Reagan and Carter', *The Journal of Politics*, Vol. 45 (August, 1983): 145–58.

Freedman, Robert, 'The Religious Right and the Carter Administration', *The Historical Journal*, Vol. 48 (March, 2005): 231–60.

Grover, William and Joseph Peschek, 'The Rehabilitation of Jimmy Carter and the Limits of Mainstream Analysis', *Polity*, Vol. 23 (1990): 139–52.

Hahn, Dan F., 'Flailing the Profligate. Carter's Energy Sermon of 1979', *Presidential Studies Quarterly*, Vol. 10 (Fall, 1980): 583–7.

Hahn, Dan F., 'The Rhetoric of Jimmy Carter', *Presidential Studies Quarterly*, Vol. 14 (Spring, 1984): 265–88.

Hill, Dilys and Phil Williams, 'The Carter Legacy: Mondale and the Democratic Party', *The World Today*, Vol. 40 (October, 1984): 413–19.

Hoxie, R. Gordon, 'Staffing the Ford and Carter Presidencies', *Presidential Studies Quarterly*, Vol. 10 (Summer, 1980): 378–401.

Jensen, Faye Lind, 'An Awesome Responsibility. Rosalyn Carter as First Lady', *Presidential Quarterly*, Vol. 20, No. 4 (1990): 769–75.

Jones, Charles O., 'Carter and Congress: From the Outside in', *British Journal of Political Science*, Vol. 15 (July, 1985): 269–98.

Kantowicz, Edward, 'Reminiscences of a Fated Presidency: Themes from Carter Memoirs', *Presidential Studies Quarterly*, Vol. 16 (Fall, 1986): 651–65.

Kaplowitz, Craig Allan, 'Struggles of the First "New Democrat": Jimmy Carter's Youth Employment Policy and the Great Society Legacy', *Presidential Studies Quarterly*, Vol. 28 (Winter, 1998): 198–206.

Kellerman, Barbara, 'Introversion in the Oval Office', *Presidential Studies Quarterly*, Vol. 13 (Summer, 1983): 383–99.

Kessel, John, '*Structures of the Carter White House*', *American Journal of Political Science*, Vol. 27 (August, 1983): 431–63.

Knott, Jack and Aaron Wildavsky, 'Jimmy Carter's Theory of Governing', *The Wilson Quarterly,* Vol. 1 (Winter, 1977): 49–67.

Krukones, Michael, 'The Campaign Promises of Jimmy Carter', *Presidential Studies Quarterly*, Vol. 15 (Winter, 1985): 136–44.

Kumar, Martha Joynt, 'The Contemporary Presidency: The Carter Communications Operations: Lessons for His Successors', *Presidential Studies Quarterly*, Vol. 37, No. 4 (December, 2007): 717–36.

Ladd, Everett Carl, 'The Brittle Mandate. Electoral Dealignment and the 1980 Election', *Political Science Quarterly*, Vol. 96 (Spring, 1981): 1–25.

Lee, David D., 'The Politics of Less. The Trials of Herbert Hoover and Jimmy Carter', *Presidential Studies Quarterly*, Vol. 13 (Spring, 1983): 305–12.

Locander, Robert, 'Carter and the Press: The First Two Years', *Presidential Studies Quarterly*, Vol. 10 (Winter, 1980): 106–20.

May, Ann Mari, 'Monetary Policy and the Carter Presidency', *Presidential Studies Quarterly*, Vol. 23 (Fall, 1993): 669–711.

Meck, Stuart and Rebecca Retzlaff, 'President Carter's Urban Policy: A Reconstruction and an Appraisal', *Journal of Planning History,* Vol. 11, No. 3 (2012): 243–80.

Morgan, Iwan, 'Jimmy Carter, Bill Clinton and the New Democratic Economics', *The Historical Journal*, Vol. 47 (December, 2004): 1015–39.

Morgan, Iwan, 'Monetary Metamorphosis: The Volcker Fed and Inflation', *Journal of Political History*, Vol. 24, No. 4 (2012): 545–71.

Mullen, William F., 'Perceptions of Carter's Legislative Successes and Failures: Views from the Hill and the Liaison Staff', *Presidential Studies Quarterly*, Vol. 12 (Fall, 1982): 522–33.

Reichard, Gary W., 'Early Returns: Assessing Jimmy Carter', *Presidential Studies Quarterly*, Vol. 20 (Summer, 1990): 603–60.

Ribuffo, Leo, 'From Carter and Clinton: The Latest Crisis of American Liberalism', *American Studies International*, Vol. 35 (June, 1997): 4–29.

Ribuffo, Leo, 'Jimmy Carter beyond the Current Myths', *Magazine of History* (Summer/Fall, 1988): 19–23.

Rozell, Mark, 'Carter Rehabilitated: What Caused the 39th President's Press Transformation?' *Presidential Studies Quarterly*, Vol. 23 (Spring, 1983): 317–30.

Rozell, Mark J., 'President Carter and the Press: Perspectives from White House Communications Advisers', *Political Science Quarterly*, Vol. 105 (Autumn, 1990): 419–34.

Sanders, Randy, 'The Sad Duty of Politics: Jimmy Carter and the Issue of Race in His 1970 Gubernatorial Campaign', *The Georgia Historical Quarterly*, Vol. LXXVI (Fall, 1992): 612–38.

Scheele, Paul E., 'President Carter and the Water Projects: A Case Study in Presidential and Congressional Decision Making', *Presidential Studies Quarterly*, Vol. 8, No. 4 (Fall, 1978): 348–54.

Stephens, David, 'President Carter, the Congressional and NEA. Creating the Department of Education', *Political Science Quarterly*, Vol. 98 (Winter, 1983–4): 641–63.

Strong, Robert A., 'Recapturing Leadership: The Carter Administration and the Crisis of Confidence', *Presidential Studies Quarterly*, Vol. 16, No. 4 (Fall, 1986): 636–50.

Sundquist, James, 'The Crisis of Competence in Our National Government', *Political Science Quarterly*, Vol. 95 (Summer, 1980): 183–208.

Sundquist, James, 'Jimmy Carter as a Public Administrator. Appraisal at Midterm', *Public Administration Review* (January/February, 1979): 3–11.

Thomas, Norman C., 'Carter Administration Memoirs', *Western Politics Quarterly*, Vol. 39 (1986): 345–60.

Wolman, Harold L. and Astrid E. Merget, 'The Presidency and Policy Formulation. President Carter and Urban Policy', *Presidential Studies Quarterly*, Vol. 10 (Summer, 1980): 402–15.

Doctoral Dissertations

Craik, David, 'US Presidents and Public Opinion: The Carter Presidency', Unpublished PhD Dissertation (University of Keele, 2005)

Harrison, Isabel D., 'State and Labour in the US: The Carter Administration and the AFL-CIO, 1976–1980: Political Strategy and the National Accord', Unpublished PhD Dissertation (Oxford University, 1989)

Abbreviations

JCPL
: *Jimmy Carter Presidential Library, Atlanta Georgia 30307-1498,* https://www.jimmycarterlibrary.gov/

JFKPL
: *John Fitzgerald Kennedy Presidential Library, Columbia Point, Boston, MA 02125.* https://www.jfklibrary.org/?gclid=EAIaIQobChMIvviu4ar0_AIVisftCh2POwZcEAAYASAAEgKNt_D_BwE

LC
: *Library of Congress Washington, DC,* http://www.loc.gov/rr/

Miller Center
: *University of Virginia, Oral History,* https://millercenter.org/the-presidency/presidential-oral-histories/jimmy-carter

NARA
: *National Archives Records Administration Washington DC,* https://www.archives.gov/college-park

PPUS
: *Papers of the President of the United States,* https://www.govinfo.gov/app/collection/PPP#:~:text=The%20Public%20Papers%20of%20the%20Presidents%2C%20which%20is%20compiled%20and,the%20National%20Historical%20Publications%20Commission

APP
: *The American Presidency Project – University of California Santa Barbara, CA 93106, USA.* https://www.presidency.ucsb.edu/

NYT
: *New York Times.*

WSJ
: *Wall Street Journal.*

WP
: *Washington Post.*

PSQ
: *Presidential Studies Quarterly.*

Index

www.ingramcontent.com/pod-product-compliance
Ingram Content Group UK Ltd.
Pitfield, Milton Keynes, MK11 3LW, UK
UKHW020705280225
455688UK00005B/248